The *New* Reading the Landscape

One of Britain's most respected landscape historians, Richard Muir has done much to make research in landscape history accessible to a wider public. In addition to *The Shell Guide to Reading the Landscape*, his many books include *Approaches to Landscape*, *History from the Air*, *Portraits of the Past*, *Villages of England* and *The Yorkshire Countryside*. Dr Muir has also written for leading journals of history, geography and landscape history. He has published on political geography and has lectured in geography at universities in England and Ireland. Richard Muir is co-founder and Editor of the journal *Landscapes*.

'This completely rewritten version of Muir's earlier book about the interpretation of landscape, originally published 20 years ago, is exciting and compulsive reading. It covers a range of aspects of landscape history (or historical geography, depending on how you look at it) in an eclectic and passionate way, combining analysis and aesthetics in a brilliantly fluid narrative.' *Times Educational Supplement*

'It allows the reader to begin to make some sense of what the landscape mutely records about the beliefs and social patterns of past societies. It is supported in this by an attractive format, clear informative diagrams and beautiful black-and-white photographs that vividly illustrate the landscape described in the text. The breadth gives a newcomer to the field a sufficiently good general introduction to the theory and practice of landscape history to be able to go out and 'try it for themselves', with the likelihood of achieving a fair initial result.' *The Local Historian*

'This latest book from Richard Muir deserves to become influential with a wide range of landscape professionals. It should also appeal to the knowledgeable amateur and be required reading by all those responsible for developing and managing change in the landscape.' *Landscape Research*

'A guide to how we can use evidence contained within the fabric of today's countryside to understand its history. It is extremely well illustrated, very reasonably priced, and will form a valuable guide for anyone who is curious about the history of our landscape.' *Devon Archaeology Society Newsletter*

'For anyone interested in learning about the landscape, particularly for anyone wanting to go forth and muddy their boots to find out more, this is an excellent introduction . . . a guide to how to understand what is all around us.' *East Midland Historian*

'The excellent presentation, the thematic arrangement and the breadth of the book means that . . . it will deservedly become a textbook for the next generation of students of the landscape. There is nothing else quite like it in combining the theoretical perspectives with practical hints for field observation and interpretation, despite a number of recent publications. It has filled a gap that needed filling.'

The Local Historian

Cover Photograph: A Wensleydale scene looking towards West Burton (Richard Muir)

The *New*
Reading the Landscape
Fieldwork in Landscape History

RICHARD MUIR

UNIVERSITY
of
EXETER
PRESS

First published in 2000 by
University of Exeter Press
Reed Hall, Streatham Drive
Exeter EX4 4QR
UK
www.exeterpress.co.uk

Corrected reprint published in 2002

Reprinted 2006, 2010

British Library Cataloguing in Publication Data
A catalogue record of this book is available
from the British Library

Paperback ISBN 978 0 85989 580 4
Hardback ISBN 978 0 85989 579 8

Typeset in 11 on 12.5 pt Palatino Light by Exe Valley Dataset Ltd, Exeter

Mixed Sources
Product group from well-managed
forests and other controlled sources
www.fsc.org Cert no. SA-COC-002112
© 1996 Forest Stewardship Council

FSC

Printed and bound in Great Britain by
Short Run Press Ltd, Exeter

*For the ordinary fieldworkers with the muddy
boots and aching joints who do most of the work,
yet see little of the credit.*

Contents

Figures

Maps

Tables

Introduction

This book is a completely rewritten and rather more advanced version of *Reading the Landscape*, which was published in 1981. It reflects the growth of serious interest in landscape history/archaeology that has occurred in the last couple of decades and the contribution that recent research has made to our understanding of the evolution of countrysides. The reasons for our growing fascination may perhaps be found in the stresses which modern living imposes on people who, in biological terms, have scarcely evolved from their hunter-gatherer forebears. Globalisation, the tyranny of economics over higher values and the phenomenon described by one geographer as 'time-space compression' magnify a longing for identity and roots. In the past, people knew who they were and where they were from, even if they were often far from happy with their lots. Now, the inner craving for stability, predictability and belonging may guide us into explorations of the bonds between past communities and their settings. Perhaps, in reconstructing the landscapes of the past, with their bounds, place-names, settlements and fieldscapes, we are piecing together new but authentic worlds of the imagination that we may wishfully inhabit?

I have never had much time for suggestions that aesthetic considerations have no place in the 'scientific' analysis of landscape evidence. It is more likely to be the case that those who decry such sensibilities are very badly placed to understand the actions of the many people who usually *did* have spiritual and artistic inclinations. This said, it is the great irony of landscape that the finest countrysides were not built by the calculating designers of parks and gardens. Instead they were made by peasants, farm hands and tenants whose mission was survival and who seldom if ever gave a thought for the visual consequences of their labours. As though guided by some hidden hand, society after society has created landscape in its own image. The contrasts between Tories and Whigs are manifested in the different sorts of parks that they built for themselves. The communal spirit of the medieval villages finds expression in surviving fragments of old commons and ridged ploughland, while the mean-spiritedness of the modern age is proclaimed by the new prairies of the barley barons and the countless countrysides which lie looted of wildlife and monuments.

Landscape history and landscape archaeology bring together researchers and enthusiasts from many different disciplinary backgrounds. This has proved to be a good and a healthy thing, since no single, self-perpetuating establishment has been able to force the subjects into any mould and determine what they should or should not be. Years of experience in and out of universities have led me to realise that the powerhouse of landscape history lies with the unsung fieldworkers, professional and amateur, the research students and the local enthusiasts. The real work is accomplished by the men and women with the muddy boots and the aching joints, even if the credit flies off in a different direction. In the pages that follow I have tried to bring together hints, field tips and guidelines and to set them in a spatial

and historical context. Useful as this may be, there is no substitute for hard-won experience. Out in the field, things are seldom as straightforward as the textbooks suggested. Usually they are harder and sometimes they are contradictory. One must always retain the flexibility needed to abandon a firmly held view if the evidence from the field is arguing otherwise. If a medieval field system appears to be the oldest facet of a countryside, with all other features superimposed upon it, then prior theories based on the greater antiquity of roads and settlements should be jettisoned. Textbooks, I suspect, may tend to encourage entrenched or stereotyped ideas, yet they should reflect the gaps in our knowledge and the variability of the processes that we do know about.

Landscape history and landscape archaeology span many disciplinary boundaries. They draw upon an amazing range of

Figure 0.1   Reading the landscape involves a careful questioning of the details of the scene. Here, a probing beneath the turf of the trough just beyond the trees showed that it was a routeway paved in stone. The trees are standing on a bank which may have been part of a deer park boundary, while stones around the foot of the trees probably come from a former building, though some may be from a wall which once stood on the bank. Faint traces of elongated, perhaps pre-Conquest buildings, lie in the area of shadows.

expertise and their followers should have no problems about asking for help. A researcher such as Steve Moorhouse, who has advanced skills in the different fields of pottery, earthworks and place-names, is quite exceptional. I certainly have no reservations about asking for expert advice—and do so quite often. The list of specialist skills associated with landscape research is a daunting one. All could systematically be learned by someone with sufficient reserves of intelligence and longevity, but I suspect that there is another gift that is crucial, even though I cannot give it a name. It concerns a special aptitude for looking at shapes and recognising how fragmentary lines in the landscape can be identified, expanded, linked and converted into shapes which emerge as former polities or furlongs or routeways or elements of settlements. I am still not sure how this skill can be taught, but I do believe that it can be cultivated.

Certainty is uncommon in landscape history, where the evidence often consists of no more than a few smeared earthworks and an ambiguous mention in an old document. Impetuousness may lead one dashing in a false direction. The hardest person to convince of a pet theory should be oneself, and ideas should be tested on the most severely critical of colleagues. Sites are never seen twice in exactly the same way and interpretations should be supported by visits in varying conditions of light and vegetation growth. Places that seem quite barren of earthworks may reveal sets of features when inspected at dawn on a January or February morning, when the grass is at its shortest and slanting rays pick up the shallowest banks and hollows. Surveying will give rise to a special familiarity, but sites should be revisited even after surveying is finished, for on certain very special occasions a whole complex of ridges and troughs may suddenly be resolved into a meaningful pattern.

The first version of *Reading the Landscape* was written in the hope that, by encouraging the processes of landscape discovery, support would be found for more effective conservational measures and improved access to the countryside. Times have changed, conservational and educational budgets have been slashed, while managers, some with fake academic titles, marketing consultants and accountants have replaced the people of real learning and vision. Rather than preserving the heritage for the generation yet to come, one now thinks in terms of recording the past before the evidence is destroyed. However, the pace of destruction makes the task of recording even more important. Perhaps generations will follow that are more concerned about the origins of our setting than we are. With little if any old countryside remaining it is even more important that we should leave records as blueprints for mental or physical reconstructions.

Publisher's Note

Sources for the references and quotations in the text of the book will be found at the end of each chapter.

CHAPTER 1

Woodlands, Forests and Parks

Woodlands form an essential component in most perceptions of the English countryside. These woods have a wide variety of ages and origins and they are amongst the most threatened of landscape features. It might be imagined that the woodlands still surviving simply represent fragments of natural countryside which persist after the expansion of agriculture and settlement into the remaining areas, but this is far from being the case. Natural woodland in Britain has been regarded as 'the wildwood'; Rackham wrote that 'In order that "wildwood" should mean something that actually existed, rather than a mere ideal, I propose to use the term to mean prehistoric vegetation as it was just before the impact of civilization, at approximately 4,000 calendar years B.C.' (1988 p.3). No remnants of the wildwood survive and there is uncertainty about the appearance and composition of the lost natural woodlands. Woods have a wide variety of origins, but almost all have existed to fulfil some particular function for the local community. Frequently, this role has been abandoned during the modern era, so that many woods endure as relics of a former system of countryside management. In such ways, the interpretation of the woodland landscapes involves as much (if not more) material of a cultural and historical nature as it does botanical evidence.

Background

The story of woodlands in Britain extends backwards to the colonisation of open tundra landscapes by trees in the aftermath of the last Ice Age. Information about the nature of this process is obtainable from pollen analysis or palynology, the outlines of which were described by Godwin in 1934. The significance of pollen evidence is easy to comprehend:

> Pollen is shed in vast amounts from vegetation and is concentrated in soils and consolidated sediments where the walls of the grains resist decay and the pollen can therefore be recovered by suitable mechanical and chemical treatments. Since pollen grains exhibit a wide range of size, shape and wall pattern, and have distinctive numbers and disposition of pores and furrows, it is possible to recognise [under high magnification] the family, genus, and sometimes even the species of plant to which a given grain belongs. (Brooks and Johannes, 1990 p.88)

The grains may be preserved indefinitely in moist, acidic conditions, though the pollen evidence retrieved from bogs and the beds of ponds needs to be treated with care, making allowance for the amounts of pollen produced by particular species and whether they were wind-pollinated or insect-pollinated. Where pollen can be sampled from a dated sequence of levels then the vegetational history of a locality may be reconstructed. In the North York Moors, for example, Simmons found that:

> If we take the introduction of agriculture in the region to have happened about 3500 bc/5500 BP, then between that date and the final traces of periglacial conditions in 8300 bc/10,250 BP, any human

occupance of the land was accompanied by rapid environmental change as climatic conditions ameliorated. The result was the fast replacement of tundra-like vegetation (and presumably the accompanying suite of animals) by forests of pine and birch and then of mixed deciduous species, with a mature forest mostly dominated by oak being established by 7000 bc/8950 BP. It seems likely that this forest left no open ground above it except where conditions were very wet, though at its lower levels it may have contained more pine. (1995 p.7)

During the last glaciation, most of Britain was covered in ice and woodland was relegated to small areas in the mountains of southern Europe. The ensuing story, as reconstructed by researchers such as Huntley and dated in radiocarbon years before present, runs roughly as follows. Tree birch was among the first species to recolonise Britain, being abundant by 12,000 years ago. Willow had also established a presence and so too may rowan and Scots pine. A rapid chilling of the climate took place 11,000 years ago, but a sustained warming was in progress by 10,000 years ago. By 9,000 years ago, Scots pine was strongly established in the south of Britain but then its northward spread was overtaken and cut off by the rapid advance of the warmth-demanding broadleaves. Elm and oak spread across the dry continental shelf to colonise south-western England, while at this time hazel had become abundant throughout Britain. Between 9,000 and 7,000 years ago, Britain gained its dominant cover of broadleafed woodland.

The composition of the woodland varied from place to place. Alder, which appeared about 9,500 years ago but was at first confined to estuarine areas, did not become widespread in Britain until about 7,000 years ago, perhaps being restricted by an absence of suitable, damp soils (Beales,

1980). Today, it is common in the wet lowlands, while ash assumes a dominant role in the dry limestone uplands. Bearing in mind that lime is insect-pollinated and does not disperse its pollen as widely as the other common forest trees, Rackham argues that 'In the Lowland Zone, to summarize a complex situation, the commonest tree . . . was almost certainly lime. This was combined with oak, hazel, and various other trees such as pine in the East Anglian Breckland and ash in Somerset' (1976 p.41). Lime remained confined in eastern Europe when the broadleaves were establishing their dominance in Britain, but it arrived about 7,000 years ago and expanded northwards, becoming abundant in some areas. Lime, ash and yew spread and helped to diversify the lowland forest. Beech does not appear to have had a presence in Britain until 3,000 years ago and it has been suggested that it was introduced by humans, though it was more probably dispersed by natural processes—perhaps with the seeds being carried by jays (Huntley, 1998). Pine, which had failed in competition with the more rapidly expanding deciduous species in northern England, established a dominance in the west of Scotland around 8,000 years ago and then expanded to colonise the Scottish Highlands.

The natural woodlands were varied: 'Recent studies in pollen analysis have shown that wildwoods were not the uniform "mixed oak forest" of earlier authors but a complex mosaic of different kinds such as limewoods, oakwoods, hazelwoods, ashwoods, elmwoods, and pinewoods. In general, oakwoods and hazelwoods predominated in north and west England, limewoods in the Midlands, east, and south' (Rackham, 1985 p.70). The processes of colonisation, competition and replacement did not necessarily culminate in the establishment of stable vegetation patterns, while human interventions distorted the natural processes. In Epping Forest, for example: 'From the Neolithic until the early Saxon period lime-dominated woodland persisted; lime underwent a dramatic decline between A.D. 600 and 840 and this is interpreted to reflect selective forest clearance during the middle Saxon period. The familiar beech–birch and oak–hornbeam associations of the Forest today developed only after this Saxon phase' (Baker *et al.*, 1978 p.645).

As the wildwood was becoming established, so it experienced interference from humans, firstly by Mesolithic hunting communities, who may have used fire to create upland hunting ranges, and then by Neolithic farmers engaged in expanding their agricultural activities. In upland areas like the South Pennines, North Yorkshire Moors, and Dartmoor, advancing trees failed to establish a natural treeline and it is now recognised that Mesolithic communities had a considerable impact on the wildwood as they sought to concentrate game in cleared upland areas: 'The creation of a clearance in this forest fringe zone would have allowed the browse plants—alder, birch, rowan, and hazel—to flourish, the ash from clearance fires increasing the fertility of the soil for a brief period. Concentrations of luxuriant browse would undoubtedly have encouraged animals to congregate: at such times they could more easily be picked off by man in comparative leisure' (Cunliffe, 1985 p.51).

Around 3700 BC, a marked decline of the elm becomes apparent in the pollen record, and this has been associated with an acceleration in the spread of farming. Troels-Smith (1960) argued that it was caused by farmers who were pollarding elms to gather leaves for use as animal fodder, and who were consequently causing a reduction in the amount of pollen that the trees could produce. More recently, there have been suspicions that the elm decline could be related to the modern Dutch elm disease epidemic, it being known that the beetles responsible were present here at that time (Girling and Grieg, 1985). The reconstruction of ancient woodland patterns has tended to rely on environmental evidence, particularly on palynology, and other techniques which are prominent in many aspects of prehistorical research are less effective: 'Certain types of past activity do not leave readily identifiable traces in the aerial photographic record. Areas of former woodland, which would have played an important role in the local economy, are difficult to identify with any certainty' (Stoertz, 1997 p.9).

The process of agricultural colonisation and woodland clearance in the Kennet valley region of Wiltshire was studied by Smith (1984). Local openings in the wildwood cover were made in the Mesolithic period, but Smith thought that 'There can be little doubt that untouched climax forest still dominated the early neolithic scene and, though sizeable inroads were being made into it over a wide front, it is clear that some clearances were only transitory' (p.114). For the next phase, one in which a regeneration of woodland seems apparent in some parts of the country, it was found that 'Snail and pollen evidence both point to continued, if uneven, opening up of the region during the mid neolithic. Selected small clearings on the periphery of the valley corridor were expanded, mainly, one suspects, to increase pastoral resources, but some ... were brought into arable use for the first time' (p.116). By the period which followed, the wildwood had been fragmented into wooded archipelagos standing in an otherwise open landscape, for 'Late neolithic pollen assemblages clearly indicate a paucity of woodland, yet many cleared areas were, to judge from the upsurge in bracken, hazel and thornscrub, being poorly maintained' (p.117). It was once imagined that ancient cultivation was confined to the light soils of the uplands, but the 'picture of neolithic valleys as oak-tangled morasses

Figure 1.1   A flint axe in a reconstructed haft. This was the tool that allowed England to become an agricultural land.

must now be finally put aside . . . valley land was preferred for both agriculture and settlement from the outset' (p.118).

The clearance of the English wildwood was essentially an achievement of the prehistoric communities, though it will frequently have been a complex process, often involving the selective removal of trees from the best quality agricultural land, phases of colonisation and expansion from such core areas, and also phases of retreat from the agricultural margins and from land damaged by destructive farming practices. The ancient communities will never have sought the total removal of woodland, and for most a time will have come when it was necessary to make decisions about the conservation of trees in order to obtain renewable supplies of timber necessary for

fencing, tool-making, house-building and many other uses.

The story of the prehistoric removal of the wildwood is one that can be read only through the ancient pollen record. When the picture is more complete it will tell of phases of confidence and prosperity when farmers cleared and farmed the more marginal areas, and also of phases of disruption and decay, when agriculture retreated and the woodland reclaimed the abandoned farmlands. Essentially, however, one must remember that the pacification of the countryside was not accomplished by Anglo-Saxons or Romans but took place well back in prehistory. Taylor wrote that:

Recent work by a new generation of scientists, using highly complex and sophisticated techniques, has shown that, far from there being dense impenetrable forests throughout prehistoric times, the great attack on woodland in England started as early as 5500 BC, and that this continued fairly steadily so that by about 1000 BC there was probably less woodland in England than there is now. Thus the primeval forests that inhibited settlement and movement in prehistoric and Roman times have been removed from our maps. (1983 p.20)

Medieval woodland

Medieval woods were normally 'natural' woodland rather than plantations; they consisted of wild trees which were managed and cropped but not cultivated. The earliest detailed indication of the extent of woodland in England is provided by Domesday Book. According to Rackham: 'Medieval England was one of the least wooded countries in Europe ... woodland in Domesday Book (including wood pasture) adds up to only 15 per cent of the land area, a smaller proportion than France has now. Woods were a small, important, and permanent part of the landscape' (1985 pp.76–7). There had not been a great deal more woodland in Saxon England, while by the fourteenth century only about 6 per cent of the English kingdom was wooded. Woods were not entirely permanent, but could advance and retreat in relation to social changes; woods seem to have advanced during the period of instability and economic decline following the collapse of Roman rule, while they retreated as swelling rural populations attempted to secure extra farmland during the eleventh, twelfth and thirteenth centuries. However, any wood that survived intact to the arrival of the Black Death in 1348 had a very good chance of surviving for the next 500 years (Rackham, 1998).

Woodland must have been managed since well back in prehistoric times, and medieval woodland was thoroughly and comprehensively organised, even though the pattern of management evolved. The primary use of woodland was as a source of fuel in the form of faggots or charcoal, while

The key notion we can employ to interprete [sic] the history of the forest is that of intensification. Open woodland populated by a scattering of deer was the least intensive of all forms of land utilisation (though whether such a pastoral paradise ever existed may be doubted). The wood also supported cattle and at some periods at least, pigs. The exploitation of woodland for coppicing compelled the enclosure of woods to allow the timber to regenerate, forcing the deer and cattle to graze within a smaller area. The competition between the two obliged the creation of parks and clearings (lawns) from which cattle were barred. But the woodland area was also progressively reduced. It was undermined by the demand for arable in the twelfth, thirteenth and early fourteenth centuries. (Hoyle, 1997 p.19)

The two essential forms of woodland management were wood-pasture, recorded in Domesday as *silva pastilis*, and coppiced woodland, known as *silva minuta*. Wood-pasture represented a very delicate balance between two normally incompatible forms of exploitation, forestry and grazing: 'The more trees there are, the less abundant and the worse will be the pasture; and the more animals there are, the less likely saplings or coppice shoots are to survive to produce a new generation of trees' (Rackham, 1986 p.120). The problems posed by livestock damaging the trees by browsing on soft leafy growth was resolved by pollarding the trees above the reach of cattle: a crop of poles would grow from the top of the permanent tree or 'bolling', yielding light timber and leaf fodder. Lennard described the 'denes' of the Weald where pannage and mast were available to herds of pigs foraging for acorns and beech nuts on the woodland floor: 'denes or denns were woodland swine pastures lying at a distance from the manors to which they belonged ...

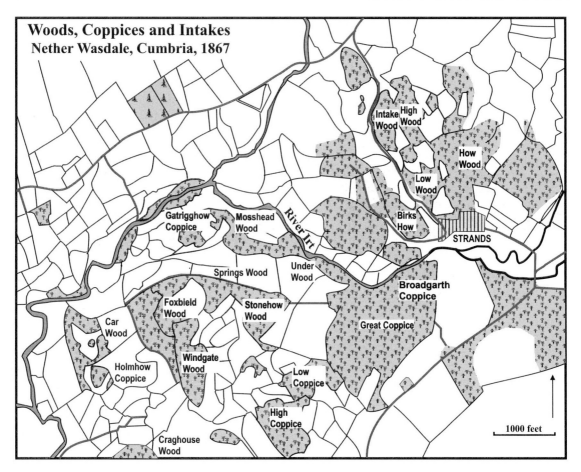

Woods, Coppices and Intakes
Nether Wasdale, Cumbria, 1867

Intake Wood
High Wood
How Wood
Low Wood
Birks How
STRANDS
Gatrigghow Coppice
Mosshead Wood
River Irt
Springs Wood
Under Wood
Broadgarth Coppice
Foxbield Wood
Stonehow Wood
Great Coppice
Car Wood
Windgate Wood
Holmhow Coppice
Low Coppice
High Coppice
Craghouse Wood
1000 feet

Map 1.1   Woods, coppices and intakes, Nether Wasdale, Cumbria. The map shows the fragmentation of an expanse of woodland by agricultural expansion and the conversion of most remaining areas into coppiced woodland. The name 'Springs Wood' probably denotes a medieval coppice, though Spring may sometimes derive from a word for a net used in catching game.

The denes were swine pastures; but they tended to develop into something more. As swineherds felled trees to build their huts and provide themselves with fuel, the clearing would tend to grow and tillage might begin' (1997 pp.14–15).

Most of the Domesday wood-pasture was found on commons, and this form of land-use covered extensive areas of Norman England—24 per cent of Derbyshire and

$10\frac{1}{2}$ per cent of Nottinghamshire (Rackham, 1986 p.121), while in the well-wooded Vale of York wood-pasture became more common as one moved towards the Dales. In the north, leafy branches that were lopped from pollards and used as fodder were known as 'green-hews', and in Wensleydale as 'deer fall', while in Tudor times the clerks of Fountains Abbey referred to them as 'watter boughs'. Some of the browse was fed to wild deer; the accounts of the grave of Tanshelf in West Yorkshire for 1420–1 include the wages of a man for felling boughs to feed the 'wild beasts' (Yorkshire Archaeological Society MS 508).

Wood-pasture was extremely sensitive to change and Rackham notes that 'By 1300 wood-pasture commons had greatly diminished. In some the grazing element had got

the upper hand and they had become heaths or grassland. Others had been en-coppiced and made into private woods. Others had become Forests or parks' (1986 p.121). In northern parts of England a revolution in woodland management appears to have come rather later, between 1400 and 1550, in both north and south Yorkshire, when there were changes from wood-pasture to coppice with standards.

In the landscape today, there are few obvious signs of the former importance of wood-pasture. In some places, like Swaledale, traces of a pollarding regime can still be recognised (Fleming, 1998). At an early stage in the medieval period here, an opening-up of the landscape created wood-pasture, and as pressure on the countryside increased the wood-pastures became pastures with pollards, which changed in turn

Figure 1.2 Although not all the trees are pollarded, this scene in the New Forest at the supposed spot where William Rufus was killed whilst hunting in 1100 resembles a medieval wood-pasture countryside.

into hay meadows. The tradition of pollarding continued after the clearance of the wood-pastures. Elms, ashes, alder and, surprisingly, hawthorn were pollarded and the elm will have produced useful leaf fodder, while evergreen winter fodder could be obtained from holly woods, often still identified by the name 'Hollins'. Fleming calculated that the tree ring evidence suggests that pollarding was abandoned in the early to mid-nineteenth century, while tree girth measurements at the rate of ½ inch per annum imply that 'almost all of the pollards were planted in the fifteenth, sixteenth and seventeenth centuries' (p.73). By exploring clues originating in the cultural landscape, in documents and in place-names, he was able to demonstrate the former existence of wood-pasture:

> In saluting the work of hill farming families, we must not lose sight of more communal farming systems, now severely attenuated, which have a much longer pedigree in Swaledale. The most obvious reminder of this is the existence of common cow pastures and common moors . . . Common pasture rights are still exercised. And since there is frequently a link between common pasture rights and wood-pasture traditions, it must be worth asking whether Swaledale, despite its 'walls and hay meadows' image, once had a tradition of wood pasture. In fact the dale is quite well wooded, and its old coppice stools, pollards and ancient tree

boles raise numerous questions about the history of woodland management here. (p.57)

Working in another dale, the author discovered a different situation (Muir, forthcoming: *Rural History*). In Nidderdale, it appears that as the common resources of wood-pasture were removed when land was enclosed by private owners in the later medieval period, the wood-pasture timber supply was replaced by poles and fodder grown on pollards planted in the expanding hedgerow network.

Coppice with standards provided a quite different system of managing woodland and producing woodland products. Most native trees are self-renewing and if coppiced or cut down close to ground level will exist as 'stools' which soon send up crops of leafy fodder and poles. When managed as a coppiced crop that is felled every few years, the trees are regularly re-envigorated and

Table 1.1   Medieval wood-management systems

System	Original appearance	Appearance after long neglect
Pollards/ wood-pasture	Short trunks or 'bollings' crowned with thickets of poles or bushy plumes of foliage. Trees were sufficiently well spaced to allow grass to grow between them in wood-pasture.	Short, gnarled trunks, often hollow, with about three to six heavy, twisted boughs all arising from the same height. Likely to be 250+ years old and pollarding may have been neglected for two centuries.
Coppice	'Stools', like tree stumps cut almost at ground level, from which slender poles and leafy rods arose. The stools were just a few feet apart and the underwood was quite dense. Wood banks were provided to exclude livestock.	A few trunks arising from the same point on the woodland floor producing an effect rather like the tentacles of an inverted octopus. The trunks can be 2 feet or more in diameter. Woodbanks eroded and sometimes indistinct.
Coppice with standards	Standards with straight, slender trunks devoid of branches at the lower level towering over a 'fuzzy' underwood of coppice stools.	The more vigorous of the upgrowths from the neglected coppice stools beginning to compete with any of the older surviving standards.
Shredding	Lower boughs stripped from the trunk of a tree, leaving a plume of foliage remaining at the top. Not a common practice.	The evidence of shredding is only occasionally seen.

Figure 1.3 This hornbeam coppice in Epping Forest could be 1,000 or more years old. A single tree was repeatedly rejuvenated by coppicing for many centuries until abandoned by the woodsmen perhaps a century or so ago.

will live virtually indefinitely: coppiced beeches in southern England could be a thousand years old. Coppice woodland was cut on rotations which varied according to the nature of the fodder, fuel or timber required: felling cycles of four, five, seven, ten and fourteen years are among those mentioned in medieval documents, while in the south of Yorkshire 20–25 year coppicing cycles are noted. In most coppice woods the interior was divided into falls, which were coppiced at different times; such woods can sometimes be recognised by 'hag' or 'fall' elements in their names. Standing at intervals among the coppice stools of the underwood one would frequently have seen trees, notably oak and elm, allowed to grow tall as 'standards' and from which heavy, constructional timber could have been harvested. In the south of Yorkshire a 'waver' was a standard that had grown through one coppice cycle', a 'blackbark' had been through two, and a 'lording' through three (Jones, 1998). It was sometimes assumed that the age of surviving woodland standards can be calculated by measuring a tree's girth and assuming one year for every $\frac{1}{2}$ inch of circumference (it was sometimes the case to allow $\frac{3}{4}$ inch for trees grown in the open and Mitchell (1966) allowed one inch). A more sophisticated, but technically complex dating technique proposed by White (1995) allows for different growth rates in different species and recognises that trees will grow rapidly until their crowns have reached their maximum extent, but will increase their girths at much slower rates as they mature and grow old.

In medieval (and prehistoric) times the demand for woodland products would have been phenomenal; they were used for fodder, fuel, house-building and ship-building and other uses not practised today. Rackham notes that 'A typical fifteenth-century Suffolk farmhouse, rather larger than average, turns out to be made of some 330 trees. Only three trees were as much as 18 inches in diameter, a usual size for a mature oak nowadays; half of them were less than 9 inches in diameter, and one in ten was as small as 6 inches' (1986 p.87). Ideas such as these are of particular interest to the landscape historian because they relate the *dwelling* to its *setting*. Similarly, Rackham (1997) notes of the two surviving thirteenth-century barns at Cressing Temple in Essex that they served an immense estate with 1,300 acres of demesne land which functioned to finance the Templars' crusading wars and support superannuated knights. About 8 per cent was woodland, of which about one-tenth was felled and sold each year. The barns were built of oak, though curved braces of elm were used in the rebuilding of the aisle walls of the Barley Barn in the fifteenth century. Rackham attempted to reconstruct the entire contents of the Barley Barn:

> These added up originally to some 4,030 cubic feet of timber from 480 trees. The diameters of these trees ranged from about seven to 24 inches, the great majority being smallish oaks nine to 10 inches in diameter at the base. Making reasonable assumptions about growth rates and the relation between timber trees and the underwood, I reckon that they amount to fifty years' growth of timber on 12.2 acres of coppice-wood. (This ignores the probability that some of the bigger trees did not come from woodland.) (p.76)

The structural timbers in most medieval buildings were small trees, which had grown swiftly, the underwood suppressing the growth of side branches below about 15 feet up the trunk, and such trees would normally be felled before reaching 100 years in age. The medieval carpenters were ingenious in their use of timbers that had grown naturally to form useful shapes; little timber was wasted and the sawing-out of shapes was avoided so far as possible, with the timber being incorporated in house frames in a green or unseasoned condition.

Coppice woodland was particularly vulnerable to damage by grazing and had to be provided with boundaries that would exclude animals. Such boundaries were also needed to deter encroachments by humans attracted by the value of woodland products and the shortage of land: 'Coppicing was all part of the trend found in the management of the medieval forest away from the idea of forest as commons towards private enclosure and exploitation' (Harvey, 1997 pp.17–18). Substantial banks and ditches were employed to exclude interlopers, with a hedge often being planted atop the bank. During the medieval period, coppice woodland succeeded wood-pasture, but it, too, was destined to vanish. Writing of Ecclesall Woods, Sheffield, Jones and Walker noted:

> The timing of the change from coppice management to high forest management has simply been based on three facts: that we know that coppicing was being carried out in Eccleshall Woods in the eighteenth century, that within living memory the woods have had their present high forest part plantation character, and that coppicing gradually disappeared as a woodland management practice in the local area between the beginning of the Victorian period and the outbreak of the First World War. (1997 p.11)

Coppice woodland tended to survive longer in the south, where it gradually became restricted to the counties ringing London.

Figure 1.4 Most pollards today are either near the end of their lives or displaying the branch growth resulting from the abandonment of pollarding for a century or more.

Today, most woods display the evidence of long-abandoned systems of management, apparent in out-grown and distorted coppice and pollard trees, though in very few of them can one find pollarding and coppicing still in operation.

The landscape archaeology of woodland

Most wooded areas have experienced a succession of uses, some or all of them leaving physical evidence after their abandonment. The woodland floor may be grooved and ridged in ways that reveal much about the history of the place. Of the Worcestershire parish of Hanbury, Dyer wrote: 'After virtually the whole area had been farmed in the Roman period, much woodland regenerated, to the point that the expansion of the early Middle Ages involved little clearance of primeval wild wood. Rather the assarters must often have encountered in their work the eroded and

Figure 1.5   This New Forest pollard must date from some time well before 1698, for it was in this year that pollarding there was made illegal since the cutting of branches to lie as deer fodder was thought to be potentially depriving the Navy of heavy timber.

overgrown banks and ditches of Romano-British farmsteads and field systems: they were recolonizing abandoned land' (1991 p.27). Woodland often covers ground which was previously settled and cultivated; wholesale advances of woodland must have taken place after the collapse of Roman power in Britain and more localised expansions will have followed the outbreaks of the Black Death. A woodland floor corrugated by plough ridges reveals the retreat of cultivation, hillforts or round barrows will probably denote an open prehistoric countryside, while other earthworks can testify to the operation of former woodland practices. They include saw pits, charcoal pans, the places where charcoal burners periodically camped to exploit the surrounding woodland, while white coal kilns were hollows which had a spout at one end. These kilns produced kiln-dried timber which was mixed with charcoal; one wood in South Yorkshire has 200 examples (Jones, 1998).

The most significant earthworks are likely to be those which bounded the wood or its components. Wood banks fronted by ditches and often crowned by hedges or pollards defined and protected the territorial integrity of the medieval wood, while inside, earthworks were needed to ensure the exclusion of livestock from the coppice divisions or panels, where tender young growth was vulnerable to browsing. Rackham wrote that 'The visitor to an unknown wood should first walk the boundary. A typical medieval wood boundary has a strong bank with an external ditch, 20 to 40 feet in total width . . . The profile is usually rounded but may be steeper on the outer face. There are often pollard trees halfway down the outer slope. Where the bank turns a sharp corner there is a corner mound' (1986 p.98). The bank normally carried a hedge, while the legal boundary of the wood could be marked by a line of pollards. The more imposing the wood bank earthworks, the older the wood is likely to be. The pattern was not standardised; some woods, particularly sections that were bordered by roads, had double wood banks, while some woods were walled rather than embanked. In most cases, the main product of a wood was the fuel produced in the coppiced underwood. The underwood was divided into panels or hags which were cut in sequence, one every year, and these panels were also defended by earthworks. The nature of woodland boundaries vary from place to place and in the southern part of the Vale of York the ancient woods can be seen to be ringed by ditches, both for drainage and for protection.

Woodland place-names

Much useful information can be gained from a survey of medieval and earlier place-names associated with woodland. These are listed in Table 1.2. The evidence of place-names should be handled with far more caution than was normal in the past. Nevertheless, within a once-wooded area the names can be informative about the nature and species of the old woodland.

In the Scandinavian parts of England, strange sounding terminations, such as *lundr*, *skogr* and *viothr* are incorporated in the place-names; all three mean 'wood.'

Table 1.2 Place-names associated with woodland

Name element	Meaning
wood (OE *wudu*) with, worth (ON *vithr*) shaw*, shay, shave (OE *sceaga*)	A wood
lund, lound or land (ON *lundr*) frith (OE *fyrhth*) beare (OE *bearu*)	These names are associated with very old woods
skew, scoe (ON *skōgr*) holt (OE *holt*)	A wood, perhaps a single-species wood
shaw* (OE *sceaga*) rewe	A band of woodland bounding a field in the Weald
grove (OE *grāfa*)	A small wood

Table 1.2   Place-names associated with woodland—continued

Name element	Meaning
ley (OE *lēah*)	A clearing *or* a wood
den, dene (OE *denn*)	A woodland swine pasture (NB OE *denu*: a valley)
copse fall hag(g) spring copy panel	These names are associated with coppiced woodland
launde	Woodland glade, lawn
ryth thwaite (ON *thveit*)	A clearing
hurst (OE *hyrst*)	A wooded hill
hanger (OE *hangra*)	A wood on a slope
hay	Hedge, sometimes an enclosure in a wood, assart or the hedge around a deer park; can be small wood in farmland
ridding rode (OE *rodu*) reed royd sart stocks stubbings	Assarted land
ovenham	Assart in the Yorkshire Wolds
hollins	Wood where holly was grown as winter fodder
storth (ON *storth*)	Brushwood, woodland plantation
stock stump	Tree stump
stubbing	Area cleared of tree stumps
field (OE *feld*)	Open ground close to woodland
coed (W *coid*)	A wood
bere (OE *bearu*)	A grove

In the Pennine valley of the Ure was the Forest of Wensleydale. The name Wensley itself means 'Waendel's clearing.' Higher up the valley there is a sequence of parish and other names that also mean wood; West Witton is the 'farm in the wood' (*wudu ton*); Ellerlands is 'alder wood' (*elri lundr*); Aysgarth is the 'open space by the oaks' (*eik skarth*); Lunds is 'wood' (*lundr*); Brindley is the 'clearing caused by fire' (*brende lēah*); Litherskew is the 'wood on the slope' (*lithr skógr*). (Darby, 1951 p. 73)

A useful discussion on place-names associated with trees, woods, forests and clearings is provided in Gelling (1993 pp.188–229).

Forests and parks

Different forms of hunting territory existed in the medieval realm. *Forests* were expanses of countryside, some parts owned directly by the Crown and some part of the realm, which were subjected to stringent laws designed to preserve the game for royal hunting parties. *Chases* were private hunting territories, often lying within larger estates, in which the owners, the greater nobles and churchmen, hunted. *Parks* were more confined and more strongly enclosed places in which deer and other game were secured until the day of the hunt. While the Saxon kings probably controlled hunting estates in various parts of the realm, it was the Normans who institutionalised the concept of a Forest as an area with its own form of law. It is important to conceptualise the Forest as an area which would probably contain a spectrum of land-uses and which was not composed solely of woodland. Thirteen townships and the town of Knaresborough shared a single vast common in the Forest of Knaresborough, though their swine were banned when young deer were vulnerable in spring and the earlier part of summer. Different experts have

---

Map 1.2   The Forest of Knaresborough. The Forest extended for many miles along the south side of the River Nidd. Developed from Jennings (1970).

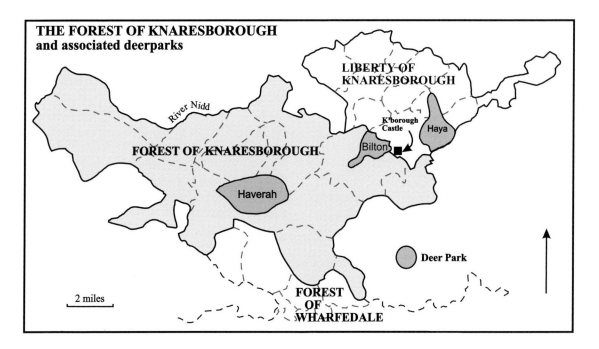

suggested vastly different estimates of the proportion of the total Forest territory which was actually wooded, and Rackham proposed a figure as low as one-fifth (1980 pp.175–9). The Forests did not correlate so much with woodland as with existing royal estates and seats of power such as castles and palaces. A maximum of about 160 Forests were created, only around half of them covering well-wooded territory. Most of Sherwood Forest was heath and Dartmoor Forest was moorland. Confusion between the *total* extent of Forests and the *wooded* forest area has resulted in the gross exaggeration of the area of England that was actually wooded under Norman and Plantagenet kings.

The term 'forest' is inherited from the Merovingian Franks and appeared in their charters in the seventh century; whatever its original meaning may have been, it came to be understood as being an area which stood outside ordinary laws (Rackham, 1989 p.38). The first mention of Forests comes in 1086, when Domesday Book recorded about 25 examples. Once introduced, the Forests not only imposed burdensome legal restrictions on the public, they also deflected patterns of landscape development. As Cantor described, 'the forceful application of the forest laws prevented landowners and farmers in the areas covered by it from agricultural improvements that involved clearing the land and extending the cultivated area. Indeed, tillage of the areas already under cultivation must have been very difficult, as the cultivator was not allowed to erect hedges to prevent the deer from gaining access to his crops' (1982 p.58). Hunting, however, seldom remained the primary use for a Forest; it was superimposed upon other uses, such as the generation of income from 'fines' on woodland users. Rather than hunting at every opportunity, the medieval kings tended to consume meat which had been killed by their huntsmen elsewhere, preserved in salt and despatched to the current royal abode.

Once a Forest had come into being it had to be administered and managed and evidence of former uses may endure in names or field monuments:

> the large areas of forest demanded administrative sub-divisions for day-to-day management. They were usually called 'walks' or 'bailiwicks': forest districts in which a keeper had charge of the game and the woods. The actual woods were often called coppices . . . Between coppices were 'ridings' and 'plains', open and often extensive zones of grass and scattered trees providing herbage for deer. 'Lawns' were enclosed plots of grassland managed to provide hay and pasture for deer and were normally situated close to the keeper's 'lodge'. Such lodges, which by the thirteenth century were often moated for defence against poachers, were scattered in the forest and thus produced a curious dispersed settlement pattern of isolated houses. (Taylor and Muir, 1983 pp.314–15).

The Forests reached their greatest extent under Henry II (1154–89) but thereafter they declined in number and extent, though during the thirteenth century about one-fifth of the realm is thought still to have been Forest (Bazeley, 1921 p.165). Areas known as 'purlieus' encompassed land removed from Forest law in the reign of Edward I or earlier, yet within which the royal deer were protected. During the centuries that followed, the Forests declined, and although they produced income from fines and various economic activities, they were costly to administer and maintain. The treasury was usually pressed for funds and the Forests were a valuable economic asset. Their resources of timber, pannage and farmland were heavily exploited, new enterprises, like vaccaries or cattle farms and horse farms were introduced, while if the Crown lands were sold they produced considerable revenues. Rackham noted that

'What the king got from his Forests varied from one to another. From Dean he had minerals, underwood, timber, red and fallow deer and wild swine, but few Forests produced more than two of these. From all Forests together he had less than a thousand deer a year, a few hundred big oaks and pollards, and some thousands of acres of underwood; these did not represent an intensive use of at least half a million acres of physical royal Forest' (Rackham, 1986 p.138).

From the fourteenth century, the waning of royal interests in the Forests became marked and the initiative passed to the local landowners and commoners, though lawns (deer pastures with hedges to exclude cattle), deer leaps and lodges were still being created in the sixteenth century. The end for several Forests arrived in the decades around 1800 in the form of Enclosure Acts: 'Their multiple land-uses, which could not be brought within the scope of cost-benefit analysis, were not understood by eighteenth-century agricultural writers: fashionable philosophy exalted conventional agriculture and despised the king's harts and the widow's geese. Forests were represented as the "nest and conservatory of sloth, idleness and misery"' (Rackham, 1986 p.139). Such sentiments were expressed by one Robert Stockdale regarding the commoners of the Forest of Knaresborough, whose commons were enclosed in 1770. The common, he claimed, 'afforded their families a little milk, yet they would attempt to keep a horse, and a flock of sheep. The first enabled them to stroll about the country in idleness, and the second, in the course of every three or four years, were so reduced by the rot, and other disasters, that upon the whole, they yielded no profit' (Brown, 1799 p.136).

Deer parks appeared in the countryside rather later than the Forests, but they became outstandingly important features, with at least 1,900 examples coming into existence during the medieval period. They take their name from the old French *parke*, which could denote both a hunting territory and an enclosure, so that 'park' names do not always reveal hunting areas. To some degree parks may have been intended to secure pasture for deer in the face of mounting grazing pressure from cattle, though in their later phases some parks became vaccaries or cattle farms. They can be regarded as private stores of game, exclusive areas of countryside, which, although they provided fresh meat for the lavish feasts and entertainments which featured so often in the lives of the medieval nobility, also supported many other activities. In contrast to the Forests, they were relatively compact—sometimes as small as 40 acres—and were strongly enclosed by earthworks, paling fences and hedges to confine their red and fallow deer (Cantor and Hatherly, 1979 p.71). Although their original boundaries could be massive, the limits of deer parks were not as fixed as many imagine, but could ebb and flow with changes in circumstance.

Cantor notes that 'deer-folds' existed in the Anglo-Saxon period and that in 1086 Domesday Book recorded the existence of 35 parks. The greatest expansion of parks came in the period 1200–1350, when population and agriculture were expanding and when surplus wealth was being produced to finance the creation of hunting parks and the purchase of the royal licences essential to their creation. The King owned the greatest number, but the great nobles and churchmen would frequently own large numbers of parks, like the Earls of Lancaster with 45, the Dukes of Cornwall with 29 and the Bishop of Winchester with 23 (Cantor, 1982 pp.76–7); a small galaxy of deer parks was associated with Richard III's castle at Middleham in Wensleydale.

The typical park of the thirteenth century had an area of 100–200 acres, but there were a few examples that exceeded 1,000 acres.

The parks were ringed by the formidable perimeter defences needed to contain the deer and exclude poachers. Earthen banks with inner ditches prevented the escape of the game and the banks might be crowned with a palisade of oak posts, a paling fence, a hedge or, as at the Royal Park at Northampton, a strong drystone wall. A wall or hedge positioned on the break of slope at the top of a steep slope was sometimes employed, as were double ditches separated by a bank and hedge or wall. Some parks had deer leaps, which were external ramps set against the boundary ramparts at a place where the pale was missing, but where the inner ditch was constructed on a grander scale, thus allowing deer access to the park while preventing their escape. Banks, palings and hedges placed on slopes could sometimes serve in a similar way. Parks tended to have oval or roughly circular

shapes and might be sited on the edge of manors, avoiding arable land, though there were exceptions, as at Newton-on-Ouse, where the deer park shared a boundary with one of the village's open fields. Sometimes parish boundaries are attached to sections of the peripheries of parks that were located at the margins of parishes. At Ripley, North Yorkshire, where the park appears to be a late example from the fifteenth century, a boundary was shared with the Forest of Knaresborough and much ridged plough-land was engulfed.

The case of Haverah Park, near Harrogate, is exceptional, for the former deer park forms a parish in its own right. The name may perhaps derive from the Old English 'hay', denoting a hedge, or perhaps 'wra' or 'roe', denoting a roe buck (Grainge, 1871 p. 339), or possibly an Old English term for 'hedgerow'. Three deer parks were established close to the castle town of Knaresborough, the administrative centre for the Forest of Knaresborough. Haverah Park was unusually large and covered 2,250

Map 1.3   Haverah Deer Park, North Yorkshire. This large park is unusual in that it constitutes an entire parish.

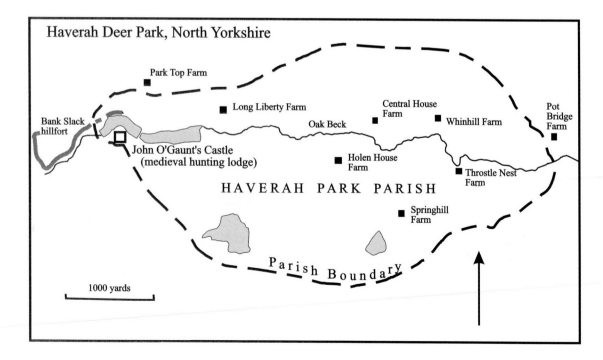

acres; it was oval in form and measured roughly 2¾ miles by 1½ miles. Close to the western boundary of the park are the ruins of a medieval hunting lodge known locally as John O' Gaunt's castle, which may date from around 1300. The land concerned appears to have been emparked shortly after 1173 by William de Stuteville, the lord of Knaresborough, with the other two parks in the locality, Bilton and Haya, being created by Richard, Earl of Cornwall, before 1244, when his brother, Henry III, provided him with deer from the Honour of Pontefract to stock the new parks (Jennings, 1970 p.47). The parks might have represented a response to a shortage of wild deer roaming free in the adjacent Forest. In the early fourteenth century Haverah Park appears, like many others, to have been used at least in part for the breeding of horses, and in 1333 the King ordered the Sheriff of Yorkshire to repair hedges, ditches and pales in the Forest of Knaresborough to prevent the escape of horses. All three parks in the vicinity of Knaresborough were employed for horse breeding in 1334. Cattle were also kept in the parks, while the existence of a forge at the start of the fourteenth century implies that adequate timber resources still existed. Some deer

Map 1.4   The former deer park at Beningbrough, near York. The name 'Coney Garth' denotes a protected medieval rabbit warren.

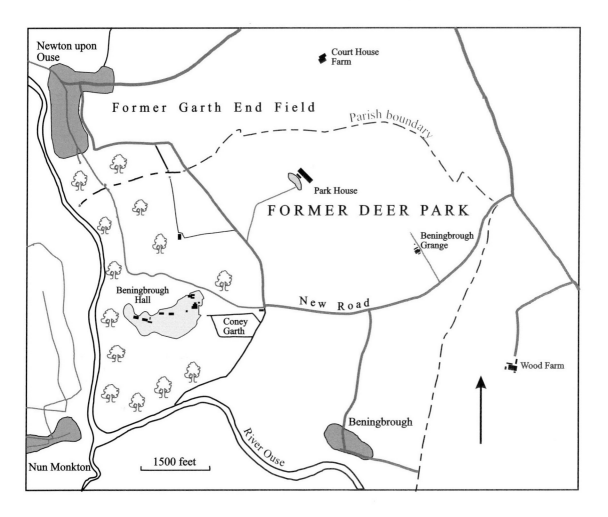

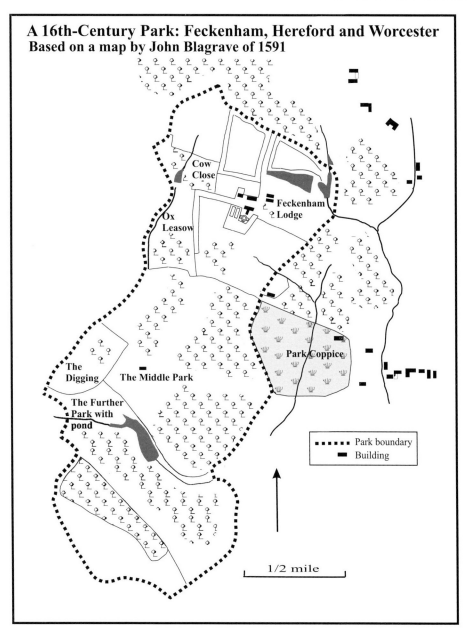

A 16th-Century Park: Feckenham, Hereford and Worcester
Based on a map by John Blagrave of 1591

Cow
Close

Ox
Leasow

Feckenham
Lodge

Park Coppice

The
Digging   The Middle Park

The Further
Park with
pond

■■■■■ Park boundary
■ Building

1/2 mile

Map 1.5   A sixteenth-century park: Feckenham,
Hereford and Worcester, based on a map by John
Blagrave of 1591. The map shows the
compartmentalisation characteristic of later parks,
with a variety of different activities being pursued.

remained in Haverah Park, and in 1499 they
numbered 160.

During the medieval period, enclosures
were made in the parks to create meadows
and horse pastures, while in the 1560s the
last of the deer disappeared owing to the
dereliction of the outer pale (Jennings, 1970
p.249). Haverah Park was sublet and some
of the four lodges were converted into
farmhouses. In 1628 the three parks were
sold by Charles I to raise money to pay off
loans; in 1639 Haverah Park was bought by

Table 1.3   The recognition of deer parks

Landscape feature	Nature of evidence
Parish boundary	Long, gently curving stretches tracing sections of the boundaries of the former park.
Bank and ditch inner earthworks	Ditto, with the ditch on the side of the curve.
Place-names	'Park' is frequently found attached to fields or farmsteads associated with a former park. Also note 'lodge' or 'hatch', a hatch being a wicket gate giving access to a wooded area, e.g. a park. 'Hay' denotes hedges, occasionally those bounding a park.

the Ingilby family of Ripley and sublet to tenants. In 1871 the parish-cum-former deer park was divided between thirteen farms, though today there are only six operational farmsteads within the boundaries of the park. Haverah parish had no substantial through-roads and no church or chapel and the community developed in a strange and exclusive manner. In mid-Victorian times Grainge noted that 'the few footpaths that necessary conveyance have made across it, are guarded, so that no stranger can enter without stating who he is, where he is going, and what he intends to do; and if the answers are not satisfactory, he is unceremoniously turned back. The motives for such conduct we cannot divine,

Table 1.4   Features associated with deer parks

Features	Evidence
Kennels	'Dog' or 'hound' place-names, like Dog Croft in Ripley park. These may reveal the kennels where hunting dogs were kept or the lanes where they were walked.
Lodges	These were the residences and offices of the parkers. The balance of functions in the park (recreational, agricultural or industrial) would influence the positioning of lodges. Frequently they were placed on the highest ground in the park, where they may be marked by 'lodge' place-names.
Hunting stands or towers	Game might be driven towards hunters positioned in a stand or tower, which could also be a venue for drinking and feasting. 'Trist' and 'stand' place-names may reveal the stands, which were normally on elevated plateaux. Platforms defined by dry moats could mark their sites.
Warrens	Square, domed or cigar-shaped pillow mounds may mark warren sites, as may 'clapper' or 'coney' place-names.
Fishponds	These may survive as earthworks, generally with low embankments on the floodplains but with substantial retaining banks when perched on slopes. Others can exist as scoops.
Quarries, mines	Stone, coal and iron were obtained from parks. Evidence is provided by the quarries, the earthworks of bell pits and the lanes used to remove the products.
Gardens	Normally these would be placed on the southern side of the manor, intervening between the house and the park. Pleasure mounts, terraces and ponds may be the more durable garden features.
Barns	Evidence can come from earthworks, normally faint, of the buildings, their entrances and the shallow mounds marking stack stands or stack garths where hay was stacked. 'Helm' and 'laithe' place-names mark barn sites.

unless it be to preserve the primitive virtues of the inhabitants from contamination by contact with the outward world' (p.344). Every year a festive meeting for the male members of the park was held at one of its farmsteads. No women were allowed to attend and Grainge thought that the custom might have derived from a ritual of the medieval park keepers and foresters (p.350).

The medieval deer park, though initially primarily a hunting reserve, served a variety of functions. The early parks were often associated with grassy lawns or laund deriving from the old French *'launde'* which then existed as clearings cut from woodland. Later, forestry could become a significant park industry. As the manor house became the venue for lavish entertainment provided for substantial parties—as occurred when a lord would progress around several of his manors, consuming surplus production at each stop—so a home park would sometimes be provided or carved out of the existing park. It would afford accommodation and pasture for the numerous draught and riding horses brought by the lord and his retinue. Monasteries had their own home parks, that of Fountains Abbey being particularly extensive (S. Moorhouse, pers. com.). Quarrying and mining were often pursued within a park, warrens could be found there and fishponds could be placed on the floodplains of streams or be perched on valley sides.

In seeking to recognise the presence of former deer parks in the rural landscape, the various types of evidence shown in Table 1.3 may be discovered. Within medieval deer parks a variety of features may be suggested by place-names or by earthworks. Some, like plough ridges or extremely old coppiced woodland or pollards, may pre-date the imposition of the park and be relics from the pre-existing countryside, while others reflect functions pursued within the old park.

Assarting and the landscape

Clearance or assarting considerably changed the woodland patterns; writing of England, Dyer noted that 'In the country as a whole the population is thought to have tripled between 1086 and 1300, and many woodland manors show a four or fivefold rise in numbers of tenants' (1991 p.27). Population growth in the period between Domesday and the arrival of the Black Death in 1348 put great pressure on the agricultural resources of the country and resulted, inevitably, in the expansion of pasture and ploughland at the expense of woodland. Darby quoted Bennett (1937 p.21): 'For a family burdened with more children than the shares in the common fields would warrant, such assart land was a godsend. Here they could utilise their spare labour, and produce something to fill the many hungry mouths at home'; and Darby added:

> The records of every county tell their own story of this spreading cultivation, and references to assarts are frequent in charters and chronicles and in the Close Rolls and Patent Rolls. Requests for permission to assart; grants of land 'with leave to assart'; gifts of land 'to be assarted as seems best'; records of 'new land recently brought into cultivation'; disputes about the 'tithes of assarts and clearings'—all these items are encountered again and again in the records of the Middle Ages. (1951 pp.78–9)

Others have questioned the efficacy of assarting as a relief from poverty and congestion. After studying the question in fourteenth-century West Yorkshire, Stinson wrote: 'assarting does nothing to redistribute wealth among those already holding land; it is possibly even more significant that it admits few others into the landholding structure' (1983 p.64). She added: 'The very poor were able to assart only when the privilege was so costly as to be itself a bane.

Such peasants probably lived in abject poverty and very probably died of starvation or the cruel diseases which attend on famine—or they died at the hands of what it pleased itself to call justice' (p.66).

Some peasants actually benefited quite considerably from assarting. Finberg (1955 pp.64–5) quoted the case of one Girold, a tenant on the manor of Bishop's Cleeve in Gloucestershire noted in a survey of 1182. His original holding was a mere 12 acres but to this were added five small assarts, three of them associated with his forebears, and one very large assart of his own making. The assarted land, amounting to 170 acres, had been taken from the woods between 1164 and 1179, but once cleared it did not form part of a 'private farm' but was absorbed into one of the village's two open arable fields where it was subject to the rules of common husbandry and rights of pasture.

Assarting took place on many scales and a variety of types of people were involved. It could take place on a grand scale as when, in 1259, Henry II charged 4d per acre for assarting in an extensive territory around Drax in the south of Yorkshire, or in 1228 when Henry III opened the Forest of Horwood, between the Severn and the Cotswolds ridgeway, to assarting. Rather than being the preserve of the hungry village peasant, assarting was frequently sanctioned and encouraged by the leading lights in medieval society and accomplished by the yeomen and petty gentry. Having explored the situation on the North York Moors, Harrison wrote:

> while seigneurial planning was an import-
> ant factor in some areas, notably in royal
> and private forests, the great lords who
> dominated the area also allowed import-
> ant freeholds to develop within their terri-
> tories partly through unrestricted assarting.
> A clientele of substantial freeholders was
> vital for the functioning of a great honour
> and for the more humble jobs in local
> administration generally . . . the one kind

of settlement for which no evidence has so far come to light in the North York Moors is the piecemeal assarting by individual peasant households which is so often held up as the norm. (1990 p.31)

At Bilsdale on the North York Moors in the years around 1300, landlords seeking to reclaim and intake the marginal uplands and their timber resources offered favourable freeholds and leaseholds to attract tenants who would assart the woodland there. This resulted in the establishment of at least four hamlets, each containing around six holdings. However, during the fourteenth century, the deterioration of the climate and the weakening of the economy resulted in the abandonment of all but one of these hamlets (McDonnell, 1986). Describing the situation in Dorset, Taylor wrote: 'All classes of society were engaged in this clearance. Only one feature distinguishes the rich from the poor and that is the amount of land cleared' (1970 p.97). Assarting was a popular activity and most levels in society engaged in it, but it did create difficulties. Not only did it reduce the amount of woodland available to communities with voracious appetites for woodland products, it also reduced the resources of pasture and pannage.

Taylor has described the countrysides associated with assarting: 'In spite of much later alteration, the modern pattern of irregularly shaped fields, often bounded by thick and botanically rich hedges perched on large banks, shows how and where medieval farmers encroached on the forests' (1975 p.95). The holders of assarts were often required to enclose them as fields; a ditch could mark the property boundary and a hedge would be planted just inside the ditch. Some of the field-names associated with assarts readily identify the origins of the fields, like ridding, royd or sart, while others can be more ambiguous. Many of the assarts in the Charnwood Forest are named 'close', a name associated with other sorts of

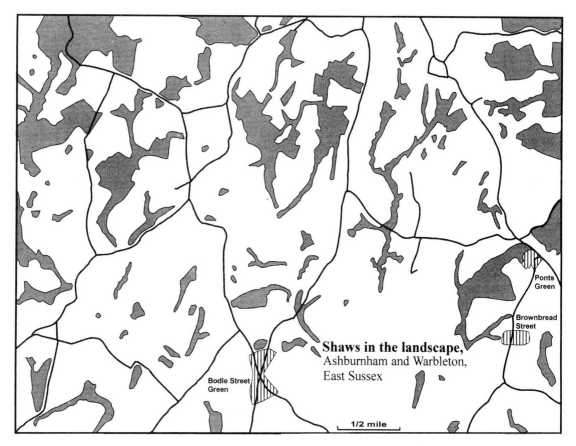

Ponts
Green

Brownbread
Street

Shaws in the landscape,
Ashburnham and Warbleton,
East Sussex

Bodle Street
Green

1/2 mile

Map 1.6   Shaws in the landscape, Ashburnham and Warbleton, East Sussex. This is an ancient or woodland type of countryside, with dispersed farm-steads and hamlets and an intricate pattern of shaws, many of which are elongated along boundaries.

enclosure too, while 'hay' denoting a hedge, small wood or a park is very commonly linked to medieval assarts, and 'ley' can be attached to them too.

A type of landscape commonly associated with woodland clearance is that charac-terised by shaws, attenuated belts of deciduous woodland that border many of the fields, as frequently seen in upland Sussex and Kent. Brandon noted that these shaws are often as much as two rods (33 feet) in width and include trees along with shrubs like hazel and field maple (1974 p.96). He wrote:

The clearing techniques of the first Wealden farmers have contributed much to the evolution of the contemporary Sussex landscape. The most distinctive feature of the Wealden landscape shaped by its pioneering medieval farmers is the patchwork of wood-bounded fields known as shaws. Similar wide borders of wood were called *rewes* on the Low Weald of west Sussex. The singular absence of narrow, crooked hedgerows in areas where the original field boundaries persist, distinguishes the field pattern of the Sussex Weald from that of other English districts enclosed directly from the wild. (p.96)

This leaves the questions of why shaws were left untouched during medieval clear-ance and why, if there were advantages in doing this, the practice was not adopted universally? The answers might lie in a heightened regional demand for timber— perhaps for the iron industry or to produce specialised timbers for shipbuilding. They could also serve as shelterbelts and field divisions, but so too could the hedgerows that were employed elsewhere in England.

Settlement studies in areas of woodland clearance

Formerly wooded areas have tended to develop their own, characteristic cultural

landscapes. Of the main *pays* of the West Midlands, Dyer wrote that:

'the feldon or champion country lay in the Avon valley and the clay plains of central Worcestershire and south-east Warwickshire. Here in the thirteenth and fourteenth centuries were nucleated

Map 1.7   Woodland clearance at Barden in Wharfedale, 1731. Information provided by Dr H.M. Beaumont, by kind permission of the Trustees of the Chatsworth Settlement.

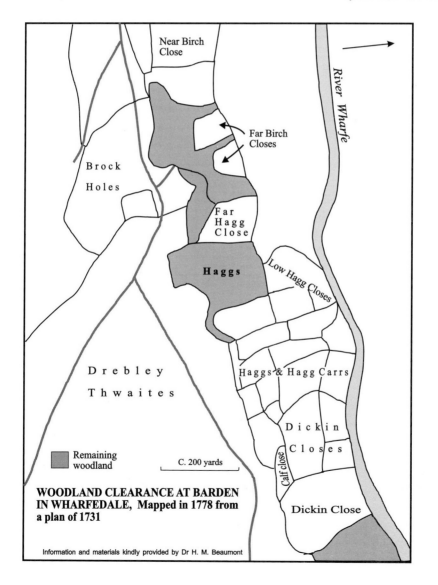

Near Birch Close

Far Birch Closes

River Wharfe

Brock Holes

Far Hagg Close

Haggs

Low Hagg Closes

Drebley Thwaites

Haggs & Hagg Carrs

Dickin Closes

Calf close

Dickin Close

Remaining woodland

C. 200 yards

WOODLAND CLEARANCE AT BARDEN IN WHARFEDALE, Mapped in 1778 from a plan of 1731

Information and materials kindly provided by Dr H. M. Beaumont

villages, open fields and peasants holding standard customary tenements who made their living primarily from corn-growing. In the woodlands of north Warwickshire and north and west Worcestershire the scattered settlements lay among wood and pasture mingled with arable. The fields were irregular and often enclosed. The landholdings were more unequal in size, the inhabitants enjoyed more free-dom, and they practised a greater variety of occupations than would be found in the feldon. (1991 pp.1–2)

Many countrysides which were wooded at the beginning of the medieval period were subsequently colonised by settlers in manners which have created distinctive landscapes of settlement. In some cases, the settlements encountered today do not derive from a process of assarting to expand the cultivated area, but rather they have evolved from woodland-related activities. The villages of Bainbridge in Wensleydale and Buckden in Wharfedale were originally established as settlements that housed small communities of foresters. Bainbridge was the chief lodge of the Forest of Wensleydale, founded early in the thirteenth century, and the twelve foresters housed there were each provided with 9 acres of ground (Raistrick, 1991). Beaumont (1996) has described how, on the Clifford estate in the Forest of Barden

in Wharfedale, six lodges were established, all situated on the valley sides occupying good vantage points. They housed keepers and officers of the Forest who were res-ponsible for managing the wildlife and woodland resources of the area, including bark for tanning and beeswax, as well as game, timber and pannage. With the passage of time, the lodge sites became farming settlements as woodland pasture was leased for grazing and cleared for cultivation; the accounts of Skipton Castle for 1322–3 show that each lodge was yielding income as a vaccary or cattle farm. Beaumont found that the lodges of Drebley and Gamsworth became farming hamlets; Gamsworth was a loose hamlet with an open field system which contracted into a single farm, while early in the eighteenth century there were seven households in Drebley hamlet which all shared an open field system.

Many more settlements resulted from the clearance rather than the management of woodland. The expansion of settlement from established village nuclei is normally associated with a movement upslope into

Figure 1.6   The Barden tower, a medieval hunting lodge owned by the Clifford family of Skipton Castle in one of their numerous hunting territories in Wharfedale.

more marginal wooded areas, though Jennings (1978) has described the situation in Calderdale, in the southern Pennines, where the occupants of villages and hamlets located at heights of around 700 to 900 feet began, after 1250, to clear the woodland from the slopes below. By 1300 they had reached the flood-prone valley bottoms and were confronted by problems of land drainage. Colonists from the older and higher settlement of Holme established Holmfirth (i.e. Holme Wood) in Holme's former common wood. Jennings considers that the 'royd' names which are common in Yorkshire and describe assarts in many cases may be dated to the period 1275–1325.

Many of the settlements which were established under the pressure of population growth and land hunger in the earlier medieval centuries would perish when the deterioration of the climate rendered the uplands inhospitable and the clay lands cold and wet. In Hanbury parish in Worcestershire, Dyer found that:

> The earthworks of now abandoned sites give us some impression of the form of peasant messuages, the term used in documents for the whole complex of houses, farm buildings, yards and gardens. The messuage was usually inhabited by a single family and stood alone beside a road or lane. It was surrounded by a ditch or bank; the roughly rectangular enclosed area usually measured between 30 and 80 metres in length. Rectangular platforms suggest the presence of two or three buildings, either accommodation for animals or a bakehouse. Sunken areas mark the sites of yards, and we can envisage a garden plot at the rear. Beyond the boundary ditch often lay the ridge and furrow of cultivated land. (1991 p.36)

Some of the messuages were grouped together in loose hamlets known as 'greens' or 'ends', and Dyer described ends where the dwellings were arranged along both sides of a road, alone or in pairs, with a croft of arable land around 100–300 yards in width separating the houses and creating an 'interrupted row' (p.40). The green settlements also formed interrupted rows, but the dwellings tended to form a line along one side of a road, sometimes along a road passing through a green or strip of common pasture, or else the houses were arranged around the edge of a green. It was thought that the ends had formed at an earlier date than the greens.

Taylor (1995 p.27) has described three essential types of dispersed settlement found in areas with villages. Firstly, there is the form found in western districts of England where a dispersed distribution, which is presumed to derive from an older pattern of settlement, is interspersed with younger nucleated villages. Secondly, there is a largely abandoned pattern of dispersed settlement associated with enduring nucleated settlement in some areas, notably the Midlands. Here, the dispersed settlements of the early to mid-Saxon eras were gradually replaced by nucleated settlement in the following four centuries. Finally, there is a dispersed settlement pattern resulting from the colonisation of woodland, moorland or estuarine areas. This has generally been ascribed to the twelfth or thirteenth centuries, though Taylor considered much of it to be earlier. Outside the main wooded areas are small settlements originating from the clearance of woodland at the extremities of parishes. Also present are the remains of early to mid-Saxon dispersed settlements, some of which survived into medieval times.

Bellamy (1994) studied the evidence for Anglo-Saxon dispersed sites and woodland in Northamptonshire's Rockingham Forest. It appears that settlements and farming were abandoned at the end of Roman rule, with the higher ground being covered by scrub and woodland. Subsequently, dis-

Table 1.5   Checklist for fieldwork in formerly wooded settings

Field-names	Sart, stocks, stocking, stubbings, bushy, reed, ridding, rode, royd, ridland and ridding denote assarted land. Shaw and hay, sometimes close, ley and field, and occasionally hag, may be associated with assarts.
Field shapes	Irregular, often thickly hedged.
Settlement	Likely to include villages, farmsteads and hamlets. Farmsteads established by assarters could expand to become hamlets, but these hamlets could often contract back to farmsteads or disappear. The earthworks of moated, ditched or unenclosed medieval farmsteads may be found. 'Greens' and 'ends' may be present, with dwellings spaced along a road in interrupted rows. Farmsteads and hamlets at the extremity of parishes may result from the assarting of the last of the woodland.
Society	More independent and individualistic than in areas with large villages and extensive open field systems.
Townships	Parishes lacking woodland and lying within generally wooded areas were sometimes extended to reach towards wooded areas for access to their valuable resources.

persed settlements which engaged in iron-working were established, with these Saxon sites of the period 400–850 AD being located on small limestone outcrops on the lower slopes (in contrast to the Romano-British sites which were situated on boulder clay above). They may have been sited on the margins of woodland covering the higher, clay soils. In the Saxo-Norman period the dispersed settlement sites were being deserted as open field farming was established.

Champion countryside and woodland countryside

Writers such as Rackham and Williamson have highlighted the distinction between two forms of countryside which exist in the English lowlands, though the terminology employed to describe the types varies. Rackham wrote:

> On the one hand, as in Essex or Herefordshire, we have the England of hamlets, medieval farms in hollows of the hills, lonely moats and great barns in the clay-lands, pollards and ancient trees, cavernous holloways and many footpaths, fords, irregularly-shaped groves with thick hedges colourful with maple, dogwood and spindle—an intricate land of mystery and surprise. On the other hand there is the Cambridgeshire type of landscape, the England of big villages, few, busy roads, thin hawthorn hedges, windswept brick farms, and ivied clumps of trees in corners of fields; a predictable land of wide views, sweeping sameness, and straight lines. These I call Ancient Countryside and Planned Countryside. (1986 pp.4–5)

Williamson referred to Homans's (1941 pp. 12–14) distinction between 'woodland' and 'champion' areas of England and described how: 'The champion landscapes of large villages and open fields dominated a broad swathe of lowland England from Yorkshire to Dorset, with a less distinct eastward projection into Hampshire and Sussex', while 'Woodland landscapes of early enclosed fields dominated the west of England, and also a large and continuous area in the south and east' (1988 p.5). These landscapes were named thus not because of the dominance of woodland over other

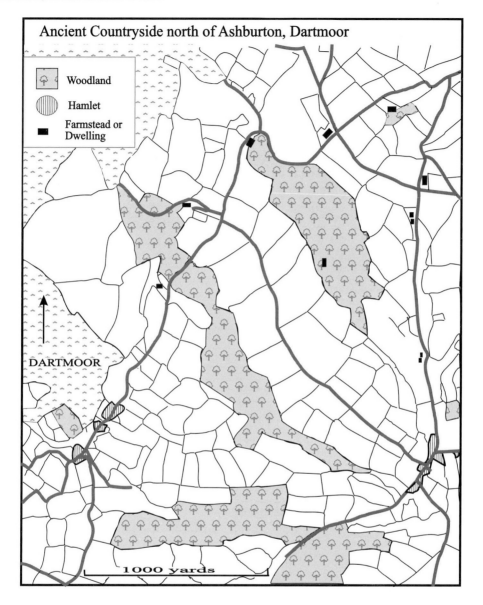

Ancient Countryside north of Ashburton, Dartmoor

Woodland

Hamlet

Farmstead or Dwelling

DARTMOOR

1000 yards

land-uses, but because of the wealth of woodland products which could be harvested from their hedgerows.

The boundary between the two forms of countryside can be very sharply defined and observers have been aware of the split personality of lowland countryside for several centuries, as when the sixteenth-century writer, William Harrison, commented: 'It is so that our soile is divided into champaigne ground and woodland, the

Map 1.8   Ancient countryside north of Ashburton, Dartmoor. The map shows the dispersed hamlets and farmsteads, numerous winding lanes, small, irregular fields and many small woods which are associated with ancient or woodland countrysides.

houses of the first lie uniformelie builded in everie town togither, with streets and lanes; whereas in the woodland countries . . . they stand scattered abroad, each one dwelling in the midst of his owne occupieng' (quoted in Williamson and Bellamy, 1987 p.13). This was an early description of the fundamental difference between the nucleated villages which characterised the settlement pattern of the champion (planned) countryside areas and the few villages and numerous dispersed farmsteads and hamlets encountered in the woodland (ancient) countryside. The large villages had been intimately associated with areas of open field farming, but whereas small, communally tilled fields might be found in woodland countryside, the emphasis here was on individually held hedged closes. The woodland areas were linked with slow, organic landscape development and with continuity between past and present, while the champion countrysides frequently have a planned appearance, the result of the traumatic and revolutionary developments associated with the Parliamentary Enclosure of the ancient open field systems.

The origins of the division into woodland and champion countrysides is still uncertain. According to Williamson, 'broad variations in the landscapes of the southern and eastern areas of medieval England must be seen in the context of a long history of distinct regional development . . . Gray may not have been entirely mistaken when he related regional variations in field systems and settlement patterns to variations in the continuity of social organisation from Roman Britain to Anglo-Saxon England' (1988 p.12). He tentatively suggested that a weakening of kin structures caused by repeated migration affected Anglo-Saxon

Table 1.6   Characteristics of champion and woodland countryside

Landscape feature	Woodland (ancient) countryside	Champion (planned) countryside
Woodlands	Numerous woods, mainly small and many ancient. Woodland place-names numerous in non-wooded sections.	Woods not common, but some large medieval woods may stand on areas of poorer soil.
Roads and trackways	Many winding and deeply hollowed lanes with numerous bridlepaths and footpaths.	Roads few but substantial and busy. Much countryside is quite far from a road. Minimal network of footpaths.
Fields	Plentiful small, irregular enclosures, normally thickly hedged. Woodland field names common.	Large, geometrical fields are common. Sometimes prairie-like fieldscapes.
Field boundaries	Thick, winding, ancient hedgerows containing species like oak, hazel, crab apple, maple and elm.	Straight hedgerows, often sparse or gappy, containing hawthorn, rose, sycamore, ash, elder and bramble.
Settlement	Few villages; hamlets and farmsteads are common. The dispersed farmsteads tend to be old and frequently stand on medieval farmstead sites.	The settlement pattern is dominated by the villages, often large, which had served as dormitories for the medieval peasant populations who worked the surrounding lands.
Other scenic aspects	Inviting, intimate countryside with plenty of visual and historical details, numerous ponds and moats, while woodland and hedgerows are prominent and ever-present features.	Countrysides may seem bare, windswept and dominated by their extensive arable fields. They lack 'secret places' and often display the angular geometry of Parliamentary Enclosure boundaries.

settlers in the north-east and Midlands of England more than it did those in the south-east. Different patterns of local social organisation may have formed in the former areas during the fifth and sixth centuries and

As population and other pressures built up during the middle and later Saxon period, solutions appropriate to such neighbourhood groups were adopted. These communal solutions facilitated the

expansion of arable at the expense of wood pasture and waste. This, however, led both to a chronic shortage of grazing and to a pattern of highly intermixed

Map 1.9   Land held by copyholders, Ingatestone, Essex, 1600–1. The map shows a dispersed pattern of farmsteads with irregular, hedged fields and land held in severalty and is typical of ancient countryside in eastern England. After Muir and Muir (1989), from Essex County Record Office Doc Ph 2/100.

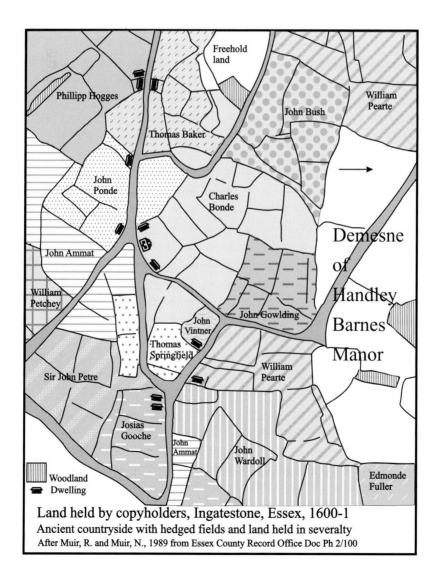

Land held by copyholders, Ingatestone, Essex, 1600-1

Ancient countryside with hedged fields and land held in severalty

After Muir, R. and Muir, N., 1989 from Essex County Record Office Doc Ph 2/100

holdings, as reclaimed land was divided between families within each neighbourhood. In time, moreover, the increasing burdens imposed from above produced a profound concern among neighbouring families over variations in the quality of land within different holdings. The ultimate outcome of all these tendencies was the regularisation of field systems. While this may have been imposed from above, the stimulus, the need arose from the structure of the farming communities themselves. (p.12).

In contrast, in the south-east the importance of extended kindreds as a major influence on the holding and allocation may have declined more slowly, as evidenced by the concentration in this region of place-names with the element '*ingas*', denoting the people of or perhaps the followers of a patriach, some form of extended kindred. 'Under the impact of increased social stratification and population growth, such large but diffuse social groupings fragmented, but not into the kind of mosaic of neighbourhood groups which had come to characterise the Midlands. In consequence, more individualistic responses were made to the problems and possibilities offered by demographic recovery and increasing social complexity' (Williamson, 1988 p.12). These are interesting suggestions, though it should be remembered that woodland countrysides are not confined to south-eastern areas like Essex or the Weald—they can also be seen in places like Herefordshire and parts of Devon. The existence of two distinct forms of lowland countryside is not at issue, but the manner of their formation will be debated for many years to come. Some may find the simple twofold classification of lowland countryside types too simplistic and prefer the concept of varied *pays* developed by the Leicester landscape historians (Everitt, 1977 and Fox, 1989).

Dyer has noted how the differences in

landscape type were associated with distinct differences in social characteristics. The woodlands were

> inhabited mainly by freeholders, who owed only light obligations to their lords. The seignorial regime of the woodland manors was less oppressive than that of the champion, partly because of the prevalence of lesser and weaker lords, such as members of the gentry. The lower densities of population freed the woodlanders from the restraints of strong village communities. They lived in isolated houses, away from interfering neighbours. They held lands in enclosures, and could use the land as arable or pasture, or employ whichever cropping system suited them best. (1991 p.48)

Field land in the woodlands was enclosed and the tenants might use it for arable or pasture as they pleased and adopt systems of farming without consulting village neighbours. There were many smallholders, and because the emphasis in woodland farming was on pastoralism, the people of the countryside tended to have more free time which could be devoted to woodland activities, such as charcoal-burning, woodturning or smelting. Their independence of spirit found expression in lawlessness and the Robin Hood ballads.

Reading the woodland landscape

In seeking to interpret woodland landscapes it is as well to be prepared for the unexpected and to base conclusions upon *all* the available evidence. The first choice to be made could concern the question of whether the wood concerned really is a wood, containing a mixture of self-regenerating hardwood species, or whether it is a plantation? Plantations have more points of contact with a crop of wheat or turnips than with woods. They may be monocultures and they comprise assemblages of alien softwood trees, generally all of one age, planted and harvested together. Thus it might seem that plantations are very uncomplicated features which offer no challenges to the landscape historian. However, Skipper and Williamson have shown that in the Brecklands near Thetford the roadside deciduous borders to the conifer plantations, dating from the 1920s and 1930s, were not planted for reasons of landscaping, as is commonly presumed. Rather, these margins, established when there were few passers-by and fewer conservationists in the region, were provided as fire barriers.

Today these strips of beech, lime, oak, chestnut and other species form a particularly distinctive and attractive element in the landscape, and it is often assumed that they were originally established mainly for aesthetic reasons, to limit the visual impact of the serried rows of conifers and thus mitigate public criticism of large scale afforestation . . . [but] the deciduous strips were mainly established as a fire protection measure. It was assumed that most fires were likely to originate from the roads running through the forest—started by lighted matches or cigarettes dropped by passers-by, or by sparks from steam-powered vehicles, which were still then a common sight. (1997 p.65)

If one takes the example of Winsley Wood in Nidderdale, one finds a small enclosure which is filled with larch and beech. Thus

Map 1.10   The pattern of small woods in Nidderdale. Note the frequent 'spring' or coppice names and the medieval 'hag' name.

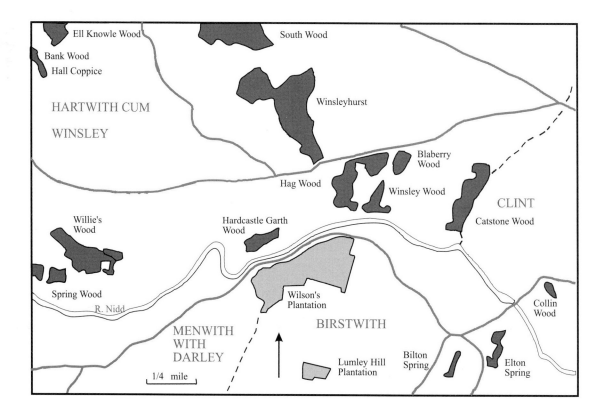

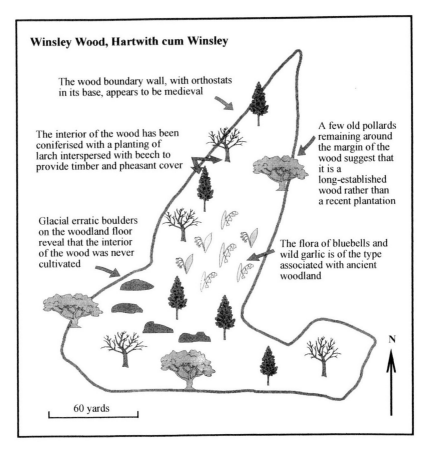

Winsley Wood, Hartwith cum Winsley

The wood boundary wall, with orthostats in its base, appears to be medieval

The interior of the wood has been coniferised with a planting of larch interspersed with beech to provide timber and pheasant cover

A few old pollards remaining around the margin of the wood suggest that it is a long-established wood rather than a recent plantation

Glacial erratic boulders on the woodland floor reveal that the interior of the wood was never cultivated

The flora of bluebells and wild garlic is of the type associated with ancient woodland

60 yards

N

Map 1.11   Winsley Wood, Hartwith cum Winsley, North Yorkshire, showing evidence of its ancient character. This is a member of a cluster of small, ancient woods; its location is shown in Map 1.10.

one might rush to the conclusion that this is a nineteenth century plantation, since both these trees, non-indigenous to northern England, were favoured in Victorian times, the beech for landscaping and pheasant cover and the larch for softwood timber production and aesthetic considerations. However, a closer familiarity with the wood will reveal that in May the woodland floor is carpeted in bluebells and wild garlic (ramsons), both plants being associated with ancient woodland, while the wall surrounding the wood contains 'orthostats'

or large boulders in its base and is of a medieval appearance. A few old pollards and coppiced hazels survive around the margins of the wood. Also, Winsley Wood is part of an 'archipelago' of small woods, some having ancient names including the 'hurst' or 'hag' elements. More interestingly, the floor of Winsley Wood is littered with very large glacial erratic boulders, while the pasture land around is clear of such rocks. This suggests that, while farmers cleared the surrounding land, the wood was never cultivated and existed, until its coniferisation, as ancient woodland. Fieldwork in woodland landscapes may be designed to interpret the evolution of the countryside concerned, but it could also be initiated for the purposes of recording rather than interpretation, for example the recording of

Table 1.7 Checklist for fieldwork in woodland landscapes

Name of Wood.........	Location.......	Owner...........
Form of boundaries	Wood banks, hedge, fence? Pollards along woodland margin or boundary bank?	
Name and its possible meaning	Pay attention to place-name elements like frith, bere, lund, hag, wood, den, grove, hurst etc. Note the names of neighbouring woods too.	
Botanical composition	Dominant species of canopy and underwood? Also significant plants of the woodland floor, including presumed indicators of long-established woodland: bluebell, herb Paris, dog's mercury, oxlip etc.?	
Former management	Evidence of coppicing, pollarding, internal partitioning by wood banks, charcoal-burning, white coal kilns, iron-working?	
Signs of ancient woodland	Note features like glacial erratics on the woodland floor, plant colonies associated with ancient woodland, place-name elements like bere, lund, land and frith.	
Map evidence	Check successive maps for evidence of woodland evolution. Check old estate maps, tithe maps etc. for woodland field names in adjacent areas showing earlier extent of the wood.	
Pre-woodland uses?	Check for traces of a pre-woodland existence: overgrown hedgebanks, ridge and furrow on the woodland floor, hillfort ramparts and ditches, pillow mounds etc.	

surviving resources of ancient woodland: 'Basically, old woodland is important in being un-recreatable. The loss of a young spruce plantation on a prepared heathland site is not serious floristically or ecologically; if necessary it can quickly be replicated. On the other hand the loss of ancient woodland means the disappearance of vegetation which has evolved gradually over hundreds of years' (Lindsay, 1980 p.88).

REFERENCES

Baker, C.A., Moxey, P.A. and Oxford, P.M. 'Woodland continuity and change in Epping Forest' *Field Studies* 4 (1978) pp.645–69.

Bazeley, M. 'The extent of English Forest in the thirteenth century' *Transactions of the Royal Historical Society* 4th ser. 4 (1921).

Beales, P.W. 'The late Devensian and Flandrian vegetational history of Crose Mere, Shropshire' *New Phytologist* 85 (1980) pp.133–61.

Beaumont, H.M. 'Tracing the evolution of an estate township: Barden in upper Wharfedale' *Local Historian* 26 (1996) pp.66–79.

Bellamy, B. 'Anglo-Saxon dispersed sites and woodland at Geddington in the Rockingham Forest, Northamptonshire' *Landscape History* 16 (1994) pp.31–7.

Bennett, H.S. *Life on the English Manor* (Cambridge: Cambridge University Press, 1937).

Brandon, P. *The Sussex Landscape* (London: Hodder and Stoughton, 1974).

Brooks, R. and Johannes, D. *Phytoarchaeology* (Portland OR: Dioscorides Press, 1990).

Brown, R. *General View of the Agriculture of the West Riding*, 2nd edn (1799).

Cantor, L. 'Forests, chases, parks and warrens' in L. Cantor (ed.) *The English Medieval Landscape* (London: Croom Helm, 1982).

Cantor, L. and Hatherly, J. 'The medieval parks of England' *Geography* 64 (1979) pp.71–85.

Cunliffe, B.W. 'Man and landscape in Britain 6000 BC–AD 400' in S.R.J. Woodell (ed.) *The English Landscape: Past, Present, and Future* (Oxford: Oxford University Press, 1985) pp.48–67.

Darby, H.C. 'The clearing of the English woodlands' *Geography* 36 (1951) pp.71–83.

Dyer, C. Hanbury: *Settlement and Society in a Woodland Landscape*, Department of English Local History Occasional Papers, Fourth Series, 4 (Leicester: University, 1991).

Everitt, A. 'River and wold: reflections on the historical origins of regions and *pays' Journal of Historical Geography* 3 (1977) pp.1–19.

Finberg, H.P.R. *Gloucestershire: The History of the Landscape* (London: Hodder and Stoughton, 1955).

Fleming, A. 'Towards a history of wood pasture in Swaledale (North Yorkshire)' *Landscape History* 19 (1998) pp.13–23.

Fox, H.S.A. 'The peoples of the wolds in English settlement history' in M. Aston, D. Austin and C. Dyer (eds) *The Rural Settlements of Medieval England* (Oxford: Blackwell, 1989) pp.77–101.

Gelling, M. *Place-names in the Landscape* (London: Dent, 1993).

Girling, M.A. and Grieg, J.R.A. 'A first fossil record for Scolytus scolytus (F.) (elm bark beetle): its occurrence in elm decline deposits from London and the implications for Neolithic elm disease' *Journal of Archaeological Science* 12 (1985) pp.347–51.

Godwin, H. 'Pollen analysis: an outline of the problems and potentialities of the method' *New Phytologist* 33 (1934) pp.278–305.

Grainge, W. *History of Harrogate and the Forest of Knaresborough* (London: John Russell Smith, 1871).

Harrison, B. 'New settlements in the North York Moors 1086–1340' in B.E. Vyner (ed.) *Medieval Rural Settlement in North-East England* (Durham: (Architectural & Archaeological Society of Durham & Northumberland), 1990) pp.19–32.

Harvey, I.M.W. 'Bernwood in the Middle Ages' in J. Broad and R. Hoyle (eds) *Bernwood: The Life and Afterlife of a Forest*, Harris Paper 2 (Preston: University of Central Lancashire, 1997).

Homans, G.C. *English Villagers of the Thirteenth Century* (Cambridge, MA: Harvard, 1941).

Hoyle, R., 'The medieval forest landscape' in J. Broad and R. Hoyle (eds) *Bernwood: The Life and Afterlife of a Forest*, Harris Paper 2 (Preston: University of Central Lancashire, 1997).

Huntley, B. 'European vegetation history: palaeovegetation maps from pollen data—13000 yr BP to present' *Journal of Quaternary Science* 5 (1990) pp.103–22.

Huntley, B. 'The Holocene history of British woodlands in a European context' in M.A. Atherton (ed.) *Woodland in the Landscape Conference Proceedings* (Leeds: Leeds University Press, 1998).

Huntley, B. and Birks, H.J.B. *An Atlas of Past and Present Pollen Maps for Europe, 0–13000 B.P.* (Cambridge: Cambridge University Press, 1983).

Jennings, B. *A History of Harrogate and Knaresborough* (Huddersfield: Advertiser Press, 1970).

Jennings, B. 'Man and the landscape' in *The Calderdale Way* (Halifax: Calderdale Way Association, 1978).

Jones, M. 'The Coal Measure woodlands of South Yorkshire: past, present and future' in M.A. Atherden (ed.) *Woodland in the Landscape Conference Proceedings* (Leeds: Leeds University Press, 1998).

Jones, M. and Walker, P. 'From coppice-with-standards to high forest: the management of Eccleshall Woods 1715–1901' in I.D. Rotherham and M. Jones (eds) *The Natural History of Ecclesall Woods* Part 1, *Peak District Journal of Natural History and Archaeology Special Publication No. 1*, (July 1997).

Lennard, R. *Rural England 1086–1153*, 2nd edn (Oxford: Oxford University Press, 1997).

Lindsay, J. 'Recording historic woodlands' in P. Brandon and R. Millman (eds) *Recording Historic Landscapes*, Department of Geography Occasional Publications 2 (London: Polytechnic of North London, 1980), pp.88–94.

McDonnell, J. 'Medieval assarting hamlets in Bilsdale, North-East Yorkshire' *Northern History* 26 (1986) pp.20–39.

Mitchell, A.F. 'Dating the "ancient oaks"' *Quarterly Journal of Forestry* 60 (1966) pp.271–6.

Muir, R. 'Pollards in Nidderdale: a landscape history' (forthcoming).

Muir, R. & Muir, N. *Fields* (London: Macmillan, 1989).

Rackham, O. *Trees and Woodland in the British Landscape* (London: Dent, 1976).

Rackham, O. *Ancient Woodland* (London: Edward Arnold, 1980).

Rackham, O. 'Ancient woodland and hedges in England' in S.R.J. Woodell (ed.) *The English Landscape: Past, Present and Future* (Oxford: Oxford University Press, 1985) pp.68–105.

Rackham, O. *The History of the Countryside* (London: Dent, 1986).

Rackham, O. 'Wildwood' in M. Jones (ed.) *Archaeology and the Flora of the British Isles* (Oxford: Oxford University Committee for Archaeology, 1988).

Rackham, O. *The Last Forest* (London: Dent, 1989).

Rackham, O. 'Cressing Temple: trees, woods and timber-framed buildings' *Local Historian* 27 (1997) pp.66–77.

Rackham, O. 'The past, present and future of woodland conservation' in M.A. Atherden (ed.) *Woodland in the Landscape Conference Proceedings* (Leeds: Leeds University Press, 1998).

Raistrick, A. *Arthur Raistrick's Yorkshire Dales* (Clapham: Dalesman, 1991).

Simmons, I. 'The history of the early human environment' in B. Vyner (ed.) *Moorland Monuments: Studies in the Archaeology of North-East Yorkshire in Honour of Raymond Hayes and Don Spratt*, CBA Research Report 101 (York: Council for British Archaeology, 1995) pp.5–15.

Skipper, K. and Williamson, T. *Thetford Forest, Making a Landscape, 1922–1997* (Norwich: Centre for East Anglian Studies, 1997).

Smith, R.W. 'The ecology of neolithic farming systems as exemplified by the Avebury region of Wiltshire' *Proceedings of the Prehistoric Society* 50 (1984) pp.99–120.

Stinson, M. 'Assarting and poverty in early-fourteenth-century western Yorkshire' *Landscape History* 5 (1983) pp.53–68.

Stoertz, C. *Ancient Landscapes of the Yorkshire Wolds* (Swindon: RCHME, 1997).

Taylor, C. *The Making of the English Landscape: Dorset* (London: Hodder and Stoughton, 1970).

Taylor, C. *Fields in the English Landscape* (London: Dent, 1975).

Taylor, C. *Village and Farmstead* (London: George Philip, 1983).

Taylor, C. 'Dispersed settlement in nucleated areas' *Landscape History* 17 (1995) pp.27–33.

Taylor, C. and Muir, R. *Visions of the Past* (London: Dent, 1983).

Troels-Smith, J. 'Ivy, mistletoe and elm: climatic indicators—fodder plants' *Danmarks Geologiske Undersøgelse*, 4th ser. 4 (1960) pp.1–32.

White, J. 'Dating the veterans' *Tree News* (Spring/Summer 1995) pp.10–11.

Williamson, T. 'Explaining regional landscapes: woodland and champion in southern and eastern England' *Landscape History* 10 (1988) pp.5–13.

Williamson, T. and Bellamy, E. *Property and Landscape* (London: Philip, 1987).

CHAPTER 2

Landscapes of Colonisation

Imagine that one could take a place on an observation platform anchored far out on the margins of space and then view the sequence of landscape colonisation in a greatly speeded up manner, so that decades might pass in seconds. One would not see the wild places of Britain overrun, one after another, in one sustained surge of cultural expansion. Instead, we would witness a pulsing pattern as settlers entered an area, enacted transformations, and then withdrew in response to climatic change or the consequences of the damage that they had inflicted on the setting. In the long term, the tendency has been for the effectively occupied territory to expand, but this expansion has not been continuous and it has experienced numerous reverses. Human settlement ebbs and flows across the face of the landscape. Once we realise that progress cannot be represented by a curve on a graph that reaches ever upwards then a greater respect for the setting may be born.

Population and climate

The progressive exploitation and manipulation of the environments can best be appreciated in an ecological context, for what happened in the inaccessible Fenland parish or the backwater upland township was part of a broader process of interaction between communities and their settings in which climatic evolution and demographic developments played central roles. Climatic change could entice or repel, with colonists being lured to colonise marginal areas in times of favourable climate (normally expressed in terms of dryness and warmth)

and evicted from them when conditions became cooler, cloudier and more cyclonic. As summarised by Parry (1975), a sustained improvement in the British climate peaked around 1200, with a severe and prolonged deterioration commencing about 1250. There was a slight improvement towards the end of the fifteenth century, but then a slump into the trough of the so-called Little Ice Age of 1600–1750. In different parts of the country the changes were experienced in different ways. For the households which had been enticed to recolonise upland moors, failure was marked by waterlogging and an acidification of the soils, with the peat blanket once more expanding. For the coastal communities in the fourteenth century, sea storms of growing intensity and the bursting of sea walls became the new reality, while for communities in the clay vales a switch from cereal cultivation to pastoralism was encouraged when the stiff, cold soils were waterlogged and slow to warm as spring dawned later and later.

Parry's research in the Lammermuir Hills in southern Scotland suggested that peasant and monastic farming had been encouraged to colonise marginal localities during the early medieval climatic optimum. But as the climate deteriorated, so the upper limit of cultivation retreated from the maximum elevation of about 1,000 feet above sea level, and between then and the end of the 'Little Ice Age' villages were abandoned and field banks and ridged ploughlands were overrun by the advancing waste. Parry believed that during the climatic optimum of 1150–1200, the climatic limit to cultivation was about 150 feet higher than in 1300, while between

1300 and 1600 there was a fall of about 450 feet:

> there is evidence in the charters of the Border abbeys that most of these traces of cultivation are the relics of longstanding, regular cropping rather than of ephemeral outfield intakes. It thus seems unlikely that they were abandoned owing to an initially unrealistic assessment of their viability for cereal cropping. Moreover it is clear that settlement existed at high levels in the study area from the early medieval period. Fifteen of these settlements were probably abandoned before 1600, two of which lay well beyond the absolute climatic limits operative in 1856–95. Of a further twelve settlements deserted between about 1600 and 1750, five lie on or above the limit. (pp.5–6)

Information relating to past climates can be gleaned from diaries, manorial records, ecclesiastical documents and a variety of other sources. Even graffiti can communicate climatic information across the ages, with a grafitto scratched into the clunch (chalk) lining the church tower at Ashwell in Hertfordshire recording: '1350, pitiful, savage and violent the dregs of people remaining become witness at last of a tempest. On St Maur's day this year 1361 it thunders on the earth.' One of the earliest references to climate is found in the *Anglo-Saxon Chronicle* (Laud E) in an entry relating to 1115: 'This was a very hard year and disastrous for the crops, because of the very heavy rains that came just before August and which proved very vexatious and troublesome until Candlemas [the following February] came', while the *Annals of Yorkshire* record that in 991 'the winter continued so long, and with such intensity, that vegetation was suspended or totally destroyed by the frost'. Research into medieval sources will require specialist abilities in Latin and palaeography, but monastic records, where they survive, can prove valuable sources of

climatic information. The records of the Bolton Priory estates, in Wharfedale, record how the harvests of 1315 and 1316 were ruined by heavy summer rains so that the community was obliged to purchase wheat marketed at five times the normal price, while waterlogged grazings and meadows reduced the priory flock from over 3,000 to 913 (Kershaw, 1973). Manor court rolls may contain information which reveals the nature of weather, if not climate. Parker (1976) quoted the following examples from the court rolls of Foxton in Cambridgeshire in the decades around 1300:

> All customary tenants fined because they refused to carry the Lady's hay out of the water on the day when they were mowing William Cock fined for contempt in saying that the tenants did not know that they were supposed to mow in a swamp. Thomas Leger fined 12d because he reaped the Lady's corn when the weather was considered too cold. Likewise six others.

One of the most recent and detailed investigation into historical records of regional climate was accomplished by Noël James Menuge in compiling a database for the North York Moors. Table 2.1 identifies the main types of material she consulted for the different periods and it is presented so as to suggest the sort of sources which could be consulted in future studies.

The researcher should not regard historical records as being absolutely accurate indicators of former climates, and chroniclers and diarists tend to record the extremes and disregard the commonplace. Thus, there are dramatic accounts of turbulent climates and flooding during the twelfth and thirteenth centuries, though the palaeoecological evidence derived from peat bogs identifies a dry period from 1150 to 1300: 'The documentary evidence does not necessarily contradict this. Peat accumulates gradually through time, consequently, the

Table 2.1   Sources of climatic information

Period	Source
Tenth century and before	Generalised mentions of conditions in Britain in Gildas, Bede and the Anglo-Saxon Chronicle.
Eleventh century	The Anglo-Saxon Chronicle, William of Malmesbury's Chronicle. Domesday shows extent of farmed area but is restricted in depth of coverage in northern England.
Twelfth century	Land charters reveal the extent and nature of agriculture and provide a wealth of indirect climatic information.
Thirteenth century	Chronicles, notably Matthew Paris's *English History*, and land charters.
Fourteenth century	Historical accounts, estate records and charters.
Fifteenth century	Estate records and charters.
Sixteenth century and seventeenth century	Court records, tithe records and Forest of Pickering records.
Eighteenth century	Meteorological records, 1788–1792, land surveys.
Nineteenth century	Meteorological reports, diaries.
Twentieth century	Meteorological reports, farming diaries, recollections.

palaeoecological evidence will not represent an individual year, but reflect the environmental conditions over two or more decades' (James Menuge, 1998 p.12). A variety of factors produce a 'smoothing' of the climatic picture derived from environmental sources.

Population growth was the other important factor in the colonisation process. Various estimates of medieval population levels exist, and accurate totals cannot be achieved. Most landscape historians have envisaged a high Roman population being drastically reduced at the end of the Roman period and then a gradual recovery towards another peak around 1300, after which adverse environmental and other factors caused a population slump. Dyer wrote that 'Numbers of people in England grew rapidly between 1086 and 1300, perhaps from about 2 to 5 or 6 million. Before 1086 demographic history is very uncertain, though the total for Roman Britain at its height is believed to have been nearer to the estimate for 1300 than that for 1086, so there must have been a great decline between c.300 and 1000'

(1989 p.45). Williams considered that a crucial factor in the expansion of colonisation after the Norman Conquest was the growth of population, 'which may have been between 1.25 and 2.25 million (probably well into the upper part of that range) in 1086, and could have risen to as great as 4.0 or 4.5 million in 1377. But if we consider the devastation of the plagues of 1348–9, 1360–2 and 1375, when probably between 30 per cent and 50 per cent of the population was wiped out, then it is possible that the population just prior to the Black Death of 1348 could have been as much as 5 or 6 million' (1982 pp.87–9).

Dyer attempted to test the hypothesis, deriving both from Postan (1972) and from archaeological work, that there was a retreat from the marginal land in the latter part of the medieval period. He noted the assumption that by about 1300 many of the inferior marginal lands into which surplus population had expanded were producing poor cereal yields and being abandoned. Three general conclusions were reached: that the retreat of the later medieval period affected settlement on all types of land, with the most dramatic consequences being felt in the long-settled villages rather than the newly settled marginal soils; that to regard the events concerned as a retreat is to place arable farming on a higher plain of achievement than the wood/pasture economy; and that concepts of long-term growth and decline in the medieval period should not be abandoned (1989 p.57).

There are grounds for believing that the woodland hamlets had a greater resilience than the villages of the champion countrysides. Also, it is not unreasonable to suppose that a population which stood at around 6 million just before the Black Death had been more than halved by the century's close and did not recover significantly for several decades. In many places, particularly in situations which could be regarded as marginal because of altitude or soils which were thin, sandy or clayey, arable farming was replaced by pastures or meadows when the pressure of supporting a swollen population eased. The evidence of these changes can be recognised in many landscapes. In the Yorkshire Dales, for example, it appears in the form of abandoned strip lynchets with their relict terraced ploughland. Also in the Dales, where ridge and furrow is found, as it commonly is, the ridges are hardly ever as developed as those of the Midlands which were built up over numerous centuries. Rather, one gets the impression of marginal ploughland worked briefly during times of high population pressure. In many other locations expansion and retreat are seen as ridge and furrow earthworks surviving on the floors of woods, beneath long-established pastures, underlying heath and moor or ascending and traversing slopes where rough upland grazing is now the only land-use. Strip lynchets are normally found in ascending sets or 'flights'. Each one is between about 60 yards (55 m) and 250 yards (229 m) in length and lynchets were formed by ploughing in a consistent direction, with the plough biting into the slope and turning the soil outwards to build up the level surface of the terrace. Cereals were grown on these level 'treads', with grazing being available to animals tethered on the steep 'risers'. A small proportion of strip lynchets in the Yorkshire Dales may belong to the Iron Age, but in England as a whole, where dating evidence is available, strip lynchets may be seen to cut hillforts and Roman and prehistoric field systems, to be underlain by Romano-British pottery and to nest together with medieval ridge and furrow systems.

Given the marginal nature of the upland limestone environments in the Yorkshire Dales or the equally uninviting nature of the lynchet-pleated slopes above Challacombe on Dartmoor, it seems reasonable to regard strip lynchets largely as a legacy of a period of intense land shortage in the decades before the eruption of the Black Death—a circumstance which lured the landless into marginal environments. Wood wrote: 'For the thirteenth century . . . there are the well-authenticated increases in England's population and in the prices of agricultural products; and there are conclusive signs of a spread of cultivation into lands previously considered marginal, not only into marsh and woodland edges but also on to the hillsides' (1961 pp.451–2).

Reclaiming the marshes

The conversion to farmland of England's woodlands began six or seven thousand years ago, but the colonisation of wetlands and coastal marshes was a much more recent development. It appears to have been almost entirely confined to the historical period and to have demanded techniques that were not available to prehistoric society. The ecological factors noted above were crucial, with population pressure in the effectively colonised territory resulting in expansion into areas which could be modified to sustain greater densities of people. Williams notes that the greatest known rates of population growth took place in those areas with the greatest potential for development as represented by the greatest expanse of 'waste':

> For example, in the Lincolnshire Fenland the number of recorded households increased by more than sixfold at Spalding, and as much as elevenfold at Pinchbeck between 1086 and 1287, and this trend continued in successive decades. Some completely new settlements such as Fleet recorded increases of over sixtyfold, and the whole area around the Wash, particularly in Holland and the Norfolk marshland, was the richest area of England in 1334. (1982 p.89)

As with the woodlands, a considerable price was paid for the reclamation and trans-

formation of wetlands. They did not exist as barren, stagnant swamps. Much of the land stood above the waters, and most of the wet areas were only seasonally inundated. They were not avoided by the country people; rather, they were exploited for wildfowl, fish, reeds and sedge for thatch, rushes for flooring, peat for fuel and for grazings. (The different land-uses in the undrained fens of eastern England and northern mosses were not necessarily compatible; free-ranging cattle damaged the drying turves, while peat digging destroyed the pasture.)

In his *Britannia* of 1586, William Camden wrote of the people of the Fens as 'a kind of people according to the nature of the place where they dwell, rude, uncivil and envious

Map 2.1   Medieval land-use in the Cambridgeshire Fen Edge, after Ravensdale (1974).

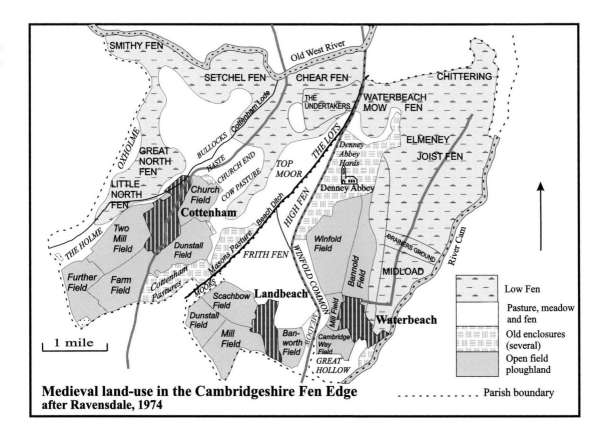

Medieval land-use in the Cambridgeshire Fen Edge
after Ravensdale, 1974

to all others whom they call Upland Men; who stalking on high upon stilts apply their minds to grazing, fishing and fowling'. Citing the respective Domesday entries for manors in the Cambridgeshire Fens, Ravensdale noted that 'the two manors in Waterbeach respectively provided 450 eels and 1000 eels and 12d from the tribute of fish. This was from very small manors, with 3 villeins and 13 bordars, and 8 bordars and 6 cottars respectively . . . In Cottenham the Manor of Crowlands provided 500 eels and 12d. from the tribute of fish, and Roger's manor 150 eels' (1974 p.48). Kipling (1972) quoted the case of the medieval Lake Windermere, where the Abbot of Furness allowed fishing by one boat and 20 nets, and where he estimated that the lake could maintain a loss of 2 tons of pike, 5 tons of perch and 2 tons of eels annually as well as contributing large amounts of trout and char. Summers wrote of some eastern localities that: 'About 1125 William of Malmesbury commented on the abundance of fish, which were so numerous"as to cause astonishment in strangers". This applied in particular to eels, and it was common for rents, tithes, even debts, to be paid with eels in lieu of money. Hence Ramsey paid annually to Peterborough Abbey 4,000 eels in return for freestone from the neighbouring quarries at Barnack' (1976 pp.34–5). Wildfowl and their eggs were highly regarded assets and rights to exploit them were jealously regarded. All forms of ducks, geese and waders were hunted, but the swan was the most valued. In the Fens, countless cygnets were eaten and swan-keeping was a significant occupation in the latter part of the medieval period (Darby, 1940). Around 1722, Defoe wrote of the duck decoys of Cambridgeshire, which were 'furnished with a breed of those they call decoy-ducks, who are taught to allure and entice their kind to the places they belong to, that it is incredible what quantities of wildfowl of all sorts, duck, mallard, teal,

widgeon, &c. they take in those duckoys every week, during the season' (1989 p.33).

Most valuable were the common grazing rights that were enjoyed in the wetlands. Often the people of different parishes inter-commoned on the fens, while

> Whatever the custom, in many places the rights tended to pass to the lord, and in time the villagers paid for the right to common. The policing of these customs was made possible by having droves from time to time to round up the cattle, the offenders getting their beasts out of the pound only by payment of a fine. Some groups of villagers and individual land-lords began to subdivide the lowlands further in an attempt to protect their rights, and almost inevitably as grazing became more regulated disputes between individual and institutions became more frequent. These were often very violent and took the form of battles of arms, the destruction of ditches and marker stones, the killing and maiming of animals, the pulling down of buildings and, in Somerset, the firing of the combustible peat moors. (Williams 1982 p.96)

Wetlands were an important part of the national heritage of resources. Most have gone, but the memory of them has persisted. Of the former Martin Mere, near Ormskirk in Lancashire, Coney wrote: 'This immense sheet of water was a dramatic landscape feature, and one not easily forgotten. Almost three centuries after Fleetwood's drainage, local people still walk "across the mere", look"over the mere"and farm"on the mere". The uninitiated may be forgiven for believing that the lake is still there' (1992 p.60).

Space does not allow a description of the drainage history of each significant area of wetland, but it can be shown that the nature of drainage, in terms of the physical environment, time, technology and tenure, could affect the appearance of the new countrysides. Williams has succinctly des-

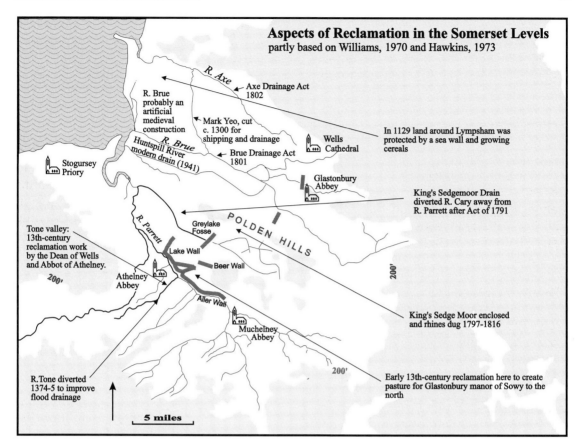

Aspects of Reclamation in the Somerset Levels
partly based on Williams, 1970 and Hawkins, 1973

R. Axe

Axe Drainage Act
1802

R. Brue
probably an
artificial
medieval
construction

Mark Yeo, cut
c. 1300 for
shipping and drainage

Wells
Cathedral

In 1129 land around Lympsham was
protected by a sea wall and growing
cereals

Huntspill River
R. Brue
modern drain (1941)

Brue Drainage Act
1801

Stogursey
Priory

Glastonbury
Abbey

King's Sedgemoor Drain
diverted R. Cary away from
R. Parrett after Act of 1791

R. Parrett

Greylake
Fosse

POLDEN HILLS

Tone valley:
13th-century
reclamation work
by the Dean of Wells
and Abbot of Athelney.

200'

Lake Wall

Beer Wall

Athelney
Abbey

200'

Aller Wall

King's Sedge Moor enclosed
and rhines dug 1797-1816

Muchelney
Abbey

200'

R.Tone diverted
1374-5 to improve
flood drainage

Early 13th-century reclamation here to create
pasture for Glastonbury manor of Sowy to the
north

5 miles

*Map 2.2   Aspects of reclamation in the Somerset
Levels, partly based on Williams (1970) and
Hawkins (1973).*

cribed the way in which environmental differences could guide the development of countryside: 'The reclamation of the second largest area of lowland waste in the country, in the Levels of central Somerset, provides some interesting comparisons with the Fens. The higher rainfall, the greater tidal range in the Bristol Channel, and the susceptibility of the region to freak, heavy downpours that trigger off almost instant floods meant that farming, then as now, was much more likely to be pastoral than arable' (1970 p.102). On the other hand, the Levels resembled the Fens in that a slightly elevated tract of country, the silt fen in the Fens and a clay belt in the Somerset Levels, lay between the lowland peat moors and the sea. In both places, too, Anglo-Saxon settlements were established on islands of higher

ground which stood above the watertable and which were often accorded 'ey' place-names, like Athelney in the Levels and Thorney, Ramsey and Bardney in the Fens. In the Levels, the building of causeways and even of floodbanks may have begun in the Anglo-Saxon period, but the documentation of land reclamation does not appear until after the Norman Conquest. In contrast to the situation in the Fens, where there were numerous peasant initiatives, in the Levels reclamation was largely accomplished by the abbeys of Muchelney, Athelney and Glastonbury and Wells Cathedral.

In 1129 land around Lympsham in the Axe valley had been reclaimed, protected by a sea wall and was said to be growing cereals (Hawkins, 1973 p.32). However, early reclamation schemes focused on the area of the Glastonbury manor of Sowy in the south-west, around the junction of the Parrett and Tone rivers. The reclamation of the Somerset marshes offered great financial advantages to the religious houses, the greatest challenge being posed by the periodic flooding of the River Parrett, which could be particularly severe when the river was high and when its current was opposed by a tidal surge driving up the channel. During the thirteenth century, the Dean of Wells and the Abbots of the Somerset abbeys introduced a succession of flood-banks to contain the waters of the Parret and its tributaries, and embankments and causeways to defend the reclaimed lands. Rivers were confined by banks, dredged and straightened to increase their efficiency as conveyors of floodwater, while the cutting of the Mark Yeo, some time around 1300, linking the River Brue to the River Axe, increased the standing of Glastonbury as a river port. At about the same time, the course of the River Brue appears to have been artificially straightened below Glastonbury. The great ecclesiastical reclamation drive of the thirteenth century was paralleled by a campaign to enclose the great commons of the Levels.

Despite the considerable progress made by the medieval engineers, much land in the Levels remained waterlogged long after the close of the Middle Ages, and around 1600 only about a third of the floodable land in the centre of the county had been reclaimed. King's Sedgemoor, to the south of the Polden Hills, presented too great a challenge and around 70,000 acres were vulnerable to winter flooding. At the Dissolution of the Monasteries this land passed from Glastonbury Abbey to the Crown. Under the Stuarts, plans to drain and enclose the moor disintegrated in chaos, but in the climate of agricultural improvement of the later eighteenth century the seasonal inundation of the moor could be regarded as a national affront. The prospect of enclosure was raised again in the 1770s, leading to an intense local debate and violent opposition. In 1791 an Act for the drainage of King's Sedgemoor was passed by Parliament, with the River Cary being diverted away from the Parrett and into a new channel that was 12 miles long and ran to an outfall on the Parrett estuary. At the start of the nineteenth century, the Brue Drainage Act of 1801 and the Axe Drainage Act of 1802 resulted in the enclosure of the wetlands, the digging of new rhines, and the selling of some of the land to defray costs. In the landscapes affected, the most characteristic features of the scene are the rhines (or rhynes). These were cut in successive lengths of 20 feet, known as 'ropes', which were 8 feet wide at the top, 4 feet wide at the bottom and 5 feet deep, and sometimes planted with willows. Since they were cut about two centuries ago, these rhines have become fringed in mature willows and have sometimes become partly silted.

As noted, there are similarities and differences between the landscapes of reclamation in the Somerset Levels and the Fens. The pastoral character of farming in the Levels, resulting from the greater dampness, endows the region with a softer, more rustic ethos, while the flat, bare, arable landscapes which lie beneath the vast skies of the Fens often seem to have a minimalist or even brutal nature.

In the Fens, too, the individual and communal efforts left a greater mark on the landscape, while institutions, both religious houses and government, dominated the colonisation of the Levels. In the Fens, Anglo-Saxon and Danish communities settled on the slightly elevated flood-free silt belt of land which lay between the salt marshes fringing the Wash and the inland

Table 2.2 Place-names associated with former wetlands

Name	Meaning
Moss (OE *mos* and ON *mosi*) and Marsh OE *mersc, merisc*)	A bog, most common in the northern half of England and Lincolnshire low-lying marshland.
Carr (ON *kjarr*)	The word denotes brushwood and describes marsh which is intermixed with woodland, often alder woodland.
Moor (OE *mōr*, ON *mōr*)	This word referred not only to upland peat, bracken and heather moors, but also to lowland heaths and infertile marshes.
Stroud/strode (OE *strōd*)	Carr-like terrain in southern England.
Mere (OE *mere*)	Enclosed expanse of water. (Some 'mere' names relate to boundaries.)
Fen (OE *fenn*)	Low-lying wetland.
Mire (ON *mýrr*)	A swamp.
Rhyne/rhine	An open drainage ditch in the Somerset Levels.
Wash/was (OE *waesse*)	Flood-prone riverside land.
Lode (ME *lode*)	A watercourse, most notably the Roman and medieval canals in the Fens/Fen edge area of Cambridgeshire.
Eau/yeo (OE *ēa*, French *eau*)	A river.
Adventurers' Land (Ground), Undertakers' Land	Fields in the Fens alotted to seventeenth-century adventurers, who put up the capital for drainage or undertakers, who did the work.
Gull/gullet	Curving bend in old floodbanks marking places where the bank has burst.
Coy	Fields associated with former duck decoys.
Holme/hulme (ON *holmr*) and -ey (OE *ēa*)	Both these names can denote firm islands surrounded by marshland.

peat fen. The pace of settlement accelerated and

between about 1150 and 1300 the ordinary men of the villages around the Wash engaged in a massive feat of reclamation that won some 16 square miles from the marshland bordering the Wash and some 90 square miles from the fenland. The reclaimed land was used mainly for arable farming to feed what seemed to be a rapidly growing population. The evidence of their youthfulness and energy in colonisation of the waste is etched indelibly on the landscape by a series of walls or dykes, and also by many additions, each dyke marking a step in the reclamation process. (Williams 1982 p.99)

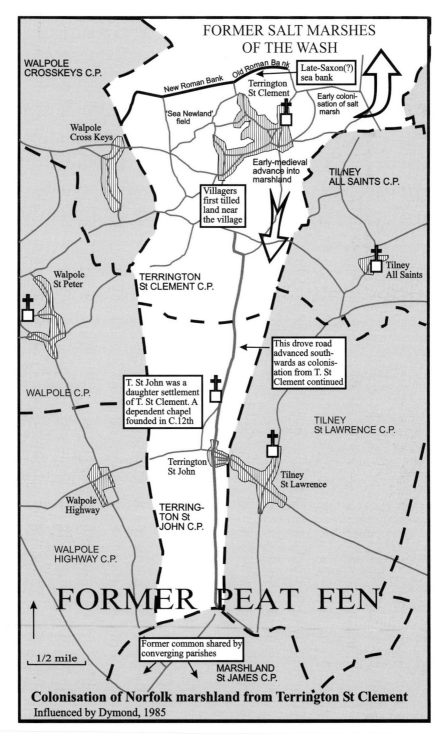

Map 2.3   Colonisation of Norfolk marshland from Terrington St Clement. Colonisation advanced southwards into the former peat fen, with neighbouring parishes converging on an area of common grazing. Influenced by Dymond (1985).

Figure 2.1   A fragment of the old Cambridgeshire fenland and a wind pump preserved at Wicken Fen in Cambridgeshire.

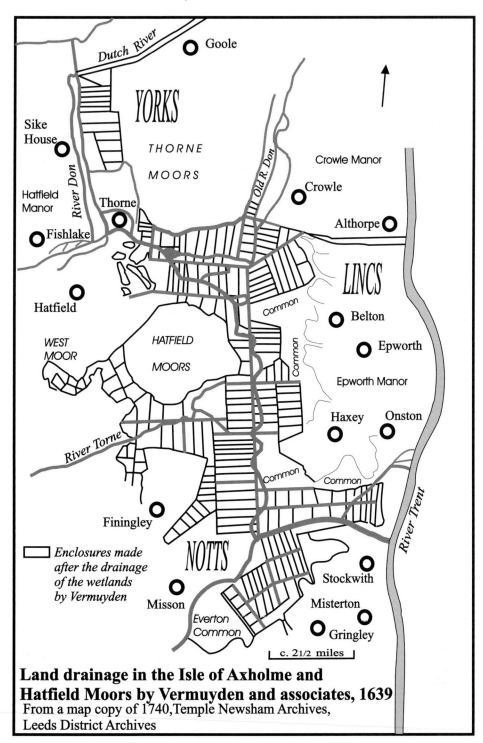

Land drainage in the Isle of Axholme and Hatfield Moors by Vermuyden and associates, 1639
From a map copy of 1740,Temple Newsham Archives,
Leeds District Archives

Map 2.4   Land drainage in the Isle of Axholme and Hatfield Moors by Vermuyden and associates, 1639. From a map copy of 1740, Temple Newsham Archives, Leeds District Archives.

Figure 2.2   The development of mechanical engineering allowed the introduction of pumps that were far more effective and reliable than the old wind pumps. This example survives at Prickwillow in Cambridgeshire.

While land was being wrested from the sea on the coastal side of the silt belt, even greater advances were being made in the peat fen to the south. The building of floodbanks may have begun before the Norman Conquest and intensified afterwards, with villagers and villages apparently co-operating in the drainage projects.

As the work progressed, so villages incorporated new lands into their parishes. Dymond wrote that inside the Roman Bank in the medieval marshland of Norfolk:

> Each township had a long, wide drove-road leading from the inhabited area to the fen. This drove road was extended southwards as new blocks of land were reclaimed, and often itself became the focus of later settlement as new houses were built along its edges. In some places this process resulted in totally new villages, served by their own chapels, as at Terrington St John or Kenwick. The outlines of these great droves are still to be seen in several parishes, and sometimes survive as broad bands of permanent grassland bounded by deep ditches. (1985 p.124)

In the Somerset Levels, as has been described, much of the landscape derives from reclamation works accomplished by the medieval Church, but in the Fens more scenes are dominated by the results of drainage initiatives dating from the seventeenth and subsequent centuries, which converted the 'summer lands', which were exploited only in the drier months of summer, into drained farmland. This involved developing systems for the speedy and reliable evacuation of water from the peat fens to the sea. Large channels were cut, running arrow-straight across the Fens, but the great initiative of the seventeenth century, involving Adventurers led by the fourth Earl of Bedford who had employed the Dutch drainage engineer, Cornelius Vermuyden, was seen by the end of the

century to have failed. As the Fenland peats were drained and dried, so they shrank, the peat surface was lowered and the gradients needed for drainage were reduced—and this caused choking beds of silt to accumulate around the rivers' mouths. The solution was found in the employment of windmills with wheels to scoop water from one drainage level to another. By 1748, 250 of these mills were working in the middle section of the Fens alone, but now the fragile timber structures have vanished from the landscape except for just one survivor at Wicken Fen. After 1820, the emphasis shifted to steam pumps, with some new drains, like the Engine Drain in Swaffham Fen of 1821, being cut to serve these engines. In the second decade of the twentieth century, diesel-powered engines took over the pumping role until replaced by electrical pumps in the second half of the century. The employment of mechanical drainage equipment is still a feature of the Fenland landscape, where brick-built engine houses which accommodated the pumping engines and scoop wheels may still retain their chimneys and stand alone in vast, featureless settings.

Both coastal and inland areas of reclaimed ground could be affected by tidal surges, but the winning of land from the sea differed from inland drainage in the significant respect that natural processes were generally heavily involved. Natural salt marshes represent a stage in the transition from sea to land. They began as sprawling, gently sloping sand flats which were exposed at low tide, and the conversion process commenced with the gradual deposition of silt and mud particles upon the sand. At first thin and localised, the mud deposits were shifted around by the tides, but in time, thicker and more permanent banks of mud could accumulate. The most significant landmark in the transition occurred when plants colonised and further stabilised the mud banks, while their foliage impeded the

currents and encouraged the deposition of silt particles held in suspension by the waters.

The first plants to arrive are eel-grass and samphire, both specialised to tolerate the brackish environment. Then other salt marsh specialists, such as the sea aster and salt-marsh grass, will colonise, and eventually a rich plant community becomes established, often including wormwood, sea pink, sea plantain and sea lavender. At this stage, the salt marsh exists as sinuous, well-vegetated

Figure 2.3   Salt marshes protected by a wall of dunes to seaward on the low, flood-prone coast of Norfolk.

banks divided by intricate networks of tidal creeks, and whenever the tides rise above the level of the creeks and inundate the banks, so additional silt deposits are trapped. The banks continue to rise until they can no longer be over-topped by the tides, though human intervention can occur at different stages during the natural tran-sition from land to sea. Sea walls may be built for flood protection, and these walls and any associated groynes serve, like the vegetation, to slow silt-laden waters and induce deposition.

The reading of the landscapes of the former wetlands involves attention to the smallest of details. The formative elements in the man-made landscape are the sea banks—floodbanks which were built to contain and exclude flood water—and drains, cut to convey the water from the land as swiftly as possible. However, the banks may be eroded and difficult or impossible to date, while the ditch networks may seem to convey no clues as to their origins. Opportunites to excavate a flood-bank are unlikely to arise, and even if they do, no obvious dating evidence, like coins or pottery, is likely to be unearthed. The so-called 'Roman Bank' running around the Wash is thought not to be Roman but is variously attributed to periods from the mid-Saxon to the mid-thirteenth century. Moreover, one bank may overwhelm and engulf the traces of another, older example in the course of the evolution of flood defence systems. Many walls now appear in the guise of causeways following their exploitation as dry, elevated platforms for roads, like the 'manor ways' of the Thames Marshes. Only rarely can a medieval (or earlier) wall be dated to a particular phase of reclamation, an example being the Morton Wall securing land near the northern end of the former sea strait of the Wantsum Channel in Kent, which is probably named after Cardinal Morton and thus datable to the 1480s. Here, the salt marshes were reclaimed by the monks of St Augustine's Priory, Canterbury, from the twelfth century onwards.

As well as excluding floods, walls also played an important role in raising the level of reclaimed ground, with the walls and groynes which obstructed and reduced the flow rate of silt-laden waters thus encouraging the deposition of soils. The silt deposits both increased fertility and elevated land above the reach of normal flooding. Wall construction could be of marsh clay dug from a ditch on its inner side (Millward and Robinson, 1971 p.133) and sometimes the clay was reinforced with brushwood and faggots. The lowest of walls were 3 or 4 feet high, and such walls would tend to become incorporated into more formidable defences as the threat of flooding increased in the course of the medieval period. In the Walland Marsh of Kent:

> Large blocks of land were usually reclaimed direct from salt marsh by erecting a bank to exclude the tides, and then making arrangements for internal drainage of the new land. Sometimes the existing winding salt marsh creeks were used for this drainage, and sometimes new, straight ditches were dug. In almost all cases there was a significant 'back ditch' running along behind the new sea embankment. An outfall, known as a 'gutt', was provided through the new embankment. (Eddison and Draper, 1997 p.77)

Later techniques of coastal defence, employed in Norfolk early in the eighteenth century, were described by Dymond: 'The main defences were sand dunes fortified with piles and rails. The latter held down faggots and were consolidated by stones and clay."Hedges"of faggots helped to catch wind blown sand, while marram grass and brambles were encouraged to stabilise the surface' (1985 p.208).

In most settings, the process of reclama-tion will not have occurred in a single phase, but over a considerable period. Thus, in the Cliffe Marshes, within the Thames Marshes, the sea level in the mid-Saxon period was around 5 feet lower than today; there was no need to construct flood

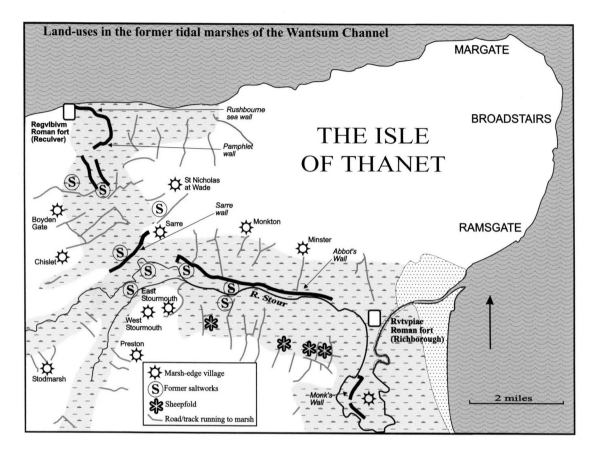

Land-uses in the former tidal marshes of the Wantsum Channel

MARGATE

Rushbourne
sea wall

Regvlbivm
Roman fort
(Reculver)

Pamphlet
wall

THE ISLE
OF THANET

BROADSTAIRS

St Nicholas
at Wade

Sarre
wall

Boyden
Gate

Sarre

Monkton

RAMSGATE

Minster

Chislet

Abbot's
Wall

East
Stourmouth

R. Stour

West
Stourmouth

Rvtvpiae
Roman fort
(Richborough)

Preston

Stodmarsh

☼ Marsh-edge village
Ⓢ Former saltworks
✳ Sheepfold
⌇ Road/track running to marsh

Monk's
Wall

2 miles

Map 2.5 Land-uses in the former tidal marshes of the Wantsum Channel. The Isle of Thanet was formerly separated from the mainland by a straits guarded at either end by Roman shore forts. Villages became established on the edges of the tidal marshes and salt-making and sheep-rearing developed in the marshes.

defences and the locality supported sub-stantial flocks. In the twelfth century sea levels rose, and from the mid-thirteenth century floods began to invade and the monks of Christchurch Priory, the owners of Cliffe manor, began to embank their marshland pastures. At first, modest banks of around 4 feet may have been sufficient. By the fourteenth century, the meadows may have stood only about 6 feet above mean tide level, which would be well below the level of the highest tides. The original sea and river walls will have been lost within larger walls (Millward and Robinson, 1971 p.133). Incorporated within the sea wall system could be sluices, tide gates and water-lets, all serving to increase human control over the flow of water.

Medieval flood walls may be prominent

features in the landscape, be masked by roads or be damaged or obliterated. Natural features in the Fens which might con-ceivably be mistaken for slumped, sinuous flood walls are 'roddons', the beds of tidal prehistoric rivers which became coated in specks of light-coloured silt, washed up-stream by the tides. The desiccation of the surrounding peat leaves the paler roddons standing as twisting, elevated ridges above the black plains of peat—and as such they were attractive platforms for medieval settlement. Other significant wetland features include the lighter patches of limey shell marl which can be seen on expanses of black fenland soil. These were produced when contact with water plants caused chalk, washed in in solution by incoming streams, to be deposited on the beds of former meres. Then there are the low mounds of residues which may mark medieval salt-making sites, the flooded pits indicating places where clay was dug for bank-building and the rectangular ponds marking reservoirs associated with Fenland windpumps.

Sand saturated in salt was filtered to produce brine, which was then heated in boiling houses, usually using peat from a nearby fen as fuel. Darby wrote that: 'Grants

Table 2.3   Wetland landscape interpretation

Wetland landscape feature	*Significance in landscape interpretation*
Parish and township boundaries	Where these are attached to linear features, like cuts, ditches or banks, those features are likely to be old, especially when they serve continuously as boundary-markers. Elongated parishes may well represent the extension of pre-existing parishes into a newly drained area, in the way that Romney Marsh parishes extended south-west into newly drained Walland Marsh territories.
Field patterns	Blocks of fields with different orientations are likely to reveal different reclamation phases.
Field/wall/ditch relationships	Walls or ditches which dog-leg around fields are likely to be respecting pre-existing, sometimes ancient enclosures.
Banks and causeways	These may be seen to be arranged in lines, each successive line marking a stage in the reclamation process.
Lanes or droves	These may stand on old floodwalls that came to serve as causeways. Broad droves often ran from the village to the fen, forming the spine of a parish/township, lengthening as the fen retreated. The droves could run to gates giving access to grazings where several villages intercommoned.
Fields and other features 1	Where a block of fields is cut by a dated feature, like a post-medieval channel, it must be older than that feature. When it conforms with it, it must be younger or of the same age.
Fields and other features 2	Small fields and field boundaries encircling or aligned along a lost feature of the landscape, like a former mere or coastal feature, must pre-date the disappearance of that feature.
Most human-made features	Some medieval features can be dated exactly from sources such as the records of abbeys and institutions responsible for drainage. Post-medieval features should be dated by successive maps, estate and parish records and specialist sources, such as the minute books of Drainage Commissions and records of the Board of Agriculture (1793–1822).

of land frequently connected coastal salt-works with the right of digging in the turbaries of the interior peatlands. The de-salted silt was left to form mounds that in time became covered with grass and fit for pasture. When the salterns of a locality grew above the level of the spring tides, the salters transferred their operations seaward' (1983 p.10). Further details about the production of brine were given by Summers: 'The method of producing salt was relatively simple, the salt water being run through three pits. After remaining in the first pit for a sufficient length of time for the mud and sand to settle, it was allowed to flow into the second until it became brine. This was then run into a third pit where it remained exposed to the sun until the water had evaporated and the salt crystals were formed' (1976 pp.35–6). Parallel, elongated ridges of desalinated silt of at least 10 feet high from saltings can be seen at sites around the Wash, like Wainfleet in Lincolnshire. Domesday Book records 180 saltings that were active in the Kings Lynn area alone.

Of the ditches of the wetlands, Taylor wrote that 'All fenland drains and cuts look alike and together with the endless flat land in which they lie give the impression of a dull, lifeless and uninteresting landscape. But for those prepared to carry out the necessary fieldwork and documentary work, the fenland landscape comes alive with history. Almost every drain and watercourse, whatever its size and form, can be dated, its original purpose ascertained and its countless alterations understood' (1973 p.191).

Factors useful in the dating of features of the wetlands landscape are shown in Table 2.3. As in other areas of landscape research, the relevant evidence relating to the development of a cultural landscape is likely to be partly concealed and dispersed between a variety of different sources. Air photographs may reveal the former drain-age patterns in an area of fenland and

Table 2.4   Place-name evidence in wetland settings

Name	Interpretation
Inning	Area of reclaimed land behind sea walls in East Anglia and the South East.
Wick	This word can have many meanings, but in southern salt marsh settings it can denote the site of the hut and milking place of a medieval shepherd.
Fleet (OE *flēot*)	An estuary or inlet.
Pool	May derive from an Old English word denoting a tidal creek or from different words denoting pools or mires.
Sea (OE *Sā*)	Sea.
Brooks	Local name for Sussex salt marshes.
Eye (OE *ēg*)	Higher island in salt marsh.
Trade	Trackway, often on a sea wall in Pevensey Levels etc.
Waller, Weller (OE *weller*)	Salt boiler, denoting medieval salt works.
Salt	These names are very common and will generally relate to salt workings rather than sea water.

display the presence of saltings; old maps, perhaps dating from the late sixteenth century onwards, may record the sequence of post-medieval drainage works; field walking might illuminate the history of settlement on fenland islands; while archaeological excavations could expose the timber trackways used in the prehistoric exploitation of a locality. In addition, place-names can provide valuable insights to former land-uses.

As Eddison and Draper note: 'The propen-

sity for change and destruction in marshland landscapes, responding to physical
problems and climatic adversity as well as to
economic factors, renders it very difficult for
either historians or geographers alone to
recover their history and evolution with

precision or certainty . . . detailed reading of
the landscape, careful scrutiny of early
maps, and extensive examination of documentary evidence can reveal highly significant information about the various phases'
(1997 p.87).

The great commons

At the time of Domesday, England had very
few unwanted places, but many localities
which were exploited in an extensive rather
than an intensive manner. For a century or
so there would be opportunities for expan-

---

*Map 2.6   Squatters on Moulsham Common, Essex,
converted into copyholders, 1591. Squatting on the
common has been legitimised by the conversion of
the squatters into copyholders. 'Tye' is a southern
word for common. Derived from a map by John
Walker held by Essex County Record Office.*

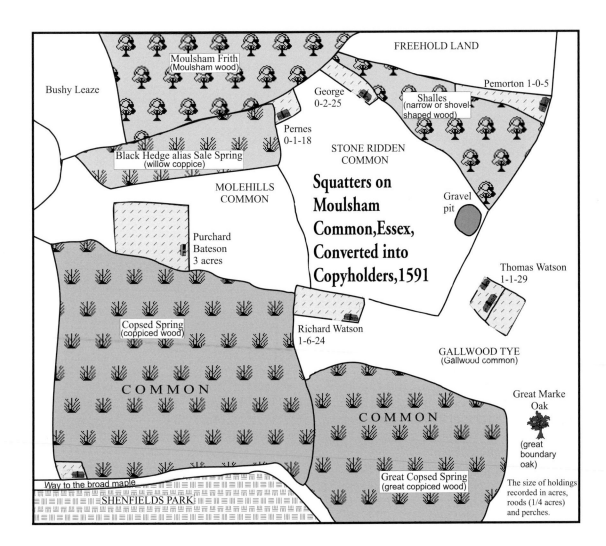

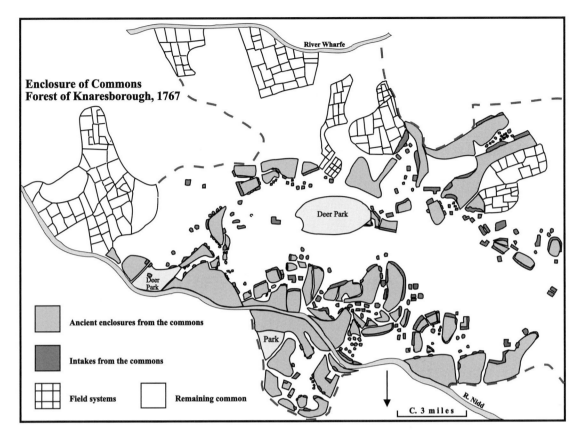

**Enclosure of Commons
Forest of Knaresborough, 1767**

River Wharfe

Deer Park

Deer Park

Park

R. Nidd

C. 3 miles

Ancient enclosures from the commons

Intakes from the commons

Field systems   Remaining common

sion into places where the pressure of human utilisation was fairly light. Gradually, however, the increases in population found expression in the landscape as common grazings and wood-pasture were converted to ploughland, adding new furlongs to the open fields, as sections of woodland were surrendered and as intakes were made in the open commons. The assault upon the waste could involve the solitary peasant household fencing and ditching morsels of woodland, moor and heath, it could involve groups of freeholders colonising an upland valley or lowland marsh, or it might concern a systematic campaign of reclamation spearheaded by a baron, bishop, abbot or prior. Much ancient common land survived until the start of the industrial age. At the start of the eighteenth century England and Wales contained 7 million to 10 million

Map 2.7   Enclosure of commons, Forest of Knaresborough, 1767. The original map, prepared prior to the enclosure award of 1778, attempted to show intakes and enclosures from the ancient commons. The portrayal of field systems is schematic. Derived from a map held by Leeds District Archives.

acres of commons, and the loss of most of these open lands has caused a profound transformation of the landscape.

The English commons must certainly have a prehistoric as well as a historic dimension and networks of enclosed pre-historic fields will frequently be seen to terminate in marginal areas loosely equiv-alent to those which served as commons in the medieval period, implying the pre-historic existence of open, communally exploited lands. Most commons may have been old by the time of Domesday, but a few are more recent, some being created to compensate communities for established commons lost in the creation of parks or other enclosures. A small common was set out at Fersfield in Norfolk around 1500 to compensate for the enlargement of Kenninghall Park (Dymond, 1985 p.108). The extent of commons varied from manor to manor and from region to region. In some southern and Midlands localities, within a few centuries of Domesday the arable acreage expanded towards the margins of the estate to leave an inadequate provision for grazing and hay and very little common. In most upland localities, however, unenclosed rough grazing was a major and crucial contributor to the farming economy and the manorial waste was the most extensive component of their landscapes. There was no simple division between upland and lowland, for many lowland communities derived enormous support from their commons or areas where they intercommoned with neighbours.

Commons were the property of the lord of the manor, but his/her rights were constrained by long-established tenant rights rooted in hallowed customs. Generally these embraced 'agistment' or rights of summer grazing; turbary, concerning rights to take turf or peat for fuel; and 'estovers', involving rights to take materials for building dwellings, ploughs or for making dead hedges. The regulation of the system was accomplished by the manor court where, in the northern uplands particularly, the principles of good neighbourhood and ancient custom prevailed. Ancient customs were revered and guided decision-making, while good neighbourhood was seen as underpinning the fabric of rural society and was supported by the allocations of the court. A complexity of regulations controlled the affairs of feudal and semi-feudal society, some of them being particular to the one manor.

Tenants were controlled in terms of what they could or could not do, the manner in which they did the things that they could do, and the times of the day or year when they could do them. Thus, 'venville' rights were attached to some farms on Dartmoor after the disafforestation of the Royal Forest in 1239. By paying small fees to the Crown or Duchy, the holders of these farms could pasture stock on the Dartmoor commons by day—but if they wished to keep the animals on at night they had to pay an extra fee. In some places, like Brown Clee Hill in Shropshire, a distinction was made between 'commoners', with full rights, and 'out-commoners', living further away, who had fewer privileges. 'Drift rolls' might exist, which specified the tracks which were to be used by different stockmen driving beasts to the common from different parts of the manor.

Many commons were 'stinted' in order to regulate the number of animals supported and prevent the over-grazing of the resource, with stinting arrangements apparently becoming widespread in the thirteenth century as population pressure on the wastes increased. Stints regulated the number of animals that could be put on the common; in articles of agreement for the use of the fen commons at Waterbeach in Cambridgeshire in 1683 it was agreed that 'for each and every common every owner or occupier shall or may feed fifteen milch cows or dry neat cattle and ten sheep, and the owner of every half commonable house proportionately. And if he or they shall not think fit to keep so many cows then he or they may keep ten cows and five mares or geldings, but not to exceed the number of five mares or horse beasts, and to abate a cow for every colt after it is a year old' (Ravensdale, 1978 p.78). In Upper Nidderdale, the stinted pastures were 'firthed' or cleared of stock on 25 March to permit a regrowth of the grass, and at the end of April the cattle were brought back in numbers which accorded to the stint. Depending on the conditions prevailing, hill sheep were let on to the commons at Michaelmas or Martinmas, and there they could graze in unlimited numbers until the spring, while the cattle were fed on hay and oat straw in the lower enclosures. In the north, commoners held 'gates', each gate relating to the right to pasture one adult animal on the common.

Problems associated with unstinted commons were modelled by Hardin (1968) to produce *The Tragedy of the Commons*, a model much loved by political scientists. It envisages an English village community in which each member is entitled to put animals on the common. The individual villagers continue to add to their livestock so long as each additional animal yields some measure of profit. Eventually, the resultant over-grazing will ruin the common for every member. Each commoner has a personal interest in continuing to add beasts to the common, but a common interest in adjusting grazing to the carrying capacity of the resource. 'Each villager also knows that if he or she adds just one more animal to the common it will not instantaneously cause the ruin of the pasture. In addition there is a "free rider" problem: if some villagers act in an ecologically responsible manner and withdraw livestock from the common then they will bear the costs of conservation, while their selfish neighbours will reap the benefits and continue to overgraze the resource to the point of its extinction' (Muir, 1997 p.260). The Hardin model found expression on scores of commons, where over-grazing could suppress the growth of grass and encourage biodiversity. Squires wrote of the commons of Charnwood Forest and described how the remaining tree cover was removed at the close of the medieval period: 'At the same time the vegetation of these areas, where land was grazed under the right of common, developed into that of upland

heath which was recognised by a distinctive flora and a characteristic open landscape. This could be clearly contrasted with another landscape that was created by the planned husbandry of private owners, to the extent that between 1500 and 1810 there existed two different Charnwoods' (1981 p.60).

The system of manors and commons was an exclusive one, being neither egalitarian nor outward-looking. In this way, a tenant household might have the right to dig peat for their own fires before May Day, but not to dig it for sale or for others. Devonians living beyond the confines of Dartmoor were 'foreigners' and could not put their stock on its commons. Common rights attached to land and properties rather than to people; cottagers on a manor might or might not be accorded the rights to pasture beasts on the common. In some cases they had such rights but were forbidden to keep dogs, owing to a fear amongst other commoners that they might 'dog-in' the stock of 'strangers' from outside the manor. The manor court did not necessarily reflect the collective will of the community and would tend to become dominated by the higher elements in farming society and support the interests of ancient freeholders rather than the smaller people.

The old commons varied hugely in their size, topography and ecology. As recently as the Napoleonic era, Exmoor resembled a vast medieval waste, with some 50 parishes in Devon and Somerset sending 25,000 sheep to graze there during the summer months. In Cumbria, Northumberland and the uplands of Yorkshire and Lancashire the open commons sprawled across most of the fell country, while in Norfolk some commons took the form of 'low commons', which followed river courses, while others existed as zones of grassland bordering tracks or 'drifts'. Intercommoning involved the sharing of a common by two or more parishes or townships and it could imply the

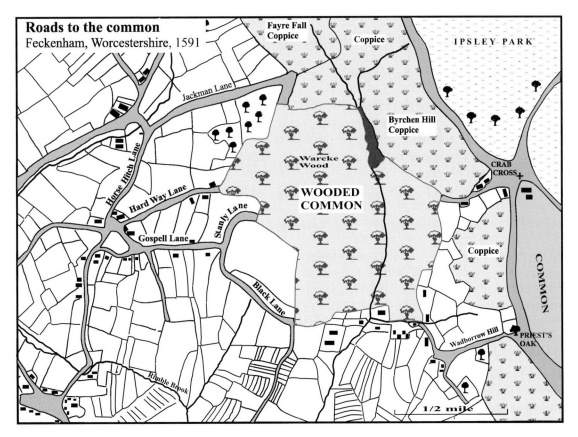

Roads to the common
Feckenham, Worcestershire, 1591

Fayre Fall Coppice
Coppice
IPSLEY PARK
Jackman Lane
Horse Hitch Lane
Byrchen Hill Coppice
Hard Way Lane
Warcke Wood
WOODED COMMON
CRAB CROSS
Stanly Lane
Gospell Lane
Coppice
COMMON
Black Lane
Wadborrow Hill
PRIEST'S OAK
Rimble Brook
1/2 mile

Map 2.8   Roads to the common, Feckenham, Worcestershire, 1591. Detail derived from a map made for Queen Elizabeth I by John Blagrave in 1591, which was redrawn in 1744 and is held by Hereford and Worcester County Council.

antiquity of the institution, with the shared common being a component of some extensive ancient estate. Writing on Norfolk, Dymond characterised commons as patches of unimproved waste left after other areas were more intensely developed. He added:

> Several characteristics point to a pre-Norman origin: for example the existence of 'intercommons' which were shared by two or more parishes: Banham and Winfarthing shared a large common of 1,200 acres, and a marsh was common to the inhabitants of Stoke Ferry, Wretton

and Wereham. In one remarkable case a thirteenth-century common was recorded as belonging to the whole hundred of Taverham. This is surely a primitive form of commoning which pre-dates the highly organised usages of medieval manors. (1985 pp.108–9)

Commons are of considerable interest to landscape archaeologists. By their nature they tended to escape medieval ploughing, which damaged or obliterated many pre-medieval monuments and earthworks. Some of the finest prehistoric settlement and field remains are associated with commons and former commons—the Iron Age field systems above Grassington in Wharfedale, most of the Bronze Age settlements and reaves on Dartmoor and a variety of Romano-British and Roman remains in the Pennines are among the numerous examples. The commons may not have been ploughed, but their character does often seem to have changed in the course of the medieval period, with the pressures of grazing leading to a replacement of woodland or wood-pasture by grassland or heath. Confirmation of this comes from woodland place-names and names associated with woodland clearance, like stocks, stubbs and royd, which often abound on commons

Though devoid of ridge and furrow, the commons preserve many earthworks of their own. Sometimes these marked the borders of the common, where double banks may be found, while holloways, known as 'outracks' or 'straker ways' in the West Midlands, radiated out from the common. Many tracks associated with droving stock to and from the common survive as motor roads today, thus the B3212 appears to coincide with a routeway used by the inhabitants of Buckland to take their cattle to pasture on Dartmoor which was mentioned in a charter of 1031 (Pearce, 1985 p.17). Describing the scene in Norfolk, Dymond wrote: 'On the heavier land especially, commons are bounded by very large earthworks, particularly deep ditches and thick hedges containing many species of shrub. These may be among the most ancient landscape features still in regular use . . . Entries to commons were often controlled by gates, which are still frequently referred to in local place names. Pits were regularly dug on common land, with or without manorial consent, to extract sand, gravel, clay and other materials' (1985 p.109). In the stone-rich lands the surfaces of commons tend to be pock-marked with little quarries. In places like the Pennines, the last enlargement of a communal quarry could have been to extract the stone needed for the walls which would enclose, privatise and partition the old common, though some communal quarries survived Parliamentary Enclosure. Other pits and gullies in the old commons of the northern fells mark the pursuit of a vein of lead, while in the lowlands commons were dug for marl and other resources. At Brill in Buckinghamshire huge pits were gouged in the extraction of clay for use in the local pottery industry.

Table 2.5   Earthworks associated with commons

Name of feature	Appearance and nature
Bell pits	Bell-shaped pits around 6 feet wide at the top and broadening at the base which lies up to 20 feet below the surface. Mainly associated with primitive forms of mining for iron ore or coal (occasionally clay), bell pits are normally seen in a back-filled state. They often exist as circular, doughnut-shaped earthworks with settlement of the dross causing central depressions which may be colonised by trees or form ponds. Filling of the shafts may produce domed mounds of dross. Bell pits usually occur in groups. Date: medieval.
Quarries	Communal quarries or clunch (chalk) pits were widespread before Parliamentary Enclosure, while in the stone-rich lands little quarries are perhaps the commonest form of earthwork and they provided materials for house-building, walling and road-making. Quarry earthworks are usually pronounced but irregular and associated with places where good-quality stone occurs near the surface. Medieval quarry workers prepared to work sideways rather than downwards and to lever and slide blocks of stone downslope from the quarry face.

Table 2.5   Earthworks associated with commons—continued

Name of feature	Appearance and nature
Clay pits	Associated with medieval pottery industries, large and small. The smaller examples may exist as depressions or ponds, but large-scale commercial pottery industries could result in a very substantial reworking of the surface of the common, as at Brill in Buckinghamshire.
Prehistoric settlements	Examples with upstanding earthworks and hut circles should be well-known, but less conspicuous examples will be numerous. Be aware of settings with sweeping views of the surrounding countryside and access to water. Scatters of stone and clumps of nettles could be significant.
Marl pits	Marl is calcareous clay or chalk which was spread to improve soils, while softer forms of limestone were sometimes dug for marl. The history of marling goes back at least to 1252 (Prince, 1964). Marl pits are normally bowl-shaped depressions, sometimes flooded, though marl was also mined from bell pits. To minimise the transport of loads, the pits were often located in the working fields rather than on the common.
Sites of dwellings	The sites of dwellings, often rather insubstantial constructions, which were built by squatters in the post-medieval period, may be marked by ruined walls, a litter of rubble or merely level house platforms cut into sloping ground.
Pillow mounds	Medieval lords had the right to set up warrens. Within the area of the warren, the rabbit breeding area could be protected by banks, while pillow mounds or 'buries' accommodated the burrows. Generally these have the form of pillow-shaped or cigar-shaped mounds measuring around 100 feet by 30 feet. Rabbits, coming from Spain, were introduced to most parts of England in the twelfth century and pillow mounds were built until the nineteenth century.
Windmill mounds	Windmills were erected in exposed situations and these were often provided by upland, downland or scarp-top commons. Windmill mounds were quite small and dome-shaped and cross-shaped depressions at their centres may mark the position of the cross trees which supported the central post on which the mill revolved so that the sails could catch the wind.
Place-names which may help to identify features	*Burgh*: usually signifying a fortification, this word could be linked to settlement sites regarded as ancient. *Coneygarth, burie, berrie*, warren: pillow mound. *Kiln*: often found in association with clay workings. *Windmill, windhill*: windmill site. Elements like *cinder, cinderhills* or *smelt* can denote metal processing sites close to mines.

REFERENCES

Coney, A. 'Fish, fowl and fen: landscape and economy on seventeenth-century Martin Mere' *Landscape History* 14 (1992) pp.51–64.

Darby, H.C. *The Draining of the Fens* (Cambridge: Cambridge University Press, 1940).

Darby, H.C. *The Changing Fenland* (Cambridge: Cambridge University Press, 1983).

Defoe, D. *A Tour Through the Whole Island of Great Britain* (Exeter: Webb and Bower, 1989), first published 1724–6.

Dyer, C. '"The retreat from Marginal Land": the growth and decline of medieval rural settlements' in M. Aston, D. Austin and C. Dyer (eds) *The Rural Settlements of Medieval England* (Oxford: Blackwell, 1989) pp.45–57.

Dymond, D. *The Norfolk Landscape* (London: Hodder and Stoughton, 1985).

Eddison, J. and Draper, G. 'A landscape of medieval reclamation: Walland Marsh, Kent' *Landscape History* 19 (1997) pp.75–88.

Hardin, G. 'The tragedy of the commons' *Science* 162 (1968) pp.1243–8.

Hawkins, D. *Avalon and Sedgemoor* (Newton Abbot: David and Charles, 1973).

James Menuge, N. *Climate Change on the North York Moors*, Research Centre Occasional Paper 1 (York: University College of Ripon and York St John, 1997).

Kershaw, I. *Bolton Priory: The Economy of a Northern Monastery, 1286–1325* (Oxford: Oxford University Press, 1973).

Kipling, C. 'The commercial fisheries of Windermere' *Transactions of the Cumberland and Westmorland Antiquarian and Archaeological Society* 72 (1972) pp.156–204.

Millward, R. and Robinson, A. *The Hoo Peninsula and the Scarplands of Mid-West Kent* (London: Macmillan, 1971).

Muir, R. *Political Geography: A New Introduction* (Basingstoke: Macmillan, 1997).

Parker, R. *The Common Stream* (St Albans: Paladin, 1976).

Parry M.L. 'Secular climatic change and marginal agriculture' *Institute of British Geographers Transactions* 64 (1975) pp.1–13.

Pearce, S. 'Early medieval land use on Dartmoor and its flanks' *Devon Archaeology* 3 (1985) pp.13–19.

Postan, M.M. (ed.), Cambridge Economic History of Europe vol. 1. (Cambridge: Cambridge University Press, 1996).

Prince, H.C. 'The origin of pits and depressions in Norfolk' *Geography* 49 (1964) pp.15–31.

Ravensdale, J.R. *Liable to Floods* (Cambridge: Cambridge University Press, 1974).

Squires, 'The two faces of Charnwood (c. 1500 AD–c. 1600 AD)' in J. Crocker (ed.) *Charnwood Forest: A Changing Landscape* (Loughborough: Loughborough Naturalists' Club, 1981) pp.60–74.

Summers, D. *The Great Level* (Newton Abbot: David and Charles, 1976).

Taylor, C.C. *The Cambridgeshire Landscape* (London: Hodder and Stoughton, 1973).

Williams, M. *The Draining of the Somerset Levels* (Cambridge: Cambridge University Press, 1970).

Williams, M. 'Marshland and waste' in L. Cantor (ed.) *The English Medieval Landscape* (London: Croom Helm, 1982) pp.86–125.

Wood, P.D. 'Strip lynchets reconsidered' *Geographical Journal* 127 (1961) pp.449–59.

CHAPTER 3

Lines in the Landscape

Boundaries are less a part of life than once they were. In modern England, people have a vague awareness of local government territories—though the most critical boundaries for many are those delimiting school catchment areas. Vital issues of worship, tenure, obligation and fealty are no longer spatially defined by revered boundaries, indeed they often do not even matter at all. Formerly, however, people were highly conscious of authorities and their jurisdictions and well-rehearsed in the disposition of local boundaries. These lines in the landscape defined the patterns of day-to-day life.

Every landscape is enmeshed in networks of boundaries. Some of these are 'living' or current and others are relics of former patterns of overlordship and partition. Some boundaries are political in character and define polities, jurisdictions and the interfaces between ethno-cultural groups. Others relate to ownership and tenancy and concern property and tenurial arrangements, while others still express arrangements for the working of the land and constitute a partitioning of countryside into fields, commons, furlongs and meadows. The physical presence of a boundary in a landscape may be emphatic, yet the origins and functions of that boundary may be uncertain and controversial, as with numerous linear earthworks. Alternatively, the material expression of a boundary may be modest and sometimes invisible and yet that boundary can effect far-reaching socio-economic consequences, as with the Anglo-Scottish boundary, which separates two national groupings, two legal systems and two educational systems, as well as having profound psychological associations.

Change, whether in the form of conquest or social evolution, frequently involves the substitution of one set of boundaries for another, so that beneath the current territorial boundaries are stratified others which express previous systems of ownership, control or division. Systems of boundaries that are relict and inconspicuous may have little or no influence on contemporary

Table 3.1   *Types of bounded space of interest to landscape historians*
(The categories are not entirely exclusive, e.g. the manor had political and economic dimensions)

	Political	Administrative	Economic
High status	Major tribal territory. Heptarchy of Saxon kingdoms.	County/shire, riding, part.	Multiple estate.
Middle status	Barony, Borders franchise.	Forest, honour, liberty, soke, hundred, rape, wapentake.	Estate, hide, carucate, virgate, farm.
Low status	Manor.	Parish, township, vill, tithing, constablewick.	Field, markland, intake.

Figure 3.1   Devil's Dyke in Cambridgeshire, a huge earthwork exemplifying the massive efforts often associated with dyke-building.

affairs, yet during their currency they may have been associated with crucial watersheds in the landscapes of governance and allegiance. In Sussex, in the centuries bracketing the Norman Conquest, both 'rapes' and 'hides' were territorial divisions with considerable significance for the population though now they are largely forgotten. In the area of landscape research one may sometimes be aware of the existence of an organised territory but be unsure of the disposition of its boundaries—as with the Iron Age territories which were subordinate to hillforts. Equally, one may be aware of the existence of boundaries, yet uncertain as to the nature of the territory which they bordered—as with pit align-

ments. Only when the core, the tributary area and its limits can be recognised can the landscape historian be confident that a basis for understanding has been established.

The evolution of boundaries: linear earthworks

The delimitation and demarcation of the first territorial boundaries must have signified a filling-up of the land and the depletion of unexploited territory that was

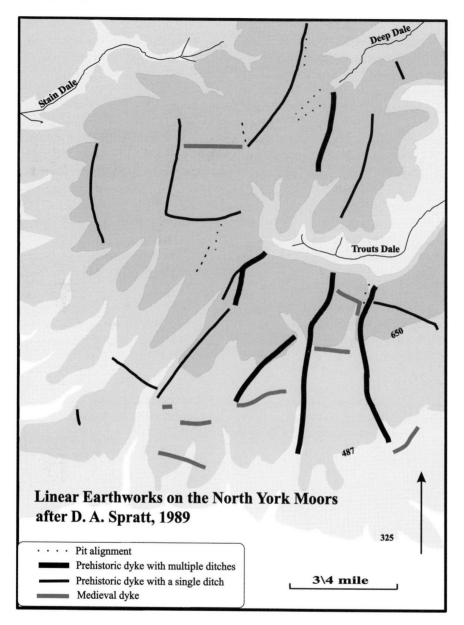

Map 3.1   *Linear earthworks on the North York Moors, after Spratt (1989).*

available for further colonisation and expansion. Similarly, as the pressure of human population upon the land resources increased, so it is evident that boundaries were made to be more prominent and insistent facets of the landscape.

Boundaries serve both instructive and symbolic roles. When manifest to the onlooker in the form of ditches, banks, chains of pits, hedgebanks and so on, they symbolise a divide that has been negotiated, imposed or claimed and perhaps, if erosion and repairs are evident, hallowed by time as well. At the same time, these and other constructions express the territorial claims of a society or dynasty. In extreme cases, as with Offa's Dyke, Devil's Dyke, Dane's Dyke and other large linear earthworks, the symbolic power is immense, with the earthworks effectively issuing threats to whoever transgresses the bounds. These boundary works, with their steep banks and deep fronting ditches, closely resemble more functional defenceworks, such as the ramparts of hillforts, so that a note of military menace is conveyed in their message. (Indeed, in 1881 General Pitt-Rivers interpreted many of the 'entrenchments' on the Yorkshire Wolds and Tabular Hills as parts of a great defensive system built to defend the territory against invaders from the west (p.690)).

Among the oldest territorial boundaries recognised are pit alignments, formerly assumed to belong to the Neolithic period, though late Bronze Age and Iron Age dates have proved to be more appropriate in some cases. Though generally regarded as boundaries, pit alignments sometimes seem ill-suited for this purpose. Pollard explored Iron Age riverside examples at St Ives, Cambridgeshire, which ran parallel to the river in places where the pits must frequently have filled with water. It was suggested that the alignments be seen in their symbolical context: 'The use of pit lines was clearly significatory, with the form carrying a commonly understood meaning related to the character of the boundary or area being defined. They clearly marked important divisions, and perhaps we might see them as a response to inter-community landscape disputes marking common rather than individual family/kin holdings or

Map 3.2   Proposed prehistoric estate boundaries on the east Tabular Hills, Yorkshire, redrawn from Spratt (1989).

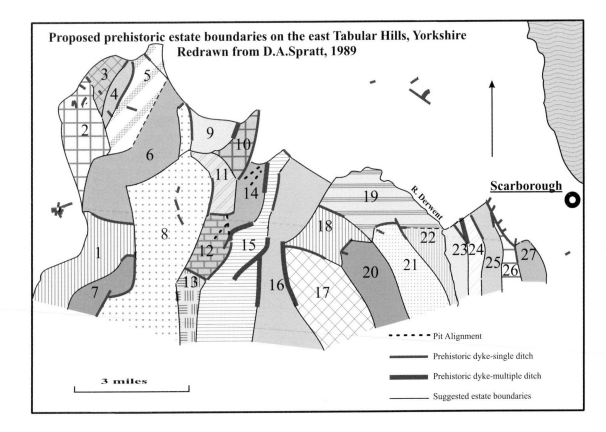

dividing different zones of resource' (Pollard, 1996 p.110). It appeared that materials of wood and bone had been symbolically deposited in the pits, perhaps in the course of some form of 'beating the bounds': 'Significantly most of the wood derives from hedges and perhaps fences. Accepting that intentional depositional practices served to situate meaning through processes of metaphor and connotation, one could envisage a metaphoric link between the placement of bits of old boundaries in a newly constructed boundary earthwork' (p.111).

These alignments are problematical features and successive air photographs taken over a considerable period of time have shown continuous linear features being converted into hyphenated ones as modern agriculture has bitten into and removed the soil blanket. Of the situation in the Yorkshire Wolds, Stoertz wrote: 'It is not uncommon to find that the most recent

Table 3.2 Place-names and boundaries

Name element	Meaning
Shire, sher, shir (OE *scir*)	A boundary, but treat carefully as a similar OE word means 'bright', 'pure'.
Row (ON *ra*)	A boundary, but 'row' may also denote 'rough'.
-mere, -more (OE *gemære*)	A boundary, but these names can easily be confused with others derived from an OE word denoting a lake or pond or one referring to a mare.
-rich, -reach, -rick, -rigg (OE *ric/raec?*)	Gelling (1993 pp.183–6) suggests the existence of an OE word which denoted a raised straight strip and which applied to linear earthworks, ridges and the raised aggers of Roman roads.
-dyke, -dike (OE *dic*)	A ditch, trench or embankment. Often associated with linear earthworks.
-hedge, -hay (OE *haga, hege, hegeræwe*)	Hedge, hedgerow; hay and haya sometimes denote hedged boundaries of deer parks.
Thorn (OE *thorn, thyrne*)	Denotes a thorn tree and often associated with thorn hedges noted in charter boundaries.
Stan, -stan (OE *stan*)	Stone, sometimes denoting a boundary stone, as in Merstham = 'boundary stone'.
Threp (OE *threap*)	Disputed land—often found in a boundary locality.
Cross (OE *cros*)	'Cross' place-names frequently signify old boundaries as crosses were commonly employed as boundary-markers.
Hare, hore, hoor (OE *har*)	Can signify a boundary, as in 'harestan' or 'boundary stone', though such words can also derive from an OE word for 'grey' or 'hoary'.
Hurrock, hurder, lad and law (OE *hlǣw*)	Northern dialect words associated with cairns or heaps of stones sometimes employed as boundary-markers ('law' generally refers to an ancient burial mound).

aerial photographs of linear ditches and earthwork banks that have been eroded by ploughing reveal pit alignments, whereas earlier photography showed the earthworks or cropmarks of continuous linear ditches' (1997 p.18). Excavations at Heslerton in the Yorkshire Wolds show that major late Bronze Age boundaries in the locality had their origins as pit alignments (Powlesland, 1986, 1988). It seems possible that the periodic recutting of the pits would have caused an enlargement which could have caused the tops of the pits to merge to form a continuous ditch—or perhaps the indivi-

dual pits could mark places where posts had been set in the bed of a ditch?

Evidence of the reorganisation of boundaries can be found on the other side of the Vale of Pickering, in the North York Moors. Detailed investigations by Spratt (1981) suggested that the early boundaries between 'estates' on the uplands of North Yorkshire were based on natural terrain

Fig. 3.2   The Tor Dyke, an undated linear earthwork which controls the pass from Upper Wharfedale into Coverdale and runs just below the breaks of slope near the top of the pass.

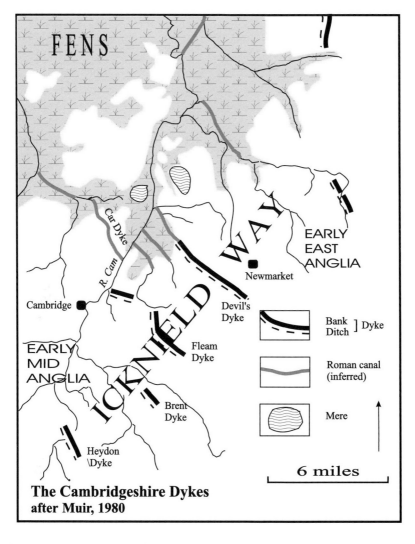

The Cambridgeshire Dykes after Muir, 1980

features, such as watercourses and watersheds, with the watershed boundaries being demarcated by round barrows which contained cremation urns of early Bronze Age date. The boundaries identified correspond remarkably well with surviving township boundaries, with differences between the two patterns often being recognisable as medieval changes. In some places in the Hambleton Hills during the middle to late Bronze Age, linear earthworks (dykes) augmented the boundaries formed by barrow chains. The Cleave Dyke, a major earthwork on the west of the Hambleton Hills, appeared to have been built in two phases,

Map 3.3   The Cambridgeshire dykes, after Muir (1980). The zone of ancient routeways known as the Icknield Way is barred by a succession of dykes of uncertain age.

the first phase being largely or entirely a pit alignment (Spratt and White, 1986) that was superseded by a continuous ditch which veered from the original alignment. Other dykes were converted from single to double forms and new dykes could be inserted into existing systems, while the Skell Dykes began as a single bank and ditch which was replaced by a double dyke on a different line. Some quite complex forms evolved. The Scamridge Dykes originally consisted of six parallel ditches and banks and the elaborate form suggested that they might have been a tribal or political boundary rather than a conventional estate boundary. The Cockmoor Dykes consist of six major dykes, probably of prehistoric origins, which are apparently joined by up to fourteen smaller parallel dykes, some perhaps the holloways of medieval tracks and some possibly pillow mounds (Spratt, 1989 pp.47–50). The major early dykes which divide the territory into estates seem to date from the end of the second millennium BC, while the estates were apparently sub-divided by 'cross-ridge dykes', some datable to the end of the first millennium BC.

Linear earthworks are widely distributed. In England there are three main concentrations: in Wessex, in the Yorkshire Wolds, and in the Tabular Hills of the North York Moors. Examples may be found in most other areas, and in the Yorkshire Dales some that are seen in Swaledale have been studied by Fleming (1994). There, the Grinton–Fremington dykes (two linear earthworks with ditches on their eastern sides that lie about 550 yards apart and that controlled the eastern approaches to Upper Swaledale and Arkengarthdale) had been regarded as Brigantian defences against the Romans. Fleming showed that they had been built across field banks associated with settlements that were almost certainly of Iron Age and Romano British dates (p.18). The dykes were also built across a Roman road serving the fort of Navio, which was still in occupation in the mid-fourth century, and consequently they could be no earlier than the final decades of the Roman occupation. He found that: 'The linear earthworks suggest the existence of a hitherto unrecognised early post-Roman polity in Upper Swaledale and Arken-garthdale—a polity which might be held to correspond, at least roughly, with the large

medieval parish of Grinton and the manor of Healaugh' (p.19). To the east of Swaledale, a boundary between Dark Age English and British territories may be marked by the Scots Dyke, while the impressive Tor Dyke controls the approaches to Coverdale from Wharfedale and is regarded by some as a frontierwork of the British Christian kingdom of Craven. Like many other ancient linear earthworks, it became a peg on which many other boundaries—township, parish, deanery, wapentake and county—could be hung (White, 1997 p.46). Plainly, ancient and even prehistoric features of the cultural landscape could influence and guide the course of medieval development.

Linear earthworks are likely to be difficult features to date, while without dating evidence it is impossible to relate them to their cultural or political-geographical contexts. Unlike so many distinctive archaeological features, they cannot readily be ascribed to a narrowly dated period. Boundary earthworks were constructed in the Neolithic period and dykes were still being built in Ireland in Norman times, with very similar earthworks being constructed during the medieval period to enclose deer parks. Unlike settlement features, with their rich accumulations of artefacts, dykes traversed expanses of largely uninhabited countryside. Only in exceptional situations are excavations likely to be rewarded, though wherever trenching and pipe-laying operations cut a linear earthwork searches may be made for datable materials lying directly upon the old land surface or at the bottom of the ditch fill. Otherwise, dating must be based on recognising older features, which are cut by the dyke, and younger features, which cut the earthwork.

Some of the difficulties and possibilities associated with such research are demonstrated by the Cambridgeshire Dykes (Muir, 1980). Four parallel dykes with north-west to south-east alignments traversed the countryside to the east of Cambridge, with Devil's Dyke, its north-western end anchored in the Fens, and Fleam Dyke still surviving as imposing earthworks. With their proximity to Cambridge University, the dykes experienced more scholarly attention than similar features elsewhere. Roman pottery of the fourth century was found beneath Heydon Dyke, the most southerly of the group, while in 1973 Professor Hope-Taylor removed a Roman coin of about AD 350 from beneath the bank of Devil's Dyke. This shows that (providing that they are contemporary) the Dykes are *younger* than the middle of the fourth century. They must also be *older* than the late Saxon period, by which time they had entered folklore and were used as frameworks on which to hang ecclesiastical boundaries.

The important questions for boundary studies such as these to solve are those of date and function. 'Function' may have important symbolic dimensions and explanations based purely on military interpretations are insupportable: Devil's Dyke is still up to 15 feet high and fronted by a ditch which can be more than 15 feet deep, but it is also about 8 miles long. Warriors could not stand more than two deep on the narrow crest of the monument, while to man it from end to end with only a single line of defenders would require a force of more than 13,000. Such would have been a much larger provincial army than could have existed in the social and environmental disruption of the post-Roman period. If the value of the dyke system was limited in strictly military terms, its importance to the society that built it must have been immense. Using data from an excavated cross-section of Devil's Dyke and experimental data from the geologically similar earthwork on Overton Down, it was calculated:

that the entire earthwork weights 1,360,090,000 kilogrammes, and if one

man with a pick and shovel can move 750 kilogrammes of solid moist chalk in one hour, then the Dyke represents the work of 1,813,453 man hours or 181,453 ten-hour man days. When we then make an extra allowance for material lost from the bank in ditch silts we arrive at the suggestion that the Dyke would have fully occupied 1000 labourers for 200 days (or 500 labourers for 400 days and so on). In addition an allowance would be needed for surveying, supervising and finishing the work and the quartering and feeding of the work force. Then again there is the opportunity cost involved since those men occupied as Dyke builders could not function as peasants or artisans. In short, the Dykes were mammoth undertakings that must have strained the resources of society. (Muir, 1980 p.204)

As obstacles to the rapid movement of cavalry, particularly to raiding parties departing with loot, the Dykes had some functional credibility, but their main role seems to have been of a symbolic nature, providing spectacular assertions of the territoriality of a post-Roman or early medieval polity. Much remains to be discovered about boundaries in the pre-Christian period. To improve our understandings we must not only discover more examples in the field, but also improve our awareness of the psychological and symbolic significance of boundaries. Also, we must learn more about the nature of the polities that boundaries delimited.

Medieval and later boundaries

Medieval people (and probably their predecessors too) were very much aware of boundaries, whether these boundaries were of an economic, legal or ecclesiastical form. Their lives were enacted within superimposed networks of overlapping authorities—authorities that controlled their beliefs, obligations and loyalties. Now, most of these authorities and institutions have declined or vanished and it is not always easy to recognise or reconstruct the old bounded territories or comprehend their functions. The tasks are made harder by the regional variations in customs which existed throughout the kingdom. Nevertheless, the old units of administration and control played vital roles in shaping the development of landscape and an understanding of their natures and extents may be essential to comprehending a passage of countryside.

Many misunderstandings in landscape history derive from attempts to impose a southern, parish-based model of organisa-tion upon other regions that it does not fit. In the areas of Midland and southern England now associated with nucleated village settlement, it seems that around AD 750–800 both the multiple estates and the organisations based on minster churches were in decline. Manorial estates and estate churches were being created, giving rise to the parish-based system, and in the most simple cases, parish, township and land-

Map 3.4   Variations in the units of community, showing the contrasting forms of local organisation in England, partly based on Winchester (1997) and Sylvester (1969).

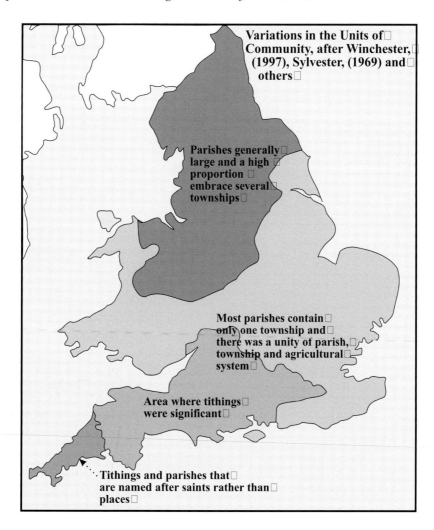

Variations in the Units of Community, after Winchester, (1997), Sylvester, (1969) and others

Parishes generally large and a high proportion embrace several townships

Most parishes contain only one township and there was a unity of parish, township and agricultural system

Area where tithings were significant

Tithings and parishes that are named after saints rather than places

working unit were defined by the one boundary. Even in the heartlands of 'village England' this model was neither universal nor stable; parts of the parish could split off and unite with neighbouring parishes or become parishes within their own rights. Some village-centred parishes contained more than one manor, and a manor which was a separate unit in terms of taxation might gain its own chapel, with the process of separation culminating in the winning of burial rights and the institution of a new parish.

In other parts of the country, the parish-based model was quite inappropriate as a basic unit of community, this role being played by the township or vill. The northern countrysides tended to be more impoverished, with more extensive pastoral farming and less intensive arable cultivation. Thus the areas needed to support a church were far more extensive. Winchester noted that:

> In the north of England the ancient ecclesiastical parish was of quite a different order of magnitude from its counterpart in the south. Most northern parishes contained more than one rural community and some were vast; Kendal parish (Westmorland) embraced 25 townships and over 68,000 acres (27,600 ha.) . . . the northern township became the basis of poor law administration; it had its own constable and frequently maintained its roads. Township meetings were held, replacing many of the functions of the parish vestry and sometimes overlapping with the manor court. In the north,

Table 3.3   Community organisation areas

Vill	Deriving from *villa*, a town/village, and *villata*, signifying a township, the vill can be an ancient territory, perhaps receding into the prehistoric period. 'Vill' is often used in a sense synonymous with 'township'. The vill generally consisted of a group of farming families who operated as neighbours, sometimes working co-operatively, within an old geographical land cell. The vill could be the fundamental unit of taxation and the constables, often elected by the manor court, linked the vill or township community and the state.
Township/constablewick	This can generally be identified with the vill; the township elected a constable who represented the community of the territory. In the north, townships gained responsibility for the poor rate after 1662. For researchers working in northern England, the township should be regarded as the fundamental unit of community.
Hamlet	These appear in Latin documents as *hameletti*. Normally regarded as settlements smaller than villages but larger than farmsteads, hamlets were also subdivisions of large northern townships and had responsibility for maintaining their own roads. The hamlets were often coherent socio-geographical territories coinciding with estates or settlement clusters and their lands—i.e. units resembling vills. They could, perhaps, have originated as vills and have later been subsumed into other vills.
Civil parish	A nineteenth century creation (1889) corresponding generally to an ecclesiastical parish in the south of England and a township in the north: a place which had responsibility for maintaining its own poor.

Table 3.3   Community organisation areas—continued

Tithing	Originally an association of ten householders, answerable to the hundred court, who shared responsibility for the arrest of criminals and the gathering of dues. It was at first a personal rather than a territorial grouping which expanded in late Saxon England but did not reach the north-eastern and western extremities. In western districts, the tithings became territorially based; in thirteenth century Cornwall tithings were sometimes territorially coincident with manors, sometimes not. In the south, tithings supported constables and corresponded to northern townships in this respect.
Hundred/wapentake	Division of Saxon England below the level of the shire. The origins of the hundred are uncertain. In the West Midlands they seem to represent areas covering 100 hides, hides being roughly the amount of land that would support a single family. Hundreds often focused on a main or hundredal manor and in Cornwall the hundreds take their names from their leading manors. In the six eastern counties of Danelaw and parts of the north the hundreds were replaced by wapentakes.
Parish (ancient)	A unit generally younger than townships and vills which was the area served by a parish church and supporting a priest who was financed by tithes collected from the population resident in the parish. These people were buried in the churchyard of their parish church when they died. In the south, parishes were often compact and coincident with manors and vills, while in the north, parishes often extended across several vills or townships. In Cornwall, parishes were not rooted in geography, tithings or manors and were named after saints. Parishes gained responsibility for poor relief and the upkeep of roads in the sixteenth century.
Chapelry	Territory lying within an ancient parish but served, often because of distance from the parish church, by a chapel of ease. Such chapels sometimes gained rights to marry and baptise. When rights of burial were gained then normally they effectively became centres of their own, new parishes.

therefore, we must construct an alternative model of local territorial organisation in which the township replaces the parish for most civil purposes and the parish, remaining essentially an ecclesiastical entity, rises above the basic level of territorial cells. (1997 p.4)

He referred to work by Sylvester (1969) that described a 'parish line' between the northern 'township country' and the southern 'parish country'. Lancashire and Cheshire have averages of over five townships per parish, Northumberland an average of more than seven, while south of a line running diagonally from Flamborough Head through Birmingham, the average is less than two. To complicate matters further, Wessex fits neither model, for here townships are replaced by tithings, which originated in personal rather than territorial associations. The main peculiarities of the system are summarised in Table 3.3.

Boundary research

Once the functions of authorities are removed, rural boundaries subside into the countryside and are gradually forgotten. Some day, an enquiring mind may spot a hedgerow that curves its way continuously across the landscape for a mile or more, or one may ramble, brushed by twigs, down a narrow, sunken lane flanked by hedge-banks, or perhaps puzzle over names like Shirburne and Mersey. In all such cases, old boundaries are being encountered. Ancient territories may not survive through their boundary features alone; in a few cases 'central places' may also be recognised. Townships will have had their meeting places, though these are generally forgotten, while those associated with ancient hundreds may sometimes be located: 'Micheldever [Hampshire] itself, the *caput* of the hundred was recorded as a king's *tun* or *villa regalis* in AD 862 when the West Saxon council purportedly met there. The church of Micheldever was recognisable as a mother church in the medieval period, retaining

authority over the eastern valley but sharing control over the region with Wonston manor to the west' (Hooke, 1994 p.86). Manor courts were not always held in the hall, and more ancient venues may sometimes have been favoured:

> At Knyttington, Berks, in the reign of Edward I, the court was held 'in a certain green place over against the house of Hugh de Gardin when it was fine, and in wet weather, by leave of the bailiff in the manor house or in that of one of the tenants'. In Essex, the Moulsham Hall Manor Court was held outside the manor

---

Map 3.5   Topography, environmental resources and parish forms. The maps portray examples of the ways in which parish forms may be influenced by the characteristics of the local environment.

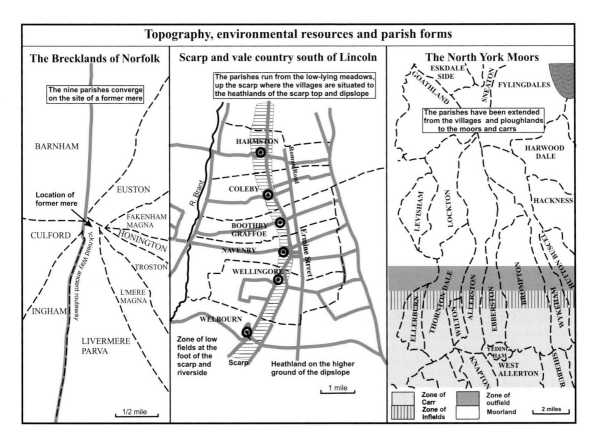

Figure 3.3   It is unclear whether stone rows, such as this one at Merrivale on Dartmoor, had territorial functions during the Bronze Age, but a variety of prehistoric monuments seem to have been connected to the establishment of land ownership between different communities.

house under the Court Oak, and in the same county at Little Leigh it was held on Court Hill. 'At Eastbourne, the name of Motcombe Lane probably marks the hollow where the moots were held', while the court of the Abbot of St Albans was held 'under the ash-tree in the middle court of the abbey . . . The 'right place' was clearly the place where long custom had decreed the meeting of the people should be held, and anything else was an assertion of the will of the lord. (Bennett, 1937 p.203)

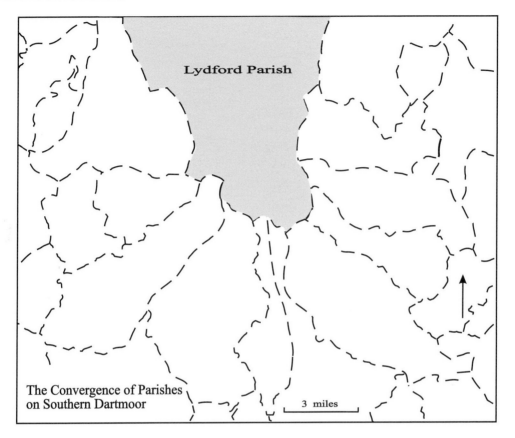

The Convergence of Parishes on Southern Dartmoor

Lydford Parish

3 miles

Boundaries of different kinds were marked in the landscape in a variety of ways. Sometimes watercourses or crestlines provided natural boundaries, while in other cases, linear earthworks, hedgerows, fences, walls, ditches or other constructions demarcated the boundary. Crosses were frequently erected to mark the boundaries of townships, monastic land-holdings, warrens, estates, sanctuary and other territories. They were also placed in non-boundary locations to mark the venues of preaching or markets, while the erection of a cross could be a condition of the holding of land from the Knights Hospitallers (Moorhouse, 1981 p.277). The Knights Hospitallers and Knights Templars enjoyed immunity from tithes and taxes on their lands, encouraging some land-holders unconnected with the military orders to erect crosses in attempts fraudulently to secure

Map 3.6   The convergence of parishes on Southern Dartmoor. Neighbouring parishes converge on the moorland commons.

these immunities. Some medieval crosses were of timber and have perished, while some of the stone crosses survive, even though their functions may be lost. The frequency of documentary references to crosses and of 'cross' place-names show that crosses occurred frequently in the medieval countrysides and townscapes.

Boundary stones were also commonplace features of the medieval countryside, and were frequently employed to mark the boundaries between adjacent landholdings. Stones were apparently sometimes used to mark the divisions between the adjacent selions in the common arable fields and could also be used for similar purposes at

Figure 3.4 Medieval crosses were frequently associated with marking routeways and the places where roads entered ecclesiastical property. This example, Bennett's Cross on Dartmoor, appears to have marked the boundary of a warren.

the ends of 'doles' in the communal meadows—where the stones must have better chances of survival and even of recognition. Some stones were fixed in place and set upright in the ground, while others seem to have been small boulders that could

be rolled out of the way of farm tackle: villagers were sometimes fined at their manor court for not replacing boundary stones. Some 'Helston' names derive from 'heel' or flat stones, set horizontally in the ground with their upper faces exposed. Cairns or piles of stones were also employed as boundary-markers, some of these probably being land clearance cairns opportunistically incorporated into a circuit of boundaries.

Manor court records tell of the disregard of boundary stones and of occasions when they were illegally moved. Given the intricate interdigitation of holdings in areas of open field farming, the demarcation of boundaries must have been important. Bennett wrote: 'such was the system . . . that it was hard for anyone to know exactly what was his own; and, even if he knew this quite well, it was harder still to be constantly on the watch to protect it against other men's carelessness or worse' (1937 p.48). He went on to quote from the fifteenth century English *Alphabet of Tales*, where the tale was related of a dying man transfixed by the vision of a burning stone that was hurtling

Figure 3.5 Prehistoric field boundaries have normally been levelled or else are only faintly visible. In some upland locations that have experienced little subsequent cultivation they may still be prominent features, as with these late-prehistoric fieldwalls at Kestor in Devon (note the silhouetted wall on the skyline).

towards his mouth: 'The priest was called, and told him to think whether he had harmed anyone with such a stone. And he thought for a while and then said, "Ah, sir! I have now a good mind of how I removed this stone in the field to the intent that I would enlarge my own ground and lessen other men's ground"' (Alphabet of Tales (E.E.T.S.),31).

Stones continued to be employed as boundary-markers after the close of the medieval period, as when a series of stones were erected around the bounds of the Forest of Knaresborough following a per-ambulation in 1767, each stone numbered and marked 'KF 1767'. The records of such perambulations can reveal invaluable information about former landscapes and provide details of the manner in which boundaries were marked. Thus, from the eighteenth century perambulation of the Forest of Knaresborough we learn that a section of the old boundary ran: 'by an old syke [ditch] (upon which syke part of a cottage standeth, and some old encroachments have been made by the owners of a township called Askwith), to a parcel of rocks upon the open common called Millstones: and so by the same syke to a place called Standing Stone, upon the Crossridge; and so up the same ridge to Dannock-bower [hedge sparrow's nest?]'. Here, the parcel of rocks, the standing stone and the cross are all suggestive of deliberately constructed boundary marks.

Stones, cairns and crosses marked points along a boundary, while ditches, hedges and walls were linear features which, to greater or lesser degrees, served as barriers and reference points on which boundaries could be hung. In some cases they pre-dated the boundaries and later provided convenient pegs when boundaries came to be made, but in other cases, as with deer parks, they were created to mark and enforce boundaries. While some walls and hedges were boundary features of the administrative and territorial landscapes, far more served only agricultural roles, such as compartmentalising a holding and keeping the horn from the corn.

Hedges have prehistoric origins. Some at least of the Bronze Age reaves of Dartmoor were probably hedgebanks; when Julius Caesar was campaigning in the (now) Franco-Belgian borderlands in 57 BC his armies encountered impenetrable networks of 'hedges that were almost like walls', and excavations at Bar Hill fort on the Antonine Wall in the 1980s revealed that bundles of brushwood cut from hedgerows had been used to fill pre-existing ditches when the fort was built around AD 142. References to hedgerows in Anglo-Saxon charters are abundant, with the hedges frequently being employed as boundary-markers.

Much has been made of the 'technique' of hedgerow dating, which has probably received more attention from amateur landscape enthusiasts than any other form of enquiry. How wonderful that one might be able to discover the age of a hedgerow simply by counting the number of species growing in a 30-yard length! Sadly, hedgerow dating does not work, and it is impossible to imagine how it *could* work (Muir, 1996). The theory proposes that the age of a 30-yard section of hedgerow equals

$$(99 \times \text{the number of shrub species}) - 16$$

with a correlation of $+0.92$ and a margin of error of 100 years either way (Pollard *et al.*, 1974). In practice the formula is generally simplified to

Age of hedge=
    number of species per 30 yards $\times$ 100

Thus, and most conveniently, researchers, teachers and enthusiasts could conclude that a five-species hedge would be 500 years old, an eight-species one would be 800 years old, and so on—allowing the salient events in the colonisation of a lowland parish to be deduced in the course of an afternoon's stroll!

The really remarkable feature of hedgerow dating was that it enjoyed such uncritical acceptance. And yet there was no known or credible biological/geographical mechanism that could function as a 'gatekeeper' to attract or restrict hedgerow colonists to the rate of one per century. More surprisingly, given the ecology credentials of the proponents, the 'theory' took no serious account of the great differences in climate, soil type, exposure, hydrology and habitats that exist between regions, districts and localities. This was despite the fact that the number of potential colonising species is far greater in a southern area of chalk geology, such as may be found in Cambridgeshire or the Weald, as compared with, say, a northern locality with acidic, ill-drained soils (Muir and Muir, 1987 pp.59–60). It was suggested that local correlations might be worked out for each area (Pollard *et al.*, p.80)—but were that to be done then what would remain would be all correlation and no theory.

Disregarding the objections which might be said to be of a logistical nature—the gross disparity in different field applications of the theory, the inaccurate employment of statistics, and the misinterpretation of the

documentary evidence relating to the ages of hedgerows—the fatal flaws in the concept can be summarised as follows. Firstly, for the theory to work then hedges would have to be planted as *single species* features and then gain new species at the rate of one per century. However, a very

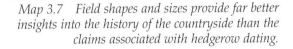

Map 3.7   *Field shapes and sizes provide far better insights into the history of the countryside than the claims associated with hedgerow dating.*

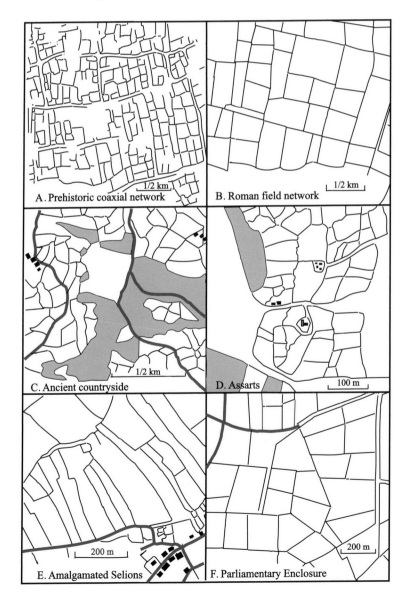

common feature of the English countryside is the post-medieval thorn hedge punctuated by oaks planted at close and regular intervals. Such hedgerows began as two-species features, but in the medieval period multi-species planting was commonplace (Johnson, 1978). At the end of the period, Fitzherbert in his *Boke of Husbandry* advised his readers to 'get thy quicksettes [live plants] in the woode countreye and let theym be of whyte thorne and crabtree for they be beste, holye and hasell be good. And if thou dwelle in the playne countrey, then mayste thou gete both ashe, oke and elm, for those wyll encrease moche woode in shorte space' (1534). Even in the Parliamentary Enclosure period of the eighteenth and nineteenth centuries when the use of hawthorn for hedging was the norm, some areas lay remote from nurseries and traditional methods of planting persisted. In the Neroche Forest of Somerset, for example, young trees were dug up in the woods and hedges began with eight to ten species

(Aston, 1985).

Secondly, the ways of Nature are not suspended within a hedgerow. The constituent species remain in constant competition for light, water and nutrients, and in this intensively competitive environment some prosper and expand at the expense of others that fail and die. In this way hedges can become species-poor rather than species-rich as they mature and as the most competitive species displace the others. Different conditions favour different competitors. In moist northern situations bird cherry, an uncommon constituent of hedgerows, can become highly competitive; blackthorn frequently advances along (and beyond) a hedge and holly appears to have expanded in northern places not too badly affected by damp or cold. But the most common competitor is elm, still flourishing as a hedgerow plant, and equipped for advancing through a hedge by suckering. It frequently converts sections of hedgerow 30 or 50 metres in length into an elm mono-

Table 3.4   Suggested stages in the destruction of a hedgerow

Stage	Appearance
Well maintained	Too dense for stock to penetrate, layed within the last 20 years. No gaps or elder.
Early neglect	Still trimmed, but by machine. Laying is overdue but has been abandoned. Gaps appear and are clumsily blocked with fence rails. Elder gains footholds.
Advanced neglect	The hedge is no longer stockproof. The thinning lower foliage reveals thickened old pleachers and 'elbows' from former laying near the base of the hedge. Cattle widen the gaps and push through the dead elder shrubs.
Relict I	The hedge now consists of a row of separate thorn bushes punctuated by tall hedgerow timber trees, such as oak or ash.
Relict II	The thorn bushes have died and only a few of the hedgerow pollards and standards remain.
Relict III	The hedgerow now exists as a linear bank or as a scarp, reflecting how the former hedge trapped soil drifting from an adjacent field. Occasional, widely separated old hedgerow trees survive.
Relict IV	The hedge bank/scarp and ditch are now only apparent when archaeological techniques are employed.

culture. Usually such sections are several centuries old, though according to hedge-row dating theory they must be less than a hundred years in age. In reality, the hedge-row constantly evolves in response to competition; in the young hedge shading by ash or elder may suppress the growth of neighbours, while in older hedges, elm, blackthorn and various other trees or shrubs

Figure 3.6   At Wasdale Head in the Lake District stones were so abundant that they were dumped in heaps which are freestanding in the fields or incorporated into the field walls.

can displace the other members of the community when the ecological conditions are favourable.

Figure 3.7   From the days of Parliamentary Enclosure through into modern times field walls have typically been built in the manner illustrated here. The 'A'-shaped frame establishes the batter of the two built faces and the space between them is packed with fragments of broken stone.

Thirdly, the history of management must play a part in influencing hedgerow composition. Elder was frequently removed because it is short-lived and on dying it leaves gaps which stock may break through. Farmers have varying ideas about the value of different hedgerow species; whether these are right or wrong does not matter, the point being that hedges are part of the cultural landscape and are affected by human choices. Hedges served different needs, some being managed as low, dense, sheep barriers, others as tall, robust bullock hedges. Different species would respond more or less favourably to different management regimes, while the neglect of trimming a mature hedge might encourage fast-growers, like ash, elm, field maple and hazel, to shade-out slower growers, like spindle or wayfaring tree, thus depressing the species account.

Hedgerow dating does not work and the dating of fields is best attempted by combining fieldwork with documentary research and studying the distinctive shape patterns associated with fields of different ages. In terms of hedgerows, it is possible to distinguish between two broad types. Firstly there are the straight hedges of the eighteenth and nineteenth centuries, which are usually of hawthorn, sometimes with oak standards, and which are often quite swiftly invaded by elder, wild rose species (mainly field and dog), sycamore, bramble and ash. Secondly, there are medieval and older hedges whose compositions vary according to geology, soil type and climate. These tend to include species like crab apple, field maple, oak (as a hedge shrub), hazel, *prunus* ssp, dogwood and various others that are lacking in younger hedges. They tend also to show the effects of invasion and the replanting of sections at various times. Where not heavily invaded they tend to be species-rich, though the degree of this richness does not reveal their ages. Many will be more than 1,200 years old, though no more than twelve mature species types can be accommodated in the 30-yard lengths favoured by hedgerow daters.

Hedgerows are among the most vulnerable features in an English setting that is under a sustained assault of unprecedented severity. As modern society created landscapes in its own debased image, the Nature Conservancy Council reported in 1984 that:

'By using air photographs, it has been estimated that, of around 500,000 miles of hedge existing in England and Wales in 1946–7, some 140,000 miles had been removed by 1974; and all but 20,000 miles of this loss was attributable to farming'. A subsequent survey by the Countryside Commission and Hunting Technical Services recorded the loss of 190,000 miles of hedgerow or 22 per cent of the network in the period 1947–85.

Stone walls are the other traditionally favoured method of enclosing land, with the distributions of hedging and walling being loosely complementary—in the sense that in the exposed northern and upland areas where hawthorn does not flourish there is a 'hard rock' geology with tough stones being readily quarried or cleared from fields. A landmark in our understanding of the value of drystone walls as evidence of landscape evolution derived from the Roystone Grange Project of 1978–86 (Wildgoose, 1986; Hodges, 1991). This produced a credible typology for walls in Derbyshire from elongated boulders laid end to end on the topsoil in periods perhaps as early as the late Mesolithic to the expertly constructed walls of the early nineteenth century. It is probable that most aspects of the Roystone Grange results can be successfully applied to other northern counties.

Orthostatic walls, displaying massive boulders laid in double rows in their bases, were attributed to the Romano-British period. The spaces between the boulder rows were filled with smaller stones and the whole wall was set in a trench with packing stones being used as props to hold the big facing stones upright. Walls with orthostats in their bases seem to have continued in use into the medieval period and even beyond in other northern localities. On the North York Moors, orthostatic walls are associated with the enclosing of intakes in the period 1550–1750, with some examples even being built after 1782 (Spratt, 1988). In looking at these walls one should remember that drystone walls are never completed: speed up the mental time frame and one encounters a succession of repairing and rebuilding. Walls blow down in gales and most walls of great age will have experienced several phases of patching and reconstruction. The only stable part of an orthostatic wall comprises the boulders at the base; above this line no original stonework may survive, so that we will not know how tall or rugged or neat the prehistoric, Roman or medieval original was.

Walls built around AD 1200 had an archaic appearance and were composed of boulders resting on a single line of massive orthostats. The mid-sixteenth-century walls at Roystone were much different. They were built in lengths that were not quite straight on a foundation of small boulders. The wall stones were irregular but the wall was built double, or of two faces, with the wall becoming narrower towards its top, where it could be capped with a single row of topstones. At the close of the medieval period, an improved craft of walling had evolved, with through-stones or 'throughs' being incorporated every fifth stone or so to bind the two faces together. Earlier walls had less sophisticated constructions and were much less stable. The post-medieval refinements were carried a stage further in the enclosure walls of the early nineteenth century. These were built in perfectly straight stretches that overrode all types of terrain. Like the walls of the preceding era, the sides were battered so that each face sloped inwards towards the topstones. Throughs were employed, the walls were set in shallow trenches and the spaces between the two faces were packed with pebbles and stone chippings. Unlike the preceding walls, these walls were built of quarried stone rather than from materials gathered from the litter in the fields.

Very similar walls were erected in other parts of the country during the Parliamentary Enclosure era, wherever the local resource base favoured walls over hedges. Generally, the wall construction standards were precisely specified by the commissioners responsible for the award: 'The enclosure act for the common fields of Linton [Wharfedale] was obtained in 1792 and makes . . . provision for walling all enclosures with walls 6 feet high, 3 feet broad at the base and battered to 14 inches wide at the top with 21 through stones per rood' (Raistrick, 1988 p.12). The rood, mentioned here, was a Yorkshire rood of 7 yards in length, the rood being the standard unit of length employed then and until quite recently by drystone wallers. It equates to the stretch of walling that a good waller could accomplish in one day.

Associated with field walls are a variety of minor landscape features which are generally known by local dialect names. Employing the Yorkshire Dales dialect, these include:

Cripple holes (or smouts or creeps). These are rectangular openings, framed by slabs in the base of walls which, when a blocking stone is rolled away, allow sheep to pass through the wall.

Gate stoups or gate posts. The stone posts set with iron hinges which carry the yats or gates.

Wallhead. The end of one ownership represented by a squared-off section of wall.

Stee, stile. Stiles had the form of steps set into the wall or of a narrow gap or squeeze. They were very common in medieval times, and probably long before.

Helms. These occur when the wall top rises to form a shallow peak. Lean-to buildings set against the wall seem to have been associated with helms or barns.

REFERENCES

Aston, M. *Interpreting the Landscape* (London: Batsford, 1985).

Bennett, H.S. *Life on the English Manor* (Cambridge: Cambridge University Press., 1937).

Countryside Commission and Hunting Technical Services, *Monitoring Landscape Change* (1986).

Fleming, A. 'Swadal, Swar (and Erechwydd?): early medieval polities in Upper Swaledale' *Landscape History* 16 (1994) pp.17–30.

Gelling, M. *Place-names in the Landscape* (London: Dent, 1993).

Hodges, R. *Wall-to-Wall History: The Story of Roystone Grange* (London: Duckworth, 1991).

Hooke, D. 'The administrative and settlement framework of early medieval Wessex' in M. Aston and C. Lewis (eds) *The Medieval Landscape of Wessex*, Oxbow Monograph 46 (Oxford: Oxbow, 1994) pp.83–96.

Johnson, W. 'Hedges—a review of some early literature' *Local Historian* (1978) pp.195–204.

Moorhouse, S.A. 'Boundaries' in M.L. Faull and S.A. Moorhouse (eds) *West Yorkshire: An Archaeological Survey to 1500* (Wakefield: West Yorkshire Metropolitan County Council, 1981) pp.265–289.

Muir, R. 'Cambridgeshire dykes retain their secrets' *Geographical Magazine* 55 (1980) pp.198–204.

Muir, R. 'Hedgerow dating: a critique' *Naturalist* 21 (1996) pp.59–64.

Muir, R. and Muir, N. *Hedgerows: Their History and Wildlife* (London: Michael Joseph, 1987).

Nature Conservancy Council, *Nature Conservation in Great Britain* (London: NCC, 1984).

Pitt-Rivers, A.H.L.F *Report of the British Association Meeting* (1881).

Pollard, E., Hooper, M.D. and Moore, N.W. *Hedges* (London: Collins, 1974).

Pollard, S.J. 'Iron Age riverside pit alignments at St Ives, Cambridgeshire' *Proceedings of the Prehistoric Society* 62 (1996) pp.93–116.

Powlesland, D.J. 'Excavations at Heslerton, North Yorkshire 1978–2' *Archaeological Journal* 143 (1986) pp.53–173.

Powlesland, D.J. 'Staple Howe in its landscape' in T.G. Manby (ed.) *Archaeology in Eastern Yorkshire: Essays in Honour of T.C.M. Brewster* (Sheffield: University of Sheffield Department of Archaeology and Prehistory, 1988).

Raistrick, A. *Pennine Walls* (Clapham: Dalesman, 1988).

Spratt D.A. 'Prehistoric Boundaries on the North Yorkshire Moors' in G.W. Barker, (ed.) *Prehistoric Communities in Northern England* (Sheffield: University of Sheffield Department of Archaeology and Prehistory, 1981) pp.87–103.

Spratt, D.A. 'Orthostatic field walls on the North York Moors' *Yorkshire Archaeological Journal* 60 (1988) pp.149–57.

Spratt D.A. *Linear Earthworks of the Tabular Hills, Northeast Yorkshire* (Sheffield: Sheffield University Department of Archaeology and Prehistory, 1989).

Spratt D.A. and White R.F. 'Further information on the Cleave Dyke system' *Yorkshire Archaeological Journal* 58 (1986) pp.195–7.

Stoertz, C. *Ancient Landscapes of the Yorkshire Wolds* (Swindon: RCHME, 1997).

Sylvester, D. *The Rural Landscape of the Welsh Borderland* (London: Macmillan, 1969).

White, R. *The Yorkshire Dales, Landscapes through Time* (London: Batsford/English Heritage, 1997).

Wildgoose, M. *The Roystone Grange Project. Wall Survey* (Derbyshire: Wildgoose, 1986).

Winchester A.J.L. 'Parish, township and tithing: landscapes of local administration in England before the nineteenth century' *Local Historian* 27 (1997) pp.3–17.

CHAPTER 4

Routeways

In one of the more reliable passages in his study of English history, Gloag wrote: 'It is difficult to travel ten miles in any direction in the country without coming across some aspect of English history, revealed to the observant by the contours of the fields, the direction of the roads, or the survival of some ancient trackway as an overgrown lane, almost impassable because of brambles and nettles, but still known by a name that, like Peddar's Way or Salt Way, recalls a vanished trading route' (1952 p.1). Roads, trackways and waterways are significant facets of the landscape, while an understanding of the means and the lines of movement pioneered by people in their efforts to communicate, socialise and trade with each other is crucial to the understanding of almost any landscape. The importance of routeways is not disputed, and yet the literature directly concerned with the interpretation of communications in historic landscapes is very small: in comparison with the published work on topics such as rural settlement or field systems, the research output is minute. The reasons for this are not hard to discover. Roads and trackways and the older waterways are generally extremely difficult to date. The great majority of winding rural tracks may well be medieval or earlier, quite possibly prehistoric, but their appearance usually offers no real clues to their precise antiquity. In studying communications one has a situation where some special examples, like Roman roads, Enclosure roads or turnpikes, are relatively easy to recognise and research, but most other routeways preserve an inscrutability in terms of their historical

origins. Given unlimited funding, practically any road or track could be dated by excavation—but with roads not being intensely occupied like settlements, one might have to expose an enormous length of road or trackway before finding any datable artefacts or materials lying upon the original surface.

In practical terms, it is by their association with other features of the cultural landscape that routeways may best be approached: 'Roads and tracks are important in that they have allowed virtually every other feature of the landscape to develop, and have themselves developed because of those features' (Hindle, 1993 p.11). Any thorough study of a village, hamlet or farmstead should include a consideration of the essential communications that linked it with the world beyond and a search for relevant earthworks. For example, a monastic lodge could not be understood without an awareness of the track that linked it to its grange and the road network which linked the grange to the abbey and to other granges. Similarly, a medieval quarry could not sensibly be studied without an appreciation of the track that connected it to building sites via rivers, roads and canals.

A routeway will only develop when sufficient people wish to travel between two points, though once established a routeway becomes a significant feature of the countryside. Its course through the landscapes helps to determine which places are accessible or 'central', with prospects for expansion, and which are remote backwaters. For example, the availability or otherwise of connections to the railway network largely determined which nineteenth century fishing villages could aspire to become holiday resorts. Having helped to establish the spatial patterns of cultural development the route may be superseded by other alignments or modes of travel and be abandoned or demoted. Thus the spectrum of communications includes many examples which are neglected or fossilised, as well as their successors. Few facets of the historic landscape are more evocative of the past than the ancient holloway: entrenched into the countryside by the passage of countless feet, wheels and hooves, yet now a lonely trough passing through parkland, woods or pasture without an obvious origin or destination.

The evolution of routeways

There can be no doubt that many routeways are prehistoric, though which and how many will probably never be known. Following the launching of the Neolithic assault on the wildwood, a lively trade in stone axes was established. It connected the few special places blessed with good axe-making materials, like flint and some volcanic rocks, with the many other places that lacked them. Axes in the grey-green volcanic ash (tuff) which were produced at a number of factory sites in the Langdale Pikes region of Cumbria were exported widely thoughout the British Isles (Fell, 1994; Plint, 1962). The roughed-out axes were probably taken down from the high fells for finishing and polishing, perhaps at Cumbrian coastal locations where gritstones were available. The distribution of recovered Great Langdale axes suggests that an organised seaborne trade was involved. In East Anglia there is a great concentration of Great Langdale axes along the north-western margin of the ancient Icknield Way, suggesting that this bundle of ancient tracks was used for importing the axes from vessels landing around north Norfolk and the Wash. Axes might also have been traded

at Cumbrian stone circle sites with herdsmen who had followed the high summer grazings of the Pennines and Lakeland fells northwards from the dales and vales of Yorkshire. Cumbrian axes may have been imported into the lower parts of Yorkshire via the Stainmore gap, while finds in the valleys of the Aire and Ribble suggest that they were used in the axe trade, perhaps with flint from the Yorkshire Wolds being traded in exchange. Some axes could have been passed from one place and society to another as tribute to influential leaders, and some could have been employed in rituals.

A Neolithic enclosure recently recognised on Gardom's Edge in the Peak District may have been a trading centre. A survey by the Peak National Park and the English Royal Commission identified a stone bank about 600 m long which was breached by seven entrances. Numerous polished axes and barbed and tanged arrowheads were found nearby and Gardom's Edge spanned two valleys offering excellent east to west communications, with flints from the Lincolnshire Wolds perhaps being brought here for trade with agriculturalists from regions poor in flint. In any event, the dispersal of the products of the Neolithic axe and pottery industries demonstrates the existence of regional and wider-ranging communications networks.

Gradually, unsupported assumptions about prehistoric routeways are being replaced by a more genuine understanding, but the conversion is only advancing slowly. It was believed that the significant ancient roads were ridgeways that followed the high ground standing above the impenetrable valley bottom swamps and densely forested slopes of the lower country. Some long-distance routeways occupying 'zones of movement' across the uplands certainly existed, but given that the lower ground in Neolithic and Bronze Age times was more likely than not to be cultivated and settled, then there will have been local, regional

Figure 4.1   Ancient trackways often consisted of a zone of branching pathways. The branching could be pronounced when the route ascended a slope, as here on Twyford Downs in Hampshire.
© *Cambridge UC (MOD).*

and, perhaps, long-distance tracks in the valleys too. Hollowed trackways are evocative and it is tempting to imagine that one may be walking in the footsteps of prehistoric predecessors. This will sometimes be the case, but the main routes were not simple linear alignments like modern roads. Instead, they existed as swarms of merging, branching, diverging and re-uniting trackways, and while the zone of movement might maintain its general line through the centuries, it could drift like a river which favours one channel and then another.

In the course of recent decades, numerous wetland trackways in various parts of the country have been discovered, demonstrating that prehistoric peoples would go to considerable lengths to secure a line of movement across difficult, waterlogged terrain (Wright, 1988). The Sweet Track in the Somerset Levels, named after its discoverer, was built of split logs from oak trees felled in the winter of 3807 to 3806 BC. The reasons for creating such tracks could variously be economic or concerned with ritual, while political motives relating to the securing of territory may not be ruled out. The evidence from the Somerset Levels suggests that in the course of the Neolithic period the technique evolved from one of pegging-down bundles of twiggy material to form a track to the construction of more sophisticated and robust routeways using piles and walkways built from poles, stakes and split logs. Such trackways, recognised in several wetlands apart from the Somerset Levels, including Corlea in Ireland, may have been associated with day-to-day movements involving the exploitation of local resources and communication between local groups (the Sweet Track linked the Polden Hills to a former island in the vicinity of Westhay Mere). Some, however, appear to have been used in ceremonies linked to votive offerings and the appease-ment of local water deities, which appear increasingly to have commanded attention as climate deteriorated in the Bronze Age. At Flag Fen, near Peterborough, in the period 1365–967 BC, a huge platform of timbers was built in what was then a bay of an inland sea. A trackway of planks, branches and piles, which was submerged in winter, led to the site and appears to have served as a platform from which people threw valuable weapons and possessions, many of them deliberately bent and broken, into the surrounding waters. The Sweet Track and the Flag Fen monuments were not unusual; in 1995 the Shinewater site was discovered in marshland east of Eastbourne. Here, a timber platform was linked to a trackway formed by a long causeway spanning a former lake. As at Flag Fen, bronze objects were cast into the waters as votive offerings.

Two Bronze Age trackways were recently explored at Bramhope Green, Bermondsey. The older consisted of parallel logs and it was thought that the junction of two separate trackways, each two logs wide, had been discovered. The second consisted of oak logs and it 'was the simplest form that a trackway can take, consisting of a single line of logs laid end to end which, whilst quite narrow, would have been perfectly adequate for walking upon. The stakes alongside it could have served in three ways. They would certainly have lent some stability to the structure; they might have acted as markers for the line of the trackway; and they could have acted as effective hand-holds' (Thomas and Rackham, 1996 p.248). The immediate environment was of open marsh fen with alder carr nearby.

The provenance of various supposed prehistoric routeways is dubious and Taylor (1979) has questioned the significance of the presumed chalk ridgeways and disputed the validity of 'ancient' trackways that display no close associations with known prehistoric settlements. Hindle wrote that: 'It can be argued that this evidence is largely irrelevant. If a suggested route is not closely related to the archaeological sites, then perhaps this may simply be because the two are largely independent of each other' (1993 pp.19–20). However, the experience of most cultural situations is that communications exist to serve communities and are quite closely related to patterns of settlement and the linking-together of adjacent communi-ties. It is remarkable how little is known about prehistoric routeways, of which only very short sections may be revealed by excavation. It would be unwise to claim prehistoric credentials for any trackway which is not associated with identifiable features, like barrows or settlement sites, or with discoveries of artefacts in concen-trations which suggest that that routeway had been used for prehistoric commerce. The most celebrated and apparently the 'safest' of Neolithic routeways was the Ridgeway in Wessex, but recent excavations on the Ridgeway near Uffington Castle hillfort revealed that: 'The compacted chalk of the path was found to run over a filled-in late Bronze Age "linear ditch" or territorial boundary, suggesting (not conclusively) that the path, at this point, dates from the early Iron Age at the earliest' (Denison, 1998a p.4).

Though some routeways appear to be less ancient than has been imagined, many others must have been in use since prehistoric times, even though this antiquity cannot be proved. It is not entirely practical to produce a typology of roads based on function and period of use since the existence of many of them will span *several* categories and periods of use. Thus a track like Clennell Street, linking Alwinton in England with Mow in Scotland, could have served traders in prehistoric and Roman times even if it can only be *proved* to have existed by the early twelfth century. At this time it was associated with transhumance and the flocks of Newminster Abbey were driven up it to reach high pastures where Kidland Forest now stands. During the Border wars, Clennell Street was used by the reivers or cattle rustlers, and with the return of more settled conditions, whisky smugglers used the tracks to take their goods furtively into England. From the sixteenth century until the railway era it was also one of the droveways associated with moving cattle and sheep across the uplands of the Borders and Pennines to English markets.

Excavations provide glimpses of prehistoric trackways, though it is generally not possible to deduce whether they existed only as field tracks linking a community with its farmland or whether they were elements in a system of regional communication. The earliest metalled road so far discovered in Britain was excavated at Yarnton, near Oxford, and it appears to belong to the Bronze Age. The roadbed was constructed of limestone fragments, imported over a distance of 5 miles, and quartzite pebbles and timber handrails ran along each side of the track. These would have been useful as the road provided a causeway or ford 5 m wide and 35 m long running across a river channel in the flood-

plain of the Thames. During the first millennium BC the causeway was remetalled with sand and gravel (Denison, 1998b p.5).

Some of the information that can be derived from excavation is apparent in the case of a late Bronze Age/early Iron Age track at Heslerton in North Yorkshire:

> This trackway, which like later trackways to the north had formed a hollow way defining its centre, was delimited by a small U-shaped ditch to the north and a second much slighter gully to the south . . . this feature, measuring 7.5 m across, was demonstrable on the basis of a complex sequence of wheel-ruts both cutting and filled by a compacted layer of aeolian material . . . a feature of the wheel ruts was both the narrowness of the individual ruts coupled with what was frequently a V-shaped profile. If the wheel ruts were very narrow and the sand was soft when they formed, the nature of the individual ruts can easily be explained as indicating intensive use by narrow wheeled vehicles during a period of aeolian deposition interspersed with wet conditions. It was difficult to isolate matching pairs of ruts since they were so tightly packed; where they could a wheel separation of 1–1.5 m was demonstrable. (Powlesland *et al.*, 1986 pp.133–4)

Bronze Age wheel ruts were also noted at Welland Bank in the Fens in 1996–7:

> Then in 1997 we found more marks and this time there could be no doubt: they were produced by a two-wheeled vehicle and the distance between the two wheels was 1.10 m . . . The thickness of the marks and the general style and scale of the vehicle would fit with a tripartite wheel we found at Flag Fen a few years ago. This wheel (diameter 900 mm) was about the size of a cycle wheel . . . The wheel ruts snaked their way around long-vanished obstacles, but seemed to be

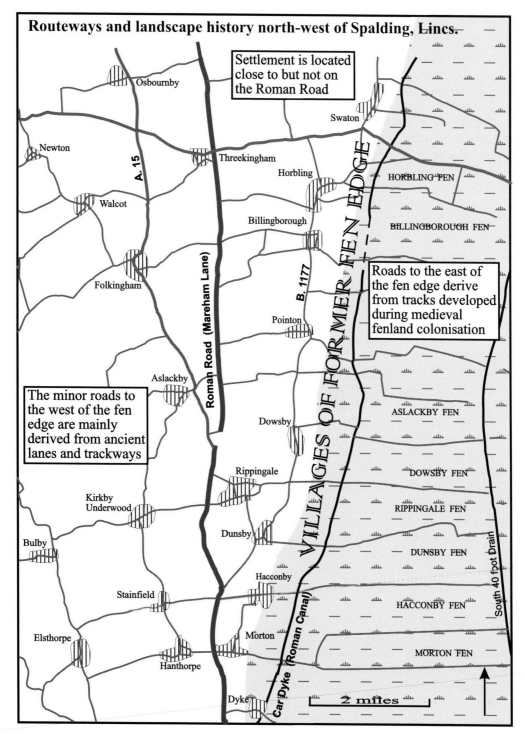

Routeways and landscape history north-west of Spalding, Lincs.

Settlement is located close to but not on the Roman Road

Osbournby

Swaton

A. 15

Newton

Threekingham

Horbling

HORBLING FEN

Walcot

Billingborough

BILLINGBOROUGH FEN

B. 1177

Roads to the east of the fen edge derive from tracks developed during medieval fenland colonisation

Folkingham

Roman Road (Mareham Lane)

Pointon

Aslackby

The minor roads to the west of the fen edge are mainly derived from ancient lanes and trackways

Dowsby

ASLACKBY FEN

VILLAGES OF FORMER FEN EDGE

Rippingale

DOWSBY FEN

Kirkby Underwood

RIPPINGALE FEN

Bulby

Dunsby

DUNSBY FEN

South 40 foot Drain

Hacconby

Stainfield

HACCONBY FEN

Car Dyke (Roman Canal)

Elsthorpe

Morton

MORTON FEN

Hanthorpe

Dyke

2 miles

Map 4.1   *Routeways and landscape history north-west of Spalding, Lincolnshire. Nucleated settlements were established at sites around a mile to the east of the Roman road, between it and the Car Dyke, and extended their territories eastwards to exploit the resources of the fens.*

heading towards one of the corner entrances into the rectangular enclosure. (Pryor, 1998 p.145)

When exposed during excavations, pre-historic trackways are frequently found to be hollowed and defined by ditches, with ruts from wheeled vehicles sometimes being apparent in the later examples. Like some medieval routeways, they could divide into a network of sub-parallel tracks when the original course became rutted or water-logged so that alternative courses were developed.

Whatever the original intentions of the Roman invaders of AD 43 may have been, subsequently the Romans became the first people to regard England and Wales as an entity to which broad military and com-mercial strategies could be applied. The roads that they built, largely during the initial expansion of the empire and paci-fication of territory, formed a coherent system, at least in the sense that major routes like Watling Street, Stane Street and Ermine Street were parts of a radial network focused on London—with Fosse Way, run-ning north-east to south-west and roughly separating the upland and lowland zones, now being thought to have provided rearward communication between several legions. In other ways, the Roman system was opportunistic, with new alignments and cross-links being added to the network as new needs arose. This could happen when the road as an element in a military strategy was superseded by the road as a highway for commerce or as a facilitator of inter-urban contact. These roads, surveyed, engineered, metalled and often still in use, were the main parts of the communication system, but neither government nor trade could have operated without the support of a multitude of lesser roads and trackways which were, and remain, indistinguishable from those of the preceding 'barbaric' eras.

In building the superior roads of Roman England, local rubble, shingle or gravel would be gathered to build a raised spine of roadway, an agger, generally between 10 and 25 feet in width, but occasionally 50 feet wide. The hard but porous materials in the agger facilitated drainage, as did the ditches dug parallel to the agger on either side. (Surviving Roman roads frequently do not have the agger and flanking ditches still recognisable, though these can be seen on sections of Ermine Street in Lincolnshire.) These roads took the most direct practical route, and would be straight where the terrain allowed, but where it was difficult they would proceed by curves, the curves often consisting of successive straight sections, or adopt less formal courses. Roman roads formed the main axes of the English transport system until the turnpike era, but in the course of the thirteen centuries between the Roman withdrawal and the launching of a vigorous new programme of road-building, the Roman routeways were largely neglected. During this long era of neglect, the system became distorted as sections of road fell into disuse and alternative routes were developed.

The sections which were abandoned could be those that traversed difficult terrain and became rutted and muddy after the maintentance of the roadbed was neglected. Different Roman engineers favoured differ-ent constructional techniques, so that some sections of road were better equipped to survive than others, while the evolution of the settlement pattern resulted in changes in priorities within the transport network. This could mean that new links were needed to connect emerging centres, while routes which served places now deserted would wither. Thus, the B6265 follows the course of a Roman road running north-westwards from York, but a couple of miles before reaching the site of the Roman town of *Isurium* (Aldborough) it abandons the Roman alignment and heads, instead, for the crossing of the Ure at Boroughbridge.

Here a bridge was built in 1145, attracting a shift of settlement from the Roman town and Saxon royal manor site to the planned medieval town which developed beside the crossing. Two miles to the north of Boroughbridge the Roman routeway is rejoined, is now seen as the A1 heading towards *Cataractonium* (Catterick). In this case, the local abandonment and substitution of the Roman route can be dated to the establishment of Boroughbridge, but in many other cases the side-tracking of an original Roman route is undated.

Roman roads may still exert a major presence in the landscape, as with the English section of Dere Street north of Hexham, where the Roman alignment is very largely followed by the A68. In other cases, Roman roads appear just as fragments within the present networks of roads and trackways. About 6 miles to the east of Harrogate, a section of Roman road just two miles long is incorporated into the A59 and it can be shown that, while surviving the decay of the adjacent sections of the Ilkley to Aldborough road, this stretch of the route was absorbed into a Dark Age or medieval saltway and much later became part of a turnpike.

Popular views on Roman roads are somewhat distorted, and two concluding points should be made to redress the balance. Firstly, the metalled, well-engineered and (generally) straight roads of the textbooks were only the top-status elements in a system that also included unsurfaced routes, winding tracks and pre-existing routeways, not to mention rivers, canals and coastal sea routes. Secondly, while the roads bound far-flung sections of territory to the capital and core and provided an integrated system of communications, these same roads sliced across established field networks for mile after mile, slighting pre-existing boundaries, political groupings and patterns of kinship and symbolising the domination by Rome and the inadequacy of indigenous arrange-

ments. (They were, however, also providing routes along which insurgents could travel as fast as could the legions.) The symbolical significance went further than this, for the roads approaching the gates of a Roman city were lined with tombs: 'It may have meant that anyone entering or leaving the town would have been reminded of its famous sons and daughters and its collective ancestry . . . they may have felt as if they were making a journey into their past and their identity as if along an avenue of remembrance; alternatively they may have felt alienated from the dominant Roman establishment' (Witcher, 1998 p.6).

After the departure of the legions, Britain sank slowly into a prolonged phase of introspection and localism, during which the economy contracted, population plummeted and insecurity became endemic. The Roman theatre of action was replaced by one which was culturally and economically centred on the North Sea, while concerted engineering operations, like those associated with building roads and bridges, were abandoned. Meanwhile, the system of regional and local central places which was established during Roman times decayed and in its place there emerged a settlement pattern of farmsteads and hamlets: there were few important destinations left for a system of transport to serve. Information about roads during this period is difficult to obtain, but the various Lives of saints written in the early Christian period suggest that travel within and between regions was accomplished without difficulty. The saints concerned were ever on the move, staying with guests or camping by the wayside at night, and the roads that they used were sometimes apparently negotiable by wheeled vehicles.

The Roman practice of engineering long distance routeways was abandoned in the years between the British defection from the empire in 410 and the Conquest of 1066. During this period, however, local and regional travel between hamlets, manors and markets as well as shorter journeys between farmsteads, fields and commons will largely have filled in the pattern of minor roads and trackways by the time of the Norman landings. If rural routeways were left to 'make themselves' during the Saxon period, some purposeful engineering work was undertaken in towns. Saxon London lay in the Covent Garden area outside the old Roman walls. One of its main roads

> was three metres wide, made of compacted gravel, but the surface was re-metalled at least ten times, so that by the mid ninth century the successive layers of metalling were nearly a metre thick. Timber drains ran along the sides, and were occasionally replaced. Running off from the road at right angles were ranges of buildings separated by alleys, with three plots on the east side and one to the west. The alleys were about as wide as the first road but they were not kept in as good repair and it has been suggested that the north–south road was the King's highway, maintained by the authorities. (Blackmore *et al.*, 1998 p.60)

Information about the local communication systems can be obtained from the Saxon charters, which frequently note ways, 'harepaths' and streets as boundary features, and from place-names, which often refer to routeways. In the charter concerning the granting of three hides of land at Abbots Bromley, Staffordshire, by King Athelred II to his thegn, Wulfric, in 996, the recitation of the bounds mentions a section running through marshy ground along a footpath, then to the street, to the red oak, and later along a brook to a ford, then to a street and along the greenway to a little barrow (Hart, 1975 pp.261–2). Sometimes the land marks listed in a charter can be related to the present landscape, allowing ancient routeways to be related to those of today.

Most of the place-names which are

invaluable to research into routeways in landscape history were established during the currency of Old English, which lasted from the English settlements to about 1150. Certain specialised roads were used during this period in association with the commerce in vital commodities. Salt was essential for the preservation of meat and fish, but was only locally available. Saltways were associated with the transport of salt from the saltings established at many places around the coast and from the salt deposits mined in Cheshire around Nantwich, Northwich and Droitwich. Names like Saltway, Psaltergate, Salter Street and Saltford recall the trade. Portways were routes particularly linked to assembling and distributing the trade goods of seaborne commerce. Like the saltways, portways were roads that could be used for a variety of purposes. The Port Way running along the crest of the Long Mynd in Shropshire was a significant droving route, particularly in the eighteenth and early nineteenth centuries, and was employed in the export of Welsh cattle to Shrewsbury market (Taylor, 1979 pp.165–6). At a more local level, a *bereford* or barley ford was a ford associated with a trackway used in the conveyance of agricultural produce. A Burton Abbey charter of 1012 mentioned land by the River Trent where the thieves hung in the middle of barley ford water meadow (Hart, 1975 p.236).

Until outlawed by Act of Parliament in 1823, there was a long tradition of burying suicides and criminals at crossroads, apparently because it was believed that the crossing road pattern would confuse the ghost of the dead and thus prevent it from discovering how to return and haunt its home. Also, the position of the graves away from settlement and by roads leading outwards perhaps underlined the status of the deceased as outcasts. During the 1920s, about 60 skeletons were excavated at a crossing known as Gallows Gate, near

Table 4.1   Place-names and the identification of routeways

Name element	Meaning and remarks
Badger or Bagger way	Old road used by dealers in corn.
Bereford, barley ford	Track used for moving farm produce.
Coldharbour, Caldecot	Often associated with Roman roads and appear to denote roadside shelters.
Gate 1 (ON *gata*)	A road or a town street in northern England.
Gate 2	Gates were also crossings and meeting points, often at the heads of burns, in the Borders, where knights responsible for maintaining the peace would meet. Later they were often adopted by droving routes.
Galloway, Galloway Gate	Relates to Galloway breed, popular as packhorses, though sometimes associated with gallows.
Harepath (OE *here-pæth*)	An 'army road'; one of the main routeways of Saxon England.
Holgate, Halgate	Possible variation of 'holloway', below, common in the northern dales.
Holloway (OE *holanweg*)	A way or road hollowed by the passage of traffic.
Jigger Lane, Jagger Way etc.	Relate to German *Jaeger* ('hunter') ponies, popular as pack horses.
Kirkgate	A road leading to a church.
Lane (OE *lane, lanu*)	A lane in the countryside or town. Generally but not always a foot track not used by wheeled traffic.
Lidgate (OE *hlid-geat*)	A gate across a road to prevent livestock from wandering, often placed at the edges of settlements, commons or open fields and on township boundaries.
Path (OE *pæth*)	A road or path, perhaps one associated with upland or heathland grazings. May be found as -path or -peth.
Road, rode, rod (OE *rodu*)	These words relate not to roads but to clearings.
Stane	Associated with Roman roads and denotes the stone or metalled construction.
Stig, sty (OE *stíg*, ON *stígr*)	Lane or path, often one ascending a hillside. *Anstig* (OE) may denote a path on which travellers walked in single file and it appears in names like Anstey.
Street (OE *stræt*)	A paved road. This name was commonly applied to Roman roads encountered by English-speakers. It occurs as 'street', 'strat' and 'stret'.
Swire (Border dialect)	A pass at a valley head in the Anglo-Scottish Borders.
Way (OE *weg*)	'Way' embraces roads of various types which existed in Saxon times.

Table 4.1   Place-names and the identification of routeways—continued

Name element	Meaning and remarks
Names associated with water and river crossings:	
Bridge (OE *brycg*)	Normally only the more important river crossings would be served by a bridge.
Ferry (ON *ferja*, ME *ferrye*)	Ferry
Ford (OE *ford*, also OW *ritu*, ON *vath* and OE *gewæd*)	These all denote fords and emerge in words like Oxford, Penrith, Wath and Biggleswade.
Hythe (OE *hŷth*) and Staithe (OE *Stæth*)	Landing places on waterways.
Lode (OE *gelād* and *lād*)	Watercourse, often associated with commerce.
Twilade, tillage (ME?)	Place where goods were transferred from one barge to another.
Whyte, waits (ME?)	Medieval dock or quay.

Fowlmere in Cambridgeshire. Some, of Anglo-Saxon date, had been beheaded, while the more recent remains had apparently been hung. In the same county, twelve skeletons unearthed at a crossroads between the villages of Dry Drayton and Oakington were found in 1977 at a place associated with a gallows maintained by Crowland Abbey (Halliday, 1997 p.6).

An impression of the nature of medieval roads can be gained by studying records of the itineraries of kings and bishops. It emerges that the Plantagenet kings led extremely mobile lives, travelling across the country from manor to manor, dispensing justice and, with their large revenues, consuming their rents in kind. Every two or three days the royal party would be on the move again, with journeys of 20 miles or more being commonplace. For most of the year there seem to have been few obstacles to travel on horseback, but the bulk movement of heavy commodities presented challenges which the road system could not meet and so the water transport network was indispensable. However, the network of natural waterways could only serve a limited range of movements, and from Roman times efforts were made to expand the opportunities.

The Roman Car Dyke was a canal designed for moving produce from the rich lands on the southern margins of the Fens firstly to the large garrison at Lincoln and then to the fortress at York. It cut across a low gravel watershed between the Rivers Cam and Ouse against the natural direction of drainage and was deeply incised and equipped with sluices. This section was still used for navigation in Saxon and medieval times, perhaps by shifting cargoes from one barge to another to compensate for the dereliction of the locks (Ravensdale and Muir, 1984 p.55). Also in the area of the Fen Edge, at least three and perhaps as many as six of the canals known as 'lodes' are Roman creations, and along with their medieval successors they provided local populations with access to the major natural waterways of the Fens, and thence to the ports of the

Figure 4.2   Artificial waterways known as 'lodes' were dug to serve the commercial needs of villages around the edges of the East Anglian fens in Roman and medieval times. This is Burwell lode, which was linked to the warehouses of the village merchants by a series of hythes.

North Sea. In the Fen Edge and elsewhere, earthworks and place-names provide clues to the former waterborne commerce. At Crowland, the medieval docks beside the three-way bridge are now overlain by broad sections of roadway, and at Ramsey, the medieval docks, the Great Whyte and Little Whyte, in front of the abbey gates are filled in. At Horningsea, the name 'Dock Lane' survives; at Burwell a waterway known as 'The Weirs' once terminated in a public wharf or 'hythe', while the village called Commercial End was a commercial river

port until the railway age.

Medieval roads served many different functions, but in appearance they may not readily be distinguished from the winding and unmetalled creations of previous and subsequent ages. Sometimes, however, historical and archaeological techniques may be helpful. At Ripley, North Yorkshire, a deep, pollard-flanked trench runs down-slope and vanishes into an artificial lake in the landscaped parkland. It appears to have run towards the still-existing village and church beyond the lake and park, suggesting that it was developed after the village had shifted from its original site early in the fourteenth century. However, its existence as a routeway may have been relatively brief, for by the end of the fifteenth century the working countryside here had been absorbed into a deer park associated with

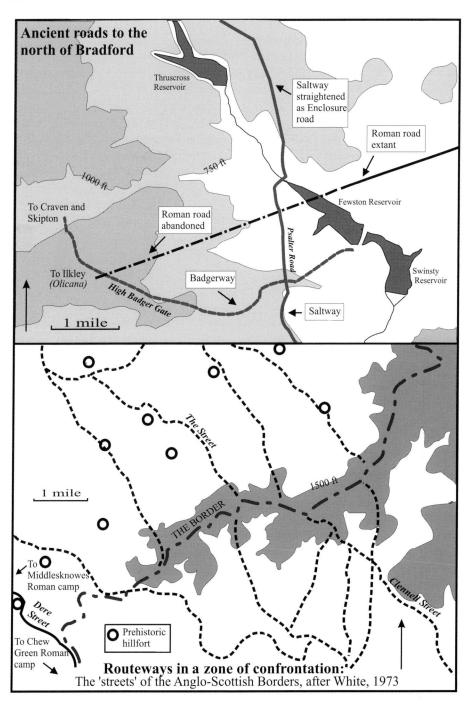

Map 4.2   Ancient roads to the north of Bradford and routeways in a zone of confrontation. To the west of Fewston reservoir three different types of ancient routeways—a Roman road, a badgerway, associated with trade in farm produce, and a saltway—are closely juxtaposed. The streets of the Anglo-Scottish Borders were used for commerce and by war bands, while the numerous hillforts suggest the antiquity of the zone of confrontation, after White (1973).

the Ingilby family at Ripley Castle. In this way, at least the main use of the holloway seems datable to the later medieval centuries. The uses made of medieval roads can be discovered in names like Portway, Maltway, Saltway, Oxdrove, as well as the Badger Gates or Ways used by the 'badger' or 'bagger' and his ponies: a man or woman licensed to buy corn at one market and sell it at another.

Such descriptive names could mask a host of other functions, though some roads were quite specialised in their uses. This was the case with some of the corpse roads associated with vast parishes in northern counties, like old Cumberland or the North Riding, where the populations of outlying hamlets and farmsteads had to carry their dead over several miles of difficult terrain for burial in the appointed churchyard. Corpse roads could have varied uses, like the Corpse Way running down Swaledale to the church at Grinton, which was used by a variety of travellers (Raistrick, 1978 p.21), though other corpse roads were followed mainly by burial parties, like the Lakeland one running over Mardale Common from the (now flooded) village of Mardale Green to the church at Shap (Hindle, 1982 p.9). In the uplands there were specialised roads developed for the extraction and distribution of resources like peat, lead or stone. High in the Pennines in the Stainmore Forest were the Tan Hill coal mines, with a main seam 4 feet in thickness; exploited since the thirteenth century, Tan Hill coal was exported to the neighbouring dales via a series of radiating trackways (Raistrick, 1978 pp.12–13). Other upland lanes had a variety of users, including monks and lay brethren visiting far-flung granges, pack horse traders, dealers in rural produce and tenants travelling to pay suit at manor courts. The Cistercian monasteries were particularly active in establishing networks of trackways to unite their far-flung holdings; important crossings on the Rivers Calder and Colne originated as bridges build by Fountains Abbey to connect estates in Bradley and Kirkheaton. 'The existence of monastic property in an area could . . . have a significant effect on a local road system, particularly where the holdings were of some size and related to others nearby . . . It would be an interesting exercise to relate the numerous granges of Kirkstall Abbey in the Leeds area to the well documented medieval road pattern in the region to see whether the road pattern was governed by the siting of the granges' (Faull and Moorhouse, 1981 p.629).

Medieval routeways associated with the movement of livestock came in a variety of forms, with some drifts or droveways being associated with short-distance movements of stock to commons and others involving long-distance or international movements. Routes in the Scottish Borders, known as 'streets', which had been used for droving Scottish cattle to markets in England, became trackways used for cross-border raiding as relations between the two kingdoms deteriorated in the fourteenth century. With the Union of the Crowns in 1603, the streets were revived as droving routes, with cattle from the Highlands and Islands being driven to markets or 'trysts' in the Central Valley, resold and then driven through the Southern Uplands and down the Pennines spine to market centres in England. By the eighteenth century, 100,000 cattle, shod like horses for crossing the hard terrain, (and much illicit whisky too) were traversing the high streets to England each year. Then the cattle were sold again at northern markets, like the one at Malham, and fattened after their arduous journeys on the pastures of Craven and West Yorkshire.

Drovers could forge new routes or adopt existing ones. The Mastiles Lane, which linked the grange of Fountains Abbey at Kilnsey in Wharfedale to the Abbey's distant estates in the Lake District, was, in medieval times, an open fell track with its course marked by crosses. Later, it was adopted by drovers moving cattle south from Scotland, and though it came to be enclosed during the decades around 1800, it remains largely a green lane. Droving was incompatible with undefended crop and the drovers took to the high ground, using the hill tracks, where herds of around 200 cattle would be divided into four parts, each in the charge of a drover and his dogs. Scottish cattle, many of them rested and fattened in northern England, were then distributed through the English lowlands. In Norfolk

> The main entry for Scots and northern cattle was through Wisbech and across the Great Ouse at Magdalen and Stow bridges. In 1750 alone, it was calculated that 20,000 Scots cattle entered Norfolk through Wisbech. Well-established droving routes also linked the grazing areas of east Norfolk to their main market at Smithfield in London. In the 1790s, a noted Norfolk drover normally took seven days to take a 'drift' of fattened beasts from St Faiths to London (112 miles). (Dymond, 1985 p.233)

By the 1880s the railways had largely extinguished this trade, but much can still be recognised in the landscape. At intervals along the old upland drove roads there are the inns and rest houses, often still bearing the 'Drovers' name. Associated with them are pastures where the herds could rest and graze overnight, while broadenings of the verges of the drove roads provided refreshment en route.

Pack horse roads were common in situations where terrain was rough and the capabilities in road-building very limited, so that wheeled traffic could not function and goods were carried in panniers slung on sturdy ponies. In the uplands, such forms of transport persisted from prehistoric times until quite an advanced stage of the railway era. Like most other types of tracks, the pack horse roads were shared with other users, so that the teams of ponies will have passed stock being moved between pastures, villagers en route to market, or wool broggers collecting and dispensing wool amongst a network of home spinners. Some pack horse roads were associated mainly with horse-borne trade, and this is apparent in the origins, courses and destinations of the tracks concerned, like the ones in upper Nidderdale which linked monastic granges to Fountains or Byland abbeys, or those used in the export of coal from Ingleton colliery to Dentdale. Most long-distance pack horse roads were furnished with stage houses, with buildings where the horsemen or 'jaggers' could sleep, safe storage for their goods and an enclosed paddock for the ponies. These way stations have now crumbled or else may be found existing as inns, farmsteads or farm buildings. 'Galloway' and 'Jagger' place-names, both relating to the ponies, are sometimes associated with the old routes.

In 1555 the first important legislation concerning roads in England was introduced. Parishes had been responsible for the upkeep of roads, but now their parishioners were required to devote four days each year to road works, under the supervision of two surveyors appointed by the parish. In the following decades, however, complaints about the condition of the system became anguished and strident. It is not clear whether the network had deteriorated or whether expectations had risen. A torrent of legislation followed, banning heavy transport and broad wheels as governments strove to discover an effective means of constructing and maintaining roads. Effective techniques of building which ensured that the roadbed was well-drained were required, and these demanding techniques could not be delivered by an unskilled, reluctant and resentful labour force. Though it was not immediately recognised, the answer was found in the creation of turnpike trusts which undertook to improve roads, build diversions or create longer sections of routeway in return for collecting an income in the form of tolls levelled on road users (Albert, 1972). The first turnpike Act appeared in 1663, allowing the collection of tolls to finance 15 miles of road between Wadesmill and Royston in Hertfordshire, but the significance of the scheme was not realised and the turnpike or bar which controlled traffic was taken down. By 1700, new Acts had created seven trusts, and during the eighteenth century there was a great proliferation of trusts and a flood of improvements. Trustees, usually worthies in the local business world, would finance road-building projects by attracting investors with offers of 4–5 per cent interest, and would hope to finance these loans and secure a profit from tolls. At first they tended to employ their own turnpikemen to man the tollbars, but later they tended to auction off the tolls to other speculators. The most rapid expansion of turnpikes came in the third quarter of the eighteenth century, while by 1820 the success of the movement was such that around 20,000 miles of improved road had been created in England and Wales—but competition from canals and railways soon became intense. As in Roman times, London became the centre of a radial system, with thirteen important routes converging on the capital by the middle of the nineteenth century. But then the roads were progressively dis-turnpiked, the last turnpike disappearing in 1895.

The impact of a successful turnpike on the territory through which it passed, and beyond, could be immense:

A . . . turnpike was opened through the centre of the forest, which afforded an easy communication between Knaresborough and Skipton in Craven, and the manufacturing towns in the north-east of Lancashire, and though scarce a single cart was before seen in the market of Skipton, not less than 200 are weekly attendant on that market at present. In consequence the product is increased beyond conception, the rents more than trebled, and the population advanced in a very high degree; indeed the lands, both ancient and those newly inclosed, being exonerated from tithe, a full scope was given to spirited cultivation. (Brown, 1799 pp.137–8)

Not all turnpikes were so successful. In 1841 the Wimborne and Puddletown Turnpike Trust spent £24,000 on converting a tangle of lanes into a new turnpike, now the A31, just when the railway was capturing traffic from the roads. As a turnpike, the new road was a failure, though it rose to prominence after the arrival of the motor car (Taylor, 1970 pp.171–2).

Turnpikes today are seen in a variety of guises. Most frequently, they form significant parts of the modern road network, but a few exist as green roads. The one from Ribblehead to Bainbridge in the Yorkshire Dales adopted the course of a Roman road, the Cam High Road, and now exists as a footpath. In some cases, substitute turnpike routes were adopted, as in Nidderdale, where part of the original turnpike from Pateley Bridge to Knaresborough crossed the steep gradients of Brimham Moor while bypassing the incipient industrial villages in the valley bottom at Dacre Banks, Summerbridge and Low Laithe. A bifurcation in the turnpike to the west of Burnt Yates marks the place where a diversion to avoid the moor and connect the new villages was begun in 1826. The presence of a former turnpike in the landscape can be obvious—as signalled by successive former toll houses, built with ticket windows pressing close towards the roadway—or subtle. Turnpiking generally involved the straightening and widening of pre-existing roads. On the Pateley Bridge to Knaresborough example, mentioned above, most traces of the earlier road were obliterated,

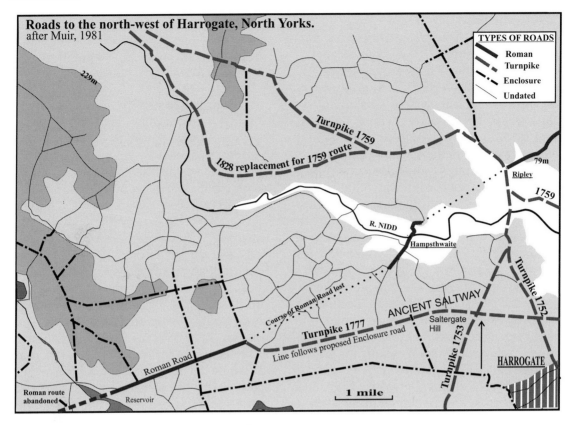

Map 4.3   Roads to the north-west of Harrogate,
North Yorkshire. A variety of different road types
are exemplified in this area, after Muir (1981).

though a short winding section west of
Ripley has an ancient roadside pollard still
in place revealing a surviving fragment of
the former route. In various places traces of
the predecessor route can be recognised
as hollows, or multiple parallel hollows
notched into the hillside beside a turnpike.
Names like 'Bar Lane' and 'Chain Bar
Lane' identify lanes that were closed-off to
prevent their use by travellers dodging a toll
house.

The Enclosure Acts resulted in the
enclosure of 21 per cent of the area of
England. In regions where the intensity of
Enclosure was much greater, like the lowland counties of the East Midlands, the
proportion of the land affected was more
than twice this level. A less heralded aspect
of the process of Enclosure was the construction of new roads. Since Enclosure
normally operated on a parochial frame-

work, these roads were created on a parish
by parish basis (except where the unit of
Enclosure embraced a cluster of parishes,
like the Forest of Knaresborough, enclosed
in 1778). Enclosure could have the effect of
fixing and straightening the course of roads
that had previously shifted and wandered as
travellers exploited the firmer routes across
open fields and commons. Confined between
hedges often 40 feet apart, the new roads
were commonly 20 feet wide and flanked by
verges, to which recourse could be made if
the stone and gravel of the roadbed became
rutted and churned. (Widths between hedges
of 30, 50 and 60 feet were also favoured.)

Enclosure provided an opportunity for the rationalisation of roads within a parish, some routes being deleted, others straightened and improved and some new alignments were provided. As a rule, however, the weakness of the system concerned the inability to affect communication patterns lying beyond the parish boundary, so that the transport remedies were strictly localised. The new roads would frequently exist as potentially useful routeways that would end abruptly at the parish boundaries. Similar routes, created in different parishes at different stages during the currency of Parliamentary Enclosure, would favour different alignments and the two roads would join at a bend, be unconnected or else would require a dog-leg section of roadway to link them together. In some cases, however, different sets of commissioners achieved broader results, as in the northern Yorkshire Wolds, where various Enclosure allocations between 1769 and 1840 succeeded in moving an east–west road, 5 miles in length, out of the bottom of a valley known as the Gypsey Race to a more northerly course which was secure from winter flooding (Allison, 1976 p.156).

Researching routeways

Within any given area, research into routeways is likely to produce a mixture of certainties and probabilities and leave a residue of mysteries. With the application of concepts of the sorts outlined here, some roads will be identified with certainty as Enclosure roads or Roman roads and so on, but others will remain undated and uncategorised, like the deep, winding lanes of the Vale of Blackmoor mentioned by Taylor: 'They wander from farm to farm in a most inexplicable way, often taking little account of the natural landscape. Are they the remains of prehistoric trackways through the forest, boundaries of Saxon estates (Saxon charters and much later estate maps

suggest that some might be) or are they merely convenient links between farmsteads that grew up in these areas over the centuries? We do not know' (Taylor, 1970 pp.170–1).

A useful approach to routeways is to examine them in their landscape context and in their relationship to other aspects of the cultural landscape. Routeways which are *superimposed* upon the countryside will cut across other, older features. In this way, Victorian railways sliced across the preexisting fieldscape, dividing fields and detaching corners as well as interrupting roads and cutting through woods. Similarly Roman roads, turnpikes and Enclosure roads could all be superimposed on countrysides, though subsequent developments would *conform* to their presence. Thus Iron Age field patterns could be disfigured by the superimposition of a Roman road, but Anglo-Saxon parish boundaries would acknowledge the presence of the same road in the landscape and conform to it. Commonly, roads will be found to conform to the field patterns in the surrounding landscape, just as an Iron Age field track would develop in association with contemporary field and settlement patterns or a medieval field lane would be seen to conform to a system of headlands as it wound its way between the packages of selions. The pattern of conformity is not always easy to recognise, and Taylor notes that some minor lanes in Wessex perhaps originated as double-ditched boundaries between farms (1970 p.171).

Despite the notion, propounded by G.K. Chesterton, that the rolling English drunkard made the rolling English road, travellers would seek to minimise their journeys and any bend in a road must have an explanation. Bends might mark places where medieval people had exercised their right to leave a swampy or impassable routeway and form a diversion through adjacent fields. The bend could relate to former terrain and

denote the avoidance of a pond or carr, or else the old road may have avoided a feature of the cultural landscape, like a houseplot or compound. The nature of a road was likely to be strongly influenced by the nature of the cultural landscapes that it traversed.

Figure 4.3   An Enclosure road cuts arrow-straight across the Nidderdale landscape; walls, farmsteads and field patterns in the area are all the products of Parliamentary Enclosure.

Table 4.2 Identifying road types

Type of road	Diagnostic features
Prehistoric roads and trackways	1. Those more important than field lanes are best regarded as zones of movement containing braided trackways. 2. Evidence can be derived from the distribution of single-source commodities, like Portland chert or Langdales tuff, and their relationship to ancient routeways, like the Icknield Way. 3. Conformity to patterns of apparently ancient fields, as in Zennor, Cornwall.
Roman roads	1. Successive sections of straight road sharing the same alignment, the Roman road having a hyphenated appearance, being interrupted by sections where the original road was abandoned and new roads developed. 2. Long sections of straightish routeway devoid of traces of pre-Norman Conquest settlement, which seems to have avoided the main thoroughfares. 3. Considerable lengths of parish boundary following a routeway. 4. The route performs a link function between Roman civil and military settlements, milestones and guardposts. 5. Rather than forming a continuous straight line, Roman roads tended to be direct and to consist, where terrain allowed, of a succession of straight sections.
Dark Age routeways	1. These are likely to be difficult to recognise, but will include many of the ancient longer-distance routeways, such as saltways, badgerways and *here-paeths*. 2. *Here-paeths* seem to have been used as military roads and seem to be associated with battlefields. 3. By the time of Domesday Book the pattern of major and minor roads in England was largely complete. It is, however, very difficult to extract the Saxon components of this network and distinguish them from those of earlier ages.
Medieval roads	1. References to ways and other routes frequently occur in manor courts, and villagers are often fined for encroachments on highways. 2. The documents of royal administration record where kings were located at the times of signing documents, allowing itineries to be reconstructed. 3. Air photographs can be particularly revealing where 'lost' medieval roads are concerned. 4. The monasteries negotiated and created numerous routes linking the outposts of their estates to the centre. Look for any wayside crosses and routes converging on abbeys and priories. Crosses might be erected where routeways entered monastic estates. 5. Market and fair charters may help to reveal the pattern of medieval centres and links.

Table 4.2   Identifying road types—continued

Type of road	Diagnostic features
Turnpikes	1. It should be quite easy to identify the turnpikes of a locality in records pre-dating the creation of the last turnpike in 1836. Frequently they were marked on maps from the late eighteenth century, mainly at a 1 inch to 1 mile scale. 2. Toll houses, often with distinctive shapes and ticket windows pressed close to the road, all now converted, occur at intervals along the road. 3. In their prime, turnpikes amounted to about a fifth of the road mileage in England. Be prepared for examples that sank into obscurity and have become minor lanes, as well as sections where an original turnpike course was superseded by an improved alignment. 4. Try to recognise sections of the pre-turnpike route enduring and running parallel to the turnpike as holloways and braided tracks and other sections where the older road alignment was adopted and preserved, along with features like old roadside hedgerows and pollards.
Enclosure roads	1. These run, mainly in straight sections, to the parish boundary and no further. 2. Look for a slight bend at parish boundary where two Enclosure roads of different dates join. 3. The form of the road may change from straight and of even width (where the road was superimposed upon open fields and commons) to narrow, winding, of varying width and with veteran trees at the roadside (where the new road picked up a track running through old enclosed countryside). 4. There should be a width between flanking hedgerows of 30, 40, 50 or 60 feet. Hedges often of hawthorn with elder, sycamore, bramble, wild roses and ash. 5. Unlike Roman roads, which also tend to be straight, these roads hardly ever follow parish boundaries, but link village and village or village and fields.

Where tightly confined by dwellings and private property defined by hedgerows the track was far more likely to develop a linear, deeply incised and rutted form than it was when traversing open, upland commons, where travellers were free to select whichever of several branches offered the easiest 'going', while stock being driven could spread unconfined across the drift or drove.

Minor prehistoric roads, or fragments of them, can be identified from their relationships to known prehistoric settlements and from their integration with ancient field systems. Major prehistoric routeways are less easy to recognise and serious consideration is reserved for those whose lines are associated with frequent discoveries of artefacts, such as stone axes. These routeways appear to have existed as 'zones of movement' and to have had a braided rather than a linear appearance. Thus, a series of fording-place settlements might form in a zone where a system of braided, sub-parallel routes encountered a river—as at

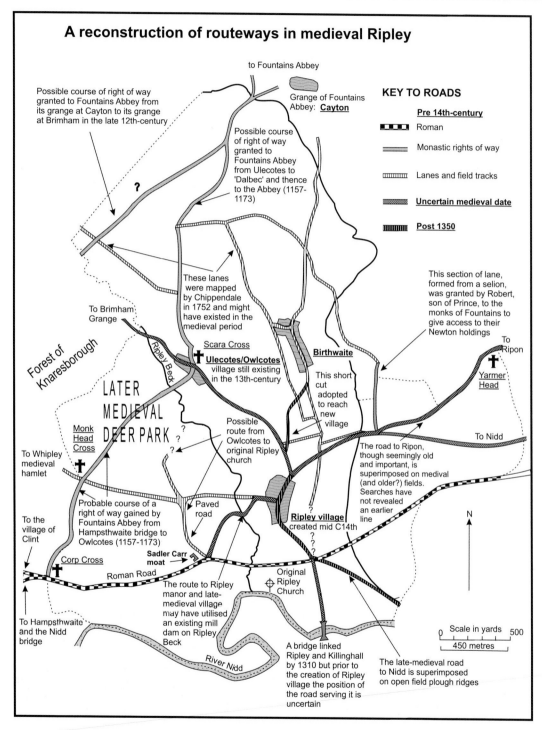

A reconstruction of routeways in medieval Ripley

to Fountains Abbey

Grange of Fountains Abbey: **Cayton**

KEY TO ROADS

Pre 14th-century

▬▬ Roman

▬▬ Monastic rights of way

▭▭▭ Lanes and field tracks

▬▬ **Uncertain medieval date**

▭▭▭ **Post 1350**

Possible course of right of way granted to Fountains Abbey from its grange at Cayton to its grange at Brimham in the late 12th-century

Possible course of right of way granted to Fountains Abbey from Ulecotes to 'Dalbec' and thence to the Abbey (1157-1173)

?

This section of lane, formed from a selion, was granted by Robert, son of Prince, to the monks of Fountains to give access to their Newton holdings

To Ripon

To Brimham Grange

These lanes were mapped by Chippendale in 1752 and might have existed in the medieval period

Ripley Beck

Scara Cross
✝ **Ulecotes/Owlcotes**
village still existing in the 13th-century

Birthwaite

Yarmer Head ✝

Forest of Knaresborough

LATER MEDIEVAL DEER PARK

?
?
?

Monk Head Cross ✝

Possible route from Owlcotes to original Ripley church

This short cut adopted to reach new village

To Nidd

The road to Ripon, though seemingly old and important, is superimposed on medival (and older?) fields. Searches have not revealed an earlier line

To Whipley medieval hamlet

Probable course of a right of way gained by Fountains Abbey from Hampsthwaite bridge to Owlcotes (1157-1173)

Paved road

?
Ripley village
created mid C14th
?
?
?

N

To the village of Clint

Corp Cross ✝

Sadler Carr moat

Roman Road

Original ⊕ Ripley Church

Scale in yards
0 ————————— 500
450 metres

To Hampsthwaite and the Nidd bridge

The route to Ripley manor and late-medieval village may have utilised an existing mill dam on Ripley Beck

River Nidd

A bridge linked Ripley and Killinghall by 1310 but prior to the creation of Ripley village the position of the road serving it is uncertain

The late-medieval road to Nidd is superimposed on open field plough ridges

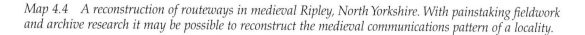

Map 4.4   A reconstruction of routeways in medieval Ripley, North Yorkshire. With painstaking fieldwork and archive research it may be possible to reconstruct the medieval communications pattern of a locality.

Figure 4.4   Clapper bridges like the Tarr Steps on Exmoor are unlikely to be very old as they would be damaged each time that there was a severe flood. However, the routeways that they serve could be very old indeed.

the junction of the Icknield Way and the River Cam, where small Saxon settlements developed at the more ancient crossing points (Taylor, 1979 pp.106–7). One might imagine that Roman roads are fully researched and understood, but in fact the *Antonine Itinerary* provides the only written list of roads, and not all of the fifteen major British routes recorded there have been identified. In most regions, especially the more peripheral ones, the potential for discovering 'lost' Roman routes are quite good. Road-hunters are quite numerous,

though the confirmation for their results may be hard to come by. Research might begin by checking the known routeways of an area in the generally reliable source, *Margary's Roman Roads in Britain*, and it could proceed to relate the information to the network portrayed on large-scale maps of the locality concerned. (Even the leading experts are capable of mistakes, and one Second World War anti-tank ditch, little more than fifteen years old at the time, was interpreted as a part of the Roman London to Chichester routeway.) The known distribution of Roman settlement traces and finds could then be incorporated, with a search being made for undiscovered transport links between significant places.

The pattern of routeways existing in a

Figure 4.5   This bridge at Crowland appears to be a pointless construction until it is realised that before drainage projects put an end to Fenland navigation, barges would have sailed under the arch.

locality during the medieval period may, to a considerable degree, be reconstructed. One might attempt a process of *landscape regression* (progressively removing the younger features from a large-scale map of the locality until the chosen period is reached) combined with *landscape replacement* (restoring, where possible, lost features to the landscape). Thus modern routes, Enclosure roads and turnpikes would be excluded, while recorded fords and former bridging points, markets and deserted settlements would be restored. Documentary and archaeological sources were employed to reconstruct the local network of routeways which served six deserted medieval villages in Norfolk, and although some ways noted in medieval sources could not be tied with confidence to the landscape, much of the old network could be reconstructed. Particular problems arose from the unstable nature of some names, so that in the case of Kilverstone, the Magdalen Way of 1471 became Grismarket Way by 1596, and the Bridgham Way of 1584 could be the Norwich Road of 1742 (Davison, 1988).

As well as mentioning the particular routeways, medieval documents contain copious references to related features. These include bridges, fords, ferries, stiles, gates, signposts, hospitals which catered for travellers or for the sick or destitute, inns and hostelries, chantry chapels, where travellers might rest, and hermitages, often sited by bridges or fords, where the occupant would offer helpful services to road users. Manor court rolls can provide information about local roads and rights of way, as with the case brought to Wakefield manor court in 1331 after Thomas Gyge and his wife had allowed their cattle to eat a neighbour's corn after breaking down a section of hedge and a stile (Faull and Moorhouse, 1981 p.643).

Bridges tend to feature quite prominently in the records, partly because of the need to pay for them and to finance repairs necessitated by neglect or flood damage. Their presence or absence exerted a considerable influence upon the development of roads, which would tend to funnel towards the few bridging points on large rivers. The most primitive of bridges were beam bridges, consisting of upright supports linked by horizontal beams of timber or stone. The clapper bridges seen in the south-western uplands, or occasionally in the north, are stone-built examples. Arched bridges are far more effective in their use of stone, a material with poor tensile strength, with the stone arch being a form with high resistance to compression. The abutments and piers of the bridge resisted the out-force generated by the arch, but as medieval bridges were built one arch at a time, during construction there would be no counter force from an adjoining span. Consequently, piers had to be very wide. This resulted in obstructions to the flow of the river, causing it to gather speed and become turbulent as it passed through the arch, which in turn could cause a deepening of the bed and the undermining of the pier (Smyth, 1998 p.6). Features seen in many medieval bridges include stone ribs on the undersides of arches, wide piers with pointed cutwaters and, sometimes, pointed arches.

With a thoughtful use of evidence of the type outlined above, an understanding of the evolution of a local system of communications may be acquired. Routeways can be studied in their own right, but an understanding of their history will normally be crucial to an appreciation of total landscapes. An awareness of routeways may also shed essential light on other areas of landscape research, particularly when the routeways concerned can be dated.

REFERENCES

Albert, W. *The Turnpike Road System of England, 1663–1840* (Cambridge: Cambridge University Press, 1972).

Allison, K.J. *The East Riding of Yorkshire* (London: Hodder and Stoughton, 1976).

Blackmore, J., Bowsher, D., Cowie, R. and Malcolm, G. 'Royal Opera House' *Current Archaeology* 158 (1998) pp.60–3.

Brown, R. *General View of the Agriculture of the West Riding*, 2nd edn (1799).

Davison, A. *Six Deserted Villages in Norfolk*, East Anglian Archaeology Report 44 (Norwich: Norwich Museums Service, 1988).

Denison, S. 'Date of Ridgeway' *British Archaeology* February (1998) p.4.

Denison, S. 'Bronze Age metalled road near Oxford' *British Archaeology* July (1998) p.4.

Dymond, D. *The Norfolk Landscape* (London: Hodder and Stoughton, 1985).

Faull, M.L. and Moorhouse, S.A. (eds) *West Yorkshire: An Archaeological Survey to A.D. 1500* (Wakefield: West Yorkshire Metropolitan County Council, 1981).

Fell, C. 'The Great Langdale stone-axe factory' *Transactions of the Cumberland and Westmorland Antiquary and Archaeological Society* new ser. 50 (1964).

Gloag, J. *2000 Years of England* (London: Cassell, 1952).

Halliday, R. 'Criminal graves at rural crossroads' *British Archaeology* June (1997) p.6.

Hart, C.R. *The Early Charters of Northern England and the North Midlands* (Leicester: Leicester University Press, 1975).

Hindle, B.P. *Medieval Roads* (Princes Risborough: Shire, 1982).

Hindle, B.P. *Roads, Tracks and Their Interpretation* (London: Batsford, 1993).

Margary, I.D. *Roman Roads in Britain*, 3rd edn (London: J. Baker, 1973).

Muir, R. *Reading the landscape* (London: Michael Joseph 1981).

Plint, R.G. 'Stone-axe factory site in the Cumbrian Fells' *Transactions of the Cumberland and Westmorland Antiquary and Archaeological Society* new ser. 62 (1962) pp.2–26.

Powlesland, D. with Haughton, C. and Hanson, J. 'Excavations at Heslerton, North Yorkshire 1972–82' *Archaeological Journal* 143 (1986) pp.53–173.

Pryor, F. 'Welland Bank Quarry, South Lincolnshire' *Current Archaeology* 160 (1998) pp.139–145.

Raistrick, A. *Green Roads in the Mid Pennines* (Buxton: Moorland, 1978).

Ravensdale, J.R. and Muir, R. *East Anglian Landscapes* (London: Michael Joseph, 1984).

Smyth, W. 'Changing materials, changing bridges', *British Archaeology* 39 (1998) pp.6–8.

Taylor, C. *Dorset* (London: Hodder and Stoughton, 1970).

Taylor, C. *Roads and Tracks of Britain* (London: Dent, 1979).

Thomas, C. and Rackham, J. 'Bronze Age trackway at Bramhope Green, Bermondsey' *Proceedings of the Prehistoric Society* 62 (1996), pp.221–54.

White, J.T. *The Scottish border and Northumberland* (London: Eyre Methuen 1973).

Witcher, R. 'Roman roads that reshaped the land' *British Archaeology* 31 (1998) pp.6–7.

Wright, G.N. *Roads and Trackways of Wessex* (Ashbourne: NPC, 1988).

CHAPTER 5

Status, Authority and the Landscape

Embedded in landscapes are the symbols of authority and power. Status was proclaimed in the construction of works which were reserved for members of an elite—moats, mottes, deer parks or duck decoys—and it was also expressed in the eviction and exclusion of the public from high-status locations, like parks, grouse moorlands and pheasant woods. One will not need to travel far in the countryside of England before encountering ample living landscape evidence of the currently dominant land-owning elite, but there is also much that is fossilised in the landscape as a legacy of former patterns of status and display. The overgrown warren, the tree mounds from a lost park now stranded in the ploughland or the terraces in the pasture which were once parts of an aristocratic garden all echo former patterns of privilege. Less obvious are the combinations of territories and boundaries which composed the ancient estates of England. These territorial units have generally vanished, but they may have exerted strong formative influences on the patterns of settlement and interaction which were established in the centuries before the Norman Conquest.

Estates and the landscape

The estate had both spatial and social dimensions; it was (and is) the vehicle through which authority found expression in the landscape. Much more in the countryside derives from the influence of the estate owner than just the rather obvious symbols of privilege already noted. Parish churches, for example, were frequently built by estate owners and situated beside their manor houses, apparently forming the double nucleus around which many villages would grow. Considerable research, much of it of a speculative nature, has concerned the antiquity of estates as features of the English landscape and some workers have detected Roman or even prehistoric aspects to the patterns of land division. That estates existed in England in prehistoric periods is now beyond dispute, their boundaries are found throughout the country in the form of linear earthworks, as has been seen. Interesting questions concern the continuing use of ancient territories through into historical or even modern times.

Questions of continuity and of Celtic and Roman survival were well entrenched in historical debate when the more modern landscape historians considered the question of estate territories and boundaries. Hoskins believed that farm units could have survived since 'Celtic times' in Cornwall and he identified a farm called Treable with a Celtic landowner, Ebell. A charter of 976 described the boundaries of the Treable estate, and Hoskins considered: 'This hollow way—"the old ditch"—was already "old" in the tenth century. It can hardly be doubted that it represents the ancient boundary between the estate of Hyple and his ancestors to the west, and that of another (unknown) Celtic landowner to the east. The two hedge-banks, still enclosing the fields of today, are thus of great age— certainly pre-Saxon' (Hoskins, 1970 p.31).

Hoskins's words were first published in 1955, and in the same year Finberg wrote of an area in Gloucestershire:

Figure 5.1   Quite often the leading figures in the making of the local landscape can be encountered in the church, as at Exton in Rutland, where the Grenes and then the Haringtons held sway.

In the valleys of the Coln and Churn there is a group of villages—Chedworth, Colesborne, Withington, Compton Abdale, and Whittington—all situated close to Roman-British villa sites. All of them bear Anglo-Saxon names, but it is difficult to think of them as wholly new creations of the Old English period. Where the settlers found an estate in working order, or but lately fallen out of cultivation, it would be natural for them to take it over before breaking new ground. Each of these parishes, therefore, may preserve in its boundaries the outlines of a Roman-British estate. (p.39).

According to Finberg, a villa-centred Roman estate in the Cotswolds became the parish of Withington, with the estate, by then centred on a minster church, being transferred to the Bishop of Worcester in the seventh century.

Other researchers claimed to have recognised the survival of elements from centuriation, the process by which Roman grainlands were set-out. It involved alignments derived from a carefully surveyed rectilinear grid. 'Boundary marks were of profound importance to the Romans, having a deep religious significance, their own god, Terminus, and being set up following an animal sacrifice' (Reed, 1984 p.266). Colchester, Lincoln, Brancaster and Ripe in Sussex were suggested, with varying degrees of controversy, to preserve such traces of Roman estates, and in 1952 Nightingale proposed that centuriated lands around Cliffe, near Rochester, were part of an estate serving Roman Rochester, with the divisions based on Watling Street and the Maidstone Roman roads. It is possible that some estates which existed in Saxon or medieval times were based on the lands or *territoria* which surrounded Roman settlements.

By the mid-1960s an awareness had been established that the estates described in Domesday may often have existed in pagan Saxon times, or earlier, while pagan Saxon burial sites were very frequently found on or near the boundaries of old ecclesiastical parishes (Bonney, 1966). More recent think-

ing was represented by Reed, who wrote: 'Anglo-Saxon England by the end of the seventh century was divided up and parcelled out into blocks of land that for want of a better word may be called estates and, if such phrases as *hunc agrum intra terminos ab antiquis possessoribus constitutos* mean anything at all, it had been so divided for a very long time' (1984 p.274). He added: 'It is equally clear that these territorial units varied enormously in size and contained their own internal subdivisions, so that it is possible to speak of a hierarchy of such

Map 5.1   Rectilinear features in the countryside near Cliffe, Kent. It was proposed that linear and rectilinear features surviving in the landscape revealed the pattern of Roman centuriation. After Nightingale (1952).

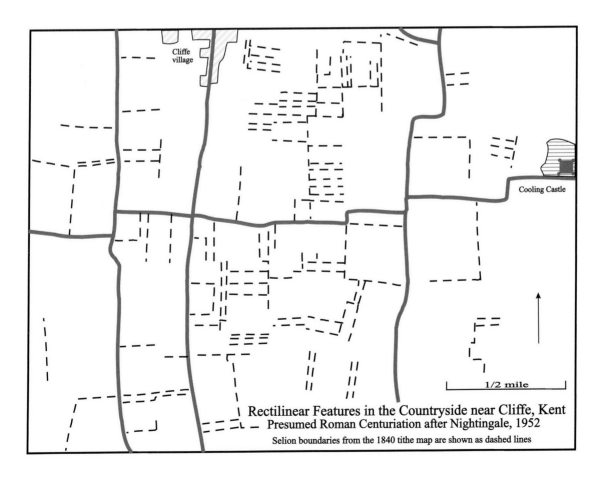

Rectilinear Features in the Countryside near Cliffe, Kent
Presumed Roman Centuriation after Nightingale, 1952
Selion boundaries from the 1840 tithe map are shown as dashed lines

units. Thus in 780 Offa, king of the Mercians, gave an estate of 35 *tributarii* in the province of the Hwicce. The estate itself was divided into four separate *villulas*, these contained in their turn five *manentes*, 10 *cassati*, 10 *mansiones* and finally another ten *manentes'* (p.294).

Similarly complicated are the interpretations concerning 'multiple estates', which involve more than the simple concept of continuity. Such estates, as described by Glanville Jones (1979), were focused on a *caput*, an important central place and power centre where the lord had his chief residence and which was surrounded by subordinate settlements. The *caput* would often be owned by an important personage, a king, bishop or abbot, and could be the administrative capital of a hundred, while its church would often be a minster, with the churches in the dependent settlements serving as daughters to the minster. Within the multiple estate there was likely to be a specialisation in production, with some vills concentrating on, say, grain production and others on stock-breeding. Certain environmental resources, like woodland, might be shared by the vills on the estate. Ford believed that 'Specialization by farms of settlements is more likely to take place in a well-ordered, planned community. Concentration on the various aspects of husbandry, such as the growth of wheat, barley, fruit and vegetables or the raising of sheep, cattle, pigs and horses as well as inland fisheries, and milling, seems more acceptable when viewed as a contribution towards a balanced economy on a considerably broader basis than that of single settlements with a supposedly subsistence economy' (1979 p.156).

During the early phases of Christianity in Saxon England a system of minster churches prevailed, but during the tenth and eleventh centuries private landowners began to build their own private churches and to appropriate ecclesiastical dues. The private churches, now serving parishes, are sometimes known as *eigenkirchen*. Roffe noted that

> it is likely that many, if not most, pre-nineteenth-century parish boundaries date from the inception of the institution in the eleventh century or earlier. Accordingly, they may tell us much about the boundaries of estates at the same time. It has already been noted that most churches were *eigenkirchen* in origin. In the past it has been argued that their parishes therefore represent the extent of the estates to which they belonged ... But it is one thing to say that all churches were *eigenkirchen* and another to say that all parishes therefore define discrete territorial interests. Once built, a church has a public life which belies its private origin since it is an amenity as well as a source of profit. (1984 p.117).

In the west of Essex a group of eight ecclesiastical parishes which cover the territory of sixteen Domesday manors are known as the Rodings and appear to have been formed from the piecemeal fission of one land unit which might be regarded as the home territory of the Hrodingas or 'people of *Hroda*'. In a recent attempt to interpret the growth and disintegration of the great estate, Bassett found that:

> Perhaps the only significant discovery has been that White Roding church was very probably an old minster and that the other churches of the Rodings were private chapels founded close to manor houses. This well exemplifies the trend seen throughout England in the tenth, eleventh and twelfth centuries whereby the local churches set up by manorial lords evolved in many cases into independent parish churches, with each one taking on pastoral responsibility for part of the area once exclusively served by an old minster. (1998 p.36)

The great estate represented by the Roding parishes conformed to the local topography, and the way in which broadly rectilinear patterns of fields or roads disregard present internal boundaries also suggests that the territory was once an integrated whole.

Gradually, during the centuries around the Norman Conquest, the granting-away of royal estates and the reorganisation and enlargement of ecclesiastical territories led to an unravelling of the ancient estate patterns. Sawyer (1974) argued that the settlement and territorial patterns of Saxon England should be interpreted as resulting from the fragmentation of large multiple estates into their small, local components. It is likely that the building blocks which were welded together to form multiple estates, and which might be recognised now as townships or tithings or vills, were older than the units they composed: 'With regard to antiquity, however, a distinction should perhaps be drawn between the multiple estate and its components. The former need not be as old-established as the latter' (Glanville Jones, 1979 p. 34). Ford wrote that:

A high proportion of the Anglo-Saxon estates that are known from charters or inferred from other evidence, were composed of numerous sub-estates and their attendant settlements, seemingly from a very early date. Such evidence as we have, again largely the accident of history, suggests a tale of subsequent fragmentation. It can be shown that many seemingly independent villages of the twelfth and thirteenth centuries were originally components of such settlement groups and the later medieval period seems to have been a time of transformation in estate pattern through the break-up of a large number of pre-Conquest land units and the creation of new estates, sometimes of a much more dispersed nature. (1979 p.152)

Information which may allow the reconstruction of ancient estate patterns may sometimes be found in the boundary clauses of Saxon charters: 'It may be possible to reconstruct, for instance, the estates of minsters, as in the case of Crediton, and to see, perhaps, the gradual breakdown of their parochiae. The emergence of the parish unit is clearly attested during this period and in many regions the smaller township community may be recognised' (Hook, 1997 p.22). Ford suggested three approaches that could lead to the discovery of the extents of early estates. They were a grouping of territories in manorial documents, the Domesday survey or Saxon charters; the linking of mother churches and dependent chapels; and the analysis of place-names. These sources of evidence, along with several others, are included in Table 5.1.

The model of the multiple estate proposed by Jones has encountered criticism on the grounds that the evidence used to support interpretations is often much later than the currency of the estate concerned (Gregson, 1985). Still, during the period since Finberg and Hoskins published their ideas on estates in 1955 an abundance of evidence has been produced to show the endurance of ancient territorial units. As noted above, Fleming considered that linear earthworks in Swaledale suggested the existence of an early post-Roman polity in Upper Swaledale and Arkengarthdale, one which might be held roughly to correspond with the large medieval parish of Grinton and the manor of Healaugh (1994 p.19). It was noted that Danelaw 'sokes' or estates described in Domesday Book were characteristically large and consisted of a central manor with outlying berewicks and sokeland, and they were regarded as relict features of earlier organisation. Though critical of some aspects of the multiple estate model, Hadley found that:

Much recent research indicates that the

Table 5.1   The recognition of early estates

Source	Evidence
Early church documents	The recognition of a minster and of dependent churches in the surrounding territories could denote a former multiple estate. The manner of grouping townships within ancient ecclesiastical parishes could also be relevant. The territory served by a minster could disintegrate into late Saxon/Norman parishes.
Pre-Conquest church documents	The territories of pre-Conquest monasteries may be identified as multiple estates.
Saxon charters, Domesday Book or manorial documents	The grouping of places together in entries in documents and surveys such as these may reveal land units that were bound together within early estates.
Pre-eleventh-century charters and early manorial documents	The existence of a multiple estate may be evidenced by the payment of rents and/or services to a *caput* by lesser units representing the dependent settlements.
Medieval manorial documents	Intercommoning arrangements shared by neighbouring parishes/townships may reveal the former existence of an estate embracing all the territories involved.
Place-names	Relevant names are those which describe a possible geographical relationship between a component of an estate and its centre. This could involve directions from the centre, as with 'North-', 'South-' etc. names, or those concerning boundary locations ('mere' names) or names associated with outlying seasonally used lands ('winter' or 'summer' names). '*Tun*' names were often associated with daughter settlements, as were names denoting their agricultural specialisations within the estate: Ryeton, Appleton and also Keswick (cheese farm) or Skipton/Shipton (sheep farm) etc. Similarities between names of adjacent parishes and localities can be suggestive, e.g. the Essex Rodings or Ripley and Ripon, North Yorkshire.
Landscape and historical evidence	Potential candidates as *caputs* include hundredal manors, the foci of old hundreds, settlements with minster churches and other ancient power centres, such as hillforts. Place-names including burgh or (in Cornwall) ker- denoting forts could be relevant.
Parish boundaries	Pre-nineteenth-century parish boundaries are quite likely to represent the boundaries of estates which existed when the parishes were created, largely in the tenth and eleventh centuries. Where different lords are known to have existed on different sides of the boundary the likelihood increases, and where the parish boundaries were fixed by medieval negotiation it diminishes.
Monuments 1	The *caputs* of Saxon estates seem frequently to be associated with places where there had been substantial Roman settlements.
Monuments 2	The association between a parish/estate boundary and pagan Saxon burials in a prehistoric barrow or a cemetery could denote the pre-Christian existence of the territorial unit.
Monuments 3	Linear earthworks are best regarded as territorial boundary-markers and they may date from prehistoric, Roman or Dark Age periods, or even the Norman period in Ireland.

provision of tribute to superior powers was effected through large territories in the early medieval period and collected through administrative centres, often royal *tuns*. A number of the large Domesday sokes owed food renders and other provisions to the king, which appear to represent a remnant of the ancient tribute system. Furthermore, it is not difficult to envisage that at an early date such territories contained inhabitants and land of varying status, and as such the Domesday sokes reflect an early type of organisation. (1996 p.12)

The multiple estates of England bore similarities to territorial units described in early medieval Welsh documents and it is suggested that they derived from Celtic patterns of land organisation. The break with the old traditions was associated not so much with the rise to positions of political authority of men bearing Saxon names, but with the Norman Conquest, which involved a suppression of the indigenous aristocracy, the frequent redistribution of land and the establishment of new administrative centres at castles and new monastic houses. Bettey noted that: 'Compared to later estates, a striking feature [was] the dispersed nature of many of the holdings, which was possibly a deliberate policy of the Conqueror to check the potential for rebellion among his most powerful adherents by preventing them from building up a strong power-base in any one area of the country' (1993 p.17).

Although the map of estates had undergone considerable changes, some aspects of territorial control survived. The significance of the hundred, its court and the hundredal manor persisted to the High Middle Ages, with three representatives from every township, tithing or vill attending meetings every third week. Sometimes the court was held in the open air, perhaps at a meeting place marked by a prehistoric monument, a

medieval mound or a geological outcrop. Sometimes the nature of its central place was encapsulated in the name of a hundred: Aston (1985) quotes cases such as Whitestone and Horethorne hundreds in Somerset. A further traumatic change in the pattern of estates was launched at the close of the medieval period, when the monastic estates were forfeit and sold to gentry and speculators, many of the estates being dismantled and resold to yeomen and tenants.

Despite all these changes, and the more recent ones resulting from the imposition of death duties, a privileged landed aristocracy and a lower stratum of smaller estate-owning petty gentry endures. In the course of many centuries small blocks of land—the territorial cells which re-emerge at different times and places bearing different names—have been combined, dismantled, re-combined and deconstructed to produce the changing patterns of rural authority which we glimpse receding into prehistoric time.

Symbols of authority

Authority carried with it the power to coerce others and to enjoy privileges and resources that were denied to them. It also enabled the favoured few to make bold and symbolic statements in the landscape by creating buildings and field monuments which would instantly be identified as signalling status, privilege and the possession of exclusive powers. Deer parks, warrens, dovecotes, fishponds and duck-decoys all contributed substantially to the material production of the manor—but all, too, could not be glimpsed by contemporary eyes without a powerful message about power and inequality being conveyed. The deer parks, warrens and dovecotes all, to a greater or lesser extent, imposed a burden on the less privileged members of the local community by exposing their crops to browsing, trampling, grazing or seed-eating, and such

Figure 5.2   Two symbols of lordly privilege are displayed in these earthworks at Harrington in Northamptonshire: on the right, a pair of fishponds, and on the left, garden terraces.
© *Cambridge UC (AEV 38).*

impositions accentuated the awareness of rural inequalities.

Deer parks, in their topographical aspects, have been described already, but it is worth noting these remarks by Stamper:

A park provided a lord with a ready supply of fresh venison, a meat that was seen, at least by the aristocracy itself, as reserved for its tables and especially the feast. As important as the meat itself was the way in which it was taken, the park being an enclosed hunting ground, where the pleasures of the chase could be enjoyed by the lord and his chosen companions. Throughout the middle ages deer hunting was the preserve of the king and the aristocracy, and the acquisition of a park was one of the marks, at least in the eyes of its creator, that he was joining their ranks. (1988 p.140)

He added that in the early medieval period the King was regarded as the owner of all deer, and so parks could only be stocked with his assistance and agreement. The King controlled the issue of the royal licences that were necessary to create a park, and the licence to empark might specifically forbid the construction of deer leaps, which would entrap the King's deer within a park. Deer parks proclaimed status by preventing more productive uses of their land and producing 'conspicuous wastage'. Possession of a deer park assisted attempts to join the ranks of

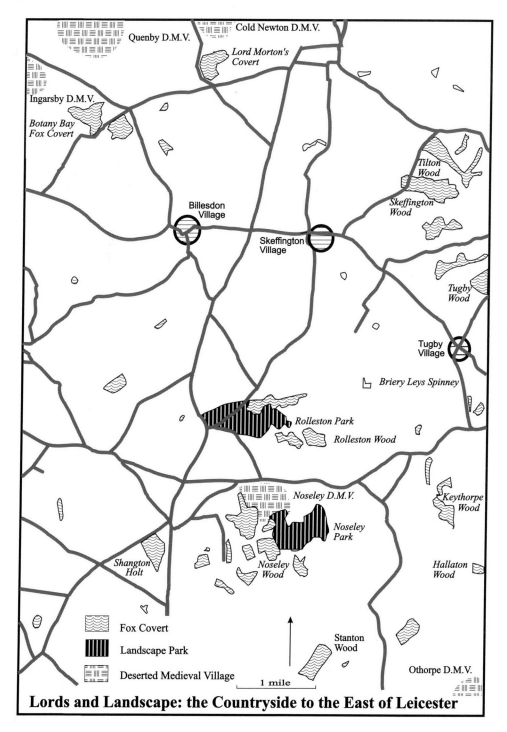

Lords and Landscape: the Countryside to the East of Leicester

Legend:
- Fox Covert
- Landscape Park
- Deserted Medieval Village

1 mile

Map 5.2   Lords and landscape: the countryside to the east of Leicester. Deserted villages, landscape park and the creation of a multitude of small woods to harbour foxes all testify to the influence of the privileged classes upon the countryside.

the landed aristocracy: 'Having made a fortune in trade, aspiring medieval families acquired parks as symbols of their new nobility. The de la Pole family were Hull merchants who became Dukes of Suffolk, and as well as building the church at Ewelme, they demonstrated their aristocratic status in the fifteenth century by constructing numerous deer parks on their estates' (Williamson and Bellamy, 1987 p.70).

Warrens, where rabbits were raised, were also symbolic of aristocratic status, the term deriving from the rights of free warren (or to hunt small game) which nobles enjoyed on their estates. Rabbits, introduced, perhaps, from Spain, were first recorded on the Isles of Scilly in 1176 (Veale, 1957 p.86) and seem initially to have been established on islands, on heathlands and in parks. At first, the animals struggled to survive in the cool, damp English climate, but gradually they became more hardy; by the middle of the thirteenth century warrens were numerous, while by the end of the century rabbit farming was making a significant contribution to the economy and warrens and their appurtenances were notable features of the countryside.

The size of the warren could vary from that of a paddock to an extensive tract of open country, and in some cases lords established warrens within commons, though situations within deer parks were popular. Frequently the areas within which the rabbits bred was enclosed in an attempt to exclude poachers, with banks and ditches, palings and hedges being employed. In 1457–8 Fountains Abbey spent 11½d on 'making hedges around the garden of the coneys', while the Duke of Lancaster's warren at Higham Ferrers in Northamptonshire, containing rabbbits, hares, pheasants and partridges, was surrounded by a wall (Stamper, 1988 p.145). At Dolebury in Avon the warren enjoyed the protection of the ramparts of the Iron Age hillfort. Not only were rabbits an expensive

form of nutrition, they also caused considerable damage to the crops of tenants and neighbours. On the larger and more vulnerable warrens, warreners were employed to protect the lord's rabbits against poachers and special lodges were built to house them. It is said that during the Peasants' Revolt the rebels at St Albans advanced behind a rabbit hung from a lance head, which symbolised their claim to the right to hunt over Abbey lands.

Place-names and earthworks allow the recognition of former warrens. 'Warren' place-names date from the post-medieval period and are frequently found; they occur repeatedly in the Norfolk Brecklands, Dartmoor or the heathlands on the dip-slopes of the Lincolnshire escarpments. In the Brecklands warrens existed for more than six centuries; eight warrens existed there during the thirteenth century, while in the nineteenth century some large warrens there were still producing around 25,000 rabbits per year. 'Rabbit' is a word that does not tend to appear in place-names; originally it was applied only to the baby rabbits, the adults being known as 'coneys' (Sheail, 1971). The latter word does appear in place-names, like Coney Hill and Coneygar, both Gloucestershire, which can be presumed to relate to medieval warrens. Similar words, including coninger, coning-erth, coneygarth and conerie, may appear in old documents or on maps to denote early warrens. Any similar names appearing in documents *pre-dating* the establishment of rabbits, like Coneysthorpe in North Yorkshire, which is mentioned in Domesday, will refer not to rabbits, but derive from Old Norse or Old English words relating to the King.

The breeding area within a warren would be enclosed with banks and ditches, palings or hedges, but such enclosures might be difficult to differentiate. More obvious are the 'pillow mounds' which accommodated the burrows, even though their function remained controversial until relatively

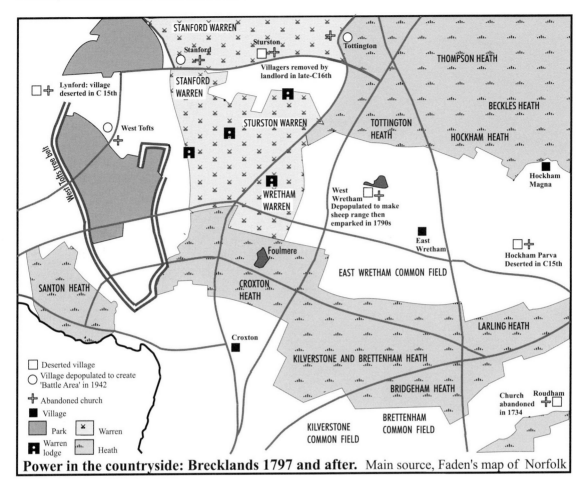

Power in the countryside: Brecklands 1797 and after. Main source, Faden's map of Norfolk

Map 5.3   Power in the countryside: the Norfolk Brecklands, 1797 and after. The depopulation of villages, the creation of warrens and parks reveal the influence of the rich landowners. Partly based on Faden's map of Norfolk of 1797.

recently. The mounds are frequently cigar- or pillow-shaped and found in groups, though circular and rarer square examples have been recorded. Some mounds have been found to contain internal structures, and a fourteenth century example from Dyfed was furnished with stone-lined tunnels. Pillow mounds may have been built from shortly after the introduction of rabbits in the twelfth century, but most of the mounds encountered are of post-medieval date. They belong to the period when the flesh and fur of the animal had become mass-produced commodities on the urban market rather than the exclusive properties of the landed nobility.

Rabbits, straying from their protected warrens to nibble the crops of the peasantry, underlined the privileged status of the rural aristocracies. Such inequalities were expressed with a more brutal clarity by the lord's exclusive right to have a dovecote— from which the birds would disperse to ravage the crops on the surrounding estate. However: 'Although doves were protected birds, in that tenants could not prevent them from feeding on their corn, there are

Figure 5.3   The cigar-shaped earthworks shown here on Huntingdon Warren, Dartmoor, are pillow mounds. © Cambridge UC (AQX 80).

few references to people being fined in the court rolls for killing or catching them, in contrast to the frequent appearance of people for catching rabbits, hares and deer' (Faull and Moorhouse, 1981 p.752). Dovecotes were common throughout much of the medieval period but it was only following an Act of 1761/2 that all landlords, freeholders and tenants who had gained the permission of their landlords were allowed to keep doves. Much remains to be learned about the form of medieval dovecotes; towards the end of the period some cylindrical towers were built, as at Garway in Herefordshire, though the finest surviving example dates from just after the Dissolution of the Monasteries, when a great lectern-shaped building was erected at Willington in Bedfordshire by Sir John Gostwick. By the end of the seventeenth century, there were around 26,000 dovecotes in England, while most of the short rectangular dovecote towers which survive were still to be built. Dovecotes are not particularly evident in place-names, though dovecotes, culveries or pigeon houses do appear on old maps and in documents. Normally a medieval dovecote would be positioned close to the manor house and its most immediate impact upon the landscape was to be found in the neighbouring grain-fields. Field-names, like Dovehouse Close, located near to the manorial building complex will reveal the former existence of a dovecote, but most 'Dove' place-names

Figure 5.4   A magnificent dovecote built around 1540 at Willington in Bedfordshire by Sir John Gostwick, who had profited from the Dissolution of the Monasteries and was proclaiming his rising status in the landscape.

derive from the Old Welsh *dubr* and the later *dwfr* and *dwr*, denoting water and streams. Some medieval dovecotes appear to have been circular buildings built upon low mounds, and these mounds may occasionally survive as earthworks.

The villager who had his crops flattened when his lord's deer were hunted across the countryside, whose corn was devoured by the lord's doves and whose sprouting crops were nibbled by his rabbits could expect to be fined if his hunger drove him to take fish from his master's fishpond. These, too, were normally built within sight of the manor house and the lord's retainers and scores of new fishpond sites and earthworks have been recognised in recent years. These ponds, stocked not with the exotic rainbow trout favoured by modern fish farmers but with carp and other coarse fish like perch, bream and young pike, provided the nobility with a reliable source of protein. River fish were caught in abundance on lines and rods and artificial ponds could serve as 'stews' to retain the catch alive for later consumption. This resource could be harvested on a grand scale for festive occasions and lavish entertainment and it furnished a food supply on Fridays, when other sources of flesh were forbidden.

The ponds vary considerably in their form, and were shallower than might be imagined. It appears that periodically they might be drained, allowing very rich crops to be grown in the fertile accumulations on their floors. Most characteristically the main ponds were rectangular or trapezoidal and they were grouped with much smaller ponds which accommodated young fish of differing sizes. Other ponds could be oval or cigar-shaped. Some ponds occupied naturally wet sites, but most were created by damming a stream, often one which had been diverted into the chosen site. Some were perched on a valley slope with the water being held by a massive containing bank. Water was generally retained by low banks, around a metre in height, and sluices were provided to regulate the water level, though some ponds existed as scoops. Within the flooded area an island was often provided as a secure roost for wildfowl. The earthworks of fishponds have frequently been mistaken for those of other kinds of monuments, even fortifications, while they often occur in association with other features. These may or may not be contemporary with the ponds; homestead moats are likely to mark the dwelling of

the fishpond owner but at Harrington in Northamptonshire the fishpond remains lie beside those of a later lost garden with its ornamental ponds, while at Wormleighton in Warwickshire the ponds were dug after the depopulation of the village in the 1490s. The banks containing fishponds tend to have a rounded profile, while those associated with garden ponds were straight-sided with a walkway along the top, giving a profile like a flat-topped 'A'. Medieval communities were ingenious in their exploitation of water resources, and the one stream might power a corn mill, fill a moat, supply a chain of fishponds and feed an ornamental lake before being harnessed by a forge or fulling mill. It is useful to remember that while the fishponds themselves served practical functions they also had aesthetic and recreational possibilities and anticipated the lakes and canals of the later formal gardens and landscape parks.

'Like deer parks, rabbit warrens, fishponds and dovecotes, the decoys for wildfowl were essentially a manorial enterprise set up by landowners, and the survival of the relic features of so many former decoys is yet further evidence of the effect of estates upon the landscape' (Bettey, 1993 p.81). Duck decoys were built from the end of the medieval period onwards. A shallow and relatively small expanse of water was used, with tame ducks being employed to entice the wild birds to land. From the extremities of the pond, narrow, tapering pipes or tunnels of water led off. A well-trained dog attracted the curiosity of the birds, perhaps by weaving a path between screens, and as they paddled closer so the ducks were lured along the pipes, where they could be trapped and caught. In the 1720s, Defoe commented on the productivity of decoys in the fenland near Spalding, which exported ducks to London in great numbers: 'some of these decoys are of so great an extent and take such great quantities of fowl, that they are let for great sums of money by the year, viz. from 100l. to 3, 4, and 500l. a year rent' (1971 p.416). Sometimes duck decoys formed part of the furnishings of a landscape park, along with lakes, kennels, temples and tree clumps, as at Escrick near York. Decoys vary in their sizes and condition, but a typical relict example might be the size of a small, rectangular field and be enclosed by hedges. If now dry, a low-lying level area would mark the extent of the pond, while narrow, slightly curving hollows leading off from the drowned area will represent the pipes.

Parks and gardens

Much has been written about parks and gardens in recent years, not all of it contributing to a better understanding of landscape development. Firstly, it is important to remember that the owner and maker of a park was not to be found draped pensively over the balustrade anticipating the philosophies of post-structuralism or the theories of M. Foucault. Rather, he would be seen scorching across the lawns on the fastest thoroughbred his money could buy or else be blasting partridge along with his friends in some corner of the estate. In short, for him and his kind, parks were about having fun and impressing one's peers.

Parks have a long history, during which they evolved considerably, acquiring new characteristics, emphasising others, while others still were being abandoned. They can also be encountered in a wide variety of forms, some being well preserved and true to the eras of their creation, while some have contracted or decayed. In many cases, the park is encountered as a relict feature, with geometrical tree mounds stranded in a sea of plough soil or the water features drained and neglected. The remains of abandoned gardens are amongst the commonest of earthworks, although their true nature is not always recognised. So long as a park or garden remained in use, as a show-

piece and status symbol it was always likely to be adapted and transformed in accordance with the changing fashions. Therefore some of the best understandings of the history of recreational landscapes have been gleaned from studying examples which experienced abandonment and whose levels and outlines were preserved beneath the turf.

Landscape parks were status symbols, ones that had clear evolutionary links with the medieval deer parks, which had also signalled the status of their aristocratic owners across the surrounding countryside. In the fifteenth and sixteenth centuries those isolated deer parks which still survived tended to be abandoned and the deer parks which survived (and the few which would still be created) were largely those which stood in close association with the house of the owner. During the next two centuries, deer tended to disappear from the lawns, though most parks survived, with sheep and cattle being introduced to crop the grass and provide an income. Hosts of new parks were created, surrounding a noble residence in a vast expanse of fashionably contrived countryside or providing a landscaped vista to the south of the mansion of a lesser lord or squire. Much has been written, largely from an aesthetic standpoint, about the transition from formal gardens, with their straight canals and geometric plantings, to the landscape parks, with their serpentine lakes, carefully positioned groves and tree belts, and lawns which swept up to the walls of the great house. Much less has been said about the socio-political significance underlying the changes, but as Everett wrote:

throughout the eighteenth century, and much of the nineteenth, arguments about the aesthetics of landscape were almost always arguments about politics. Intervention in the landscape was understood as making explicit and readable state-

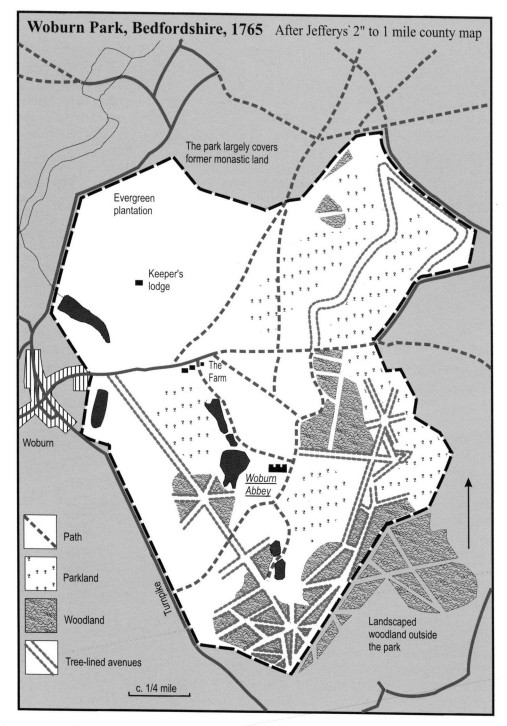

Woburn Park, Bedfordshire, 1765 After Jefferys' 2" to 1 mile county map

The park largely covers
former monastic land

Evergreen
plantation

Keeper's
lodge

The
Farm

*Woburn
Abbey*

Woburn

Turnpike

Path

Parkland

Woodland

Tree-lined avenues

c. 1/4 mile

Landscaped
woodland outside
the park

Map 5.4   Woburn Park, Bedfordshire, 1765. The park occupies medieval monastic land. Note how the landscaped woodland divided by geometrical avenues extends beyond the confines of the park to the south-east. Based on Jefferys' 2 inches to 1 mile county map.

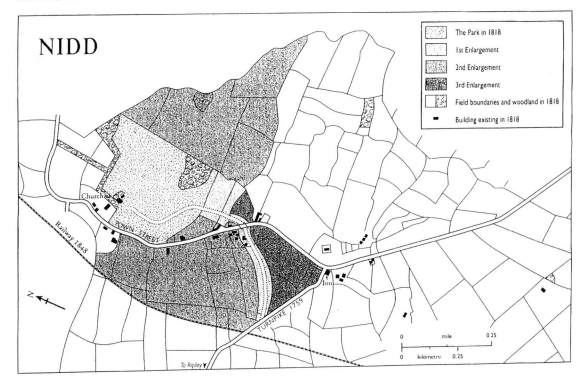

The Park in 1818

1st Enlargement

2nd Enlargement

3rd Enlargement

Field boundaries and woodland in 1818

Building existing in 1818

Map 5.5   Nidd, North Yorkshire, showing how the village aligned along Town Street was destroyed by successive enlargements to the park. Note how a selion from the old open fields was commandeered to accommodate a carriageway, giving a more impressive approach to the hall, which had previously been reached by a short track leaving Town Street near the church. From Muir and Amos (1998).

ments about the political history, the political constitution, the political future of England, and about the relations that should exist between its citizens. In the Tory view, those who abandoned the landscape to the market were also abandoning the order of civil society to fragmentation. (1994 p.7)

Parks and gardens were extensive expressions of the political affiliations of their owners. They were created for pleasure and to impress peers, clients and potential supporters, to overawe the tenantry and to establish their master's affiliation with a particular political grouping. Large and intricate geometrical plantings of flowers defined by low shrubby hedges or the later landscape park of the Brownian type, with its exclusion of the lower elements in rural society, vast acreages of taxable land and triumphal displays of ownership were identified with the corrupt Whig ascendancy. The traditional class of rural Tory

squires, excluded from power and favour under Walpole, looked to the more 'affordable magnificence' of the simpler park, where an income could be derived from the grazings, woods and plantations (Taigel and Williamson, 1993 p.77).

One does not need to become mired in iconography to appreciate that parks had important social, symbolic and psychological roles and provided their owners with unrivalled opportunities to proclaim their gentlemanly rank. In countrysides still mostly untransformed by Parliamentary

Enclosure: 'the status landscapes of the élite were clearly divorced from the environment produced by the community and by work' (Williamson and Bellamy, 1987 p.140). In the late seventeenth and early eighteenth centuries, networks of arrow-straight pathways radiating outwards across the park from the site of the great house drew the eye towards the horizon and announced the extent of lands which the owner could afford to remove from more intensive cultivation. The broad, uncluttered panorama was associated with noble status and the freedom to ride fast and at will, while architectural icons and embellishments punctuated the scene. Statuary associated with Classical themes made statements about the refinement and nobility of the owner; his stables, elegant and imposing, were prominently displayed and proclaimed his wealth and sporting prowess. Palladian architecture, adopted for many great Whig houses, like Walpole's Houghton in Norfolk, was associated with the majesty of classical Rome, though Baroque architecture was linked to the supposed decadence of France and Spain (Taigel and Williamson, 1993 p.54).

Very few could afford to create or maintain a park, even though its lawns raised venison, beef, mutton and wool. In terms of status, the whole point about a park was its exclusivity. Parks were private landscapes, and this privacy was created or enhanced by the eviction of intruding villagers, the diversion of country roads, the building of 6 feet tall surrounding walls and the planting of curtains of trees to prevent those within from seeing out and vice versa. In the case of the village of Nidd in North Yorkshire, destroyed in three consecutive phases of emparking during the first half of the nineteenth century, the old village High Street, now only part of a lane, was excavated and entrenched into the countryside to prevent passers-through from being seen and from seeing into the park (Muir and Amos, 1998).

The removal of villages sometimes revealed the lord as a despot. These were not isolated and unusual instances for in park after park in England one can see a scene repeated: the great house standing beside an otherwise isolated church, and the church presiding over the surrounding earthworks of a deserted village. However harsh and exploitative the medieval feudal aristocracy may have been, no group can have shown a greater detachment from the affairs of their rural neighbours than the Whig ascendancy of the Georgian period. The evictions had a history extending back to the decline of the castle and rise of the mansion at the close of the Middle Ages. The late-medieval removal of villages to create sheep runs had scarcely ended when the assault on settlements by the makers of parks began. At Wilstrop, in North Yorkshire, in 1498, the village was emparked and depopulated, but on this unusual occasion the evictor found his displaced tenants in an alliance with members of the gentry that he had also offended. Large-scale assaults were mounted upon the paling and quicksetts surrounding the new park, and on one occasion the mob broke in and cut down 100 recently planted walnut trees and apple trees (Beresford, 1971 pp.205–7).

In 1579 Sir Christopher Hatton initiated the construction of gardens at Holdenby in Northamptonshire. A section settlement there intruding upon the works was removed, but rebuilt as a landscaping feature nearby:

The gardens were intended to be laid out on the slopes of the hill and on the flat ground to the east. However, an obstacle to this was the existence of the village of Holdenby, which was in effect two villages, one with a parish church on the hillside, the other just north-east of the new house. Hatton swept both away, leaving only the church to be incorporated into the garden. The upper village

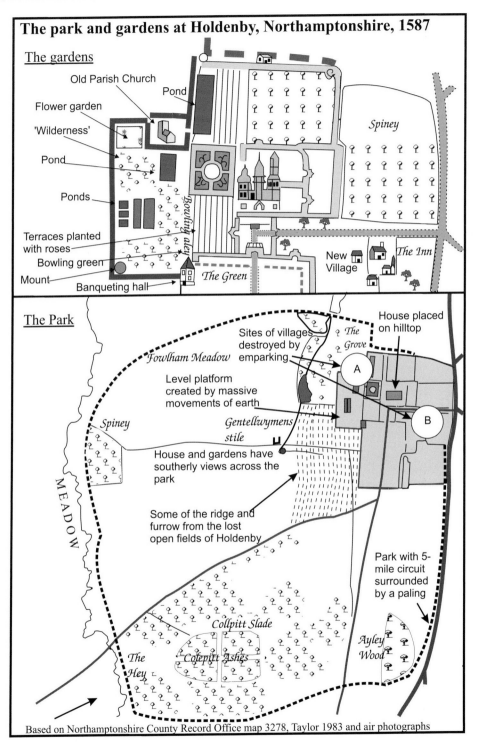

The park and gardens at Holdenby, Northamptonshire, 1587

The gardens

Old Parish Church
Pond
Flower garden
'Wilderness'
Pond
Ponds
Terraces planted with roses
Bowling green
Mount
Banqueting hall

Spiney

Bowling alley

New Village
The Inn
The Green

The Park

Sites of villages destroyed by emparking
House placed on hilltop

Fowlham Meadow
The Grove

Level platform created by massive movements of earth

Spiney

Gentellwymens stile

House and gardens have southerly views across the park

Some of the ridge and furrow from the lost open fields of Holdenby

MEADOW

Park with 5-mile circuit surrounded by a paling

Collpitt Slade
Colepitt Ashes

Ayley Wood

The Hey

Based on Northamptonshire County Record Office map 3278, Taylor 1983 and air photographs

Map 5.6 The park and gardens at Holdenby, Northamptonshire, 1587. Developed from Northamptonshire County Record Office map 3278, Taylor (1983) and air photographs.

Table 5.2   The impact of a park on the neighbouring countryside

Type of impact	Character of the intervention
Woodland	The partial landscaping of the area *beyond* the park with the introduction of geometrical tree clumps. Provision of cover for pheasants or foxes. Medieval parks in the north were often associated with 'outwoods', though these outlying woods tend not to be found in the south.
Settlement	Building of model estate villages at approaches to the park, often to replace settlements demolished in the creation and enlargement of the park.
Routeways	Diversion around the park of routeways which formerly ran through it. Conversion of old routes or building of new ones to create imposing tree-lined carriage drives running towards the great house.
Boundaries	The perimeter of the park was normally walled in ashlar, which would contrast with any drystone walls in the neighbouring fieldscape. The uniform wall would traverse the landscape, with gatehouses or lodges being provided where roads entered the park.

was then recreated with a rectangular plan, laid out axially to the garden, which had views from the main courtyard through an arch to the new square village green. (Taylor, 1983 p.44)

Sir Christopher was a great landowner and politician, and in the two centuries and more that followed, position and prestige were no barriers to the displacement of rural communities, with the decision of whether or not to rehouse the victims of emparking being left to the landlord's discretion. At Houghton it was the Prime Minister who was responsible. Here, the village was depicted lying on the southern fringes of the park in 1719, but by the early 1730s it had been removed, displaced by the expansion of the park, and a model village built outside the park had replaced it. However, not all the abandoned village earthworks encountered within a park equate with communities evicted by emparking. Villages could perish before a park was created, while settlements which were already in decline were more likely to be targeted for removal. At Houghton an arm of the settlement appears already to have been abandoned when the park was created (Taigel and Williamson, 1993 p.74). New Houghton, a street of 24 unpretentious estate houses and eight almshouses, was built outside the park gates at Houghton in 1729 and was one of the first model villages to be created to replace predecessors destroyed by emparking. Later, model villages were evolved in a spectrum of different architectural styles, sometimes used in combination, to provide settlements which could serve as conversation pieces for guests approaching the park and which would articulate the humanitarian concerns and artistic sensibilities of the master. At Edensor near Chatsworth in Derbyshire the sensibilities were more those of the magpie than the connoisseur, for early nineteenth century cottages in Georgian, Tudor, Swiss and other styles gained a Gothic church in the 1860s.

In the creation of model villages or the rebuilding of labourers' cottages on their estates, the motives of landowners ranged from a benevolent desire to see their workers well-housed and contented, to a concern that an attractive village with picturesque cottages and suitably subservient tenants should, like elegant lodges, grand entrance gates or long

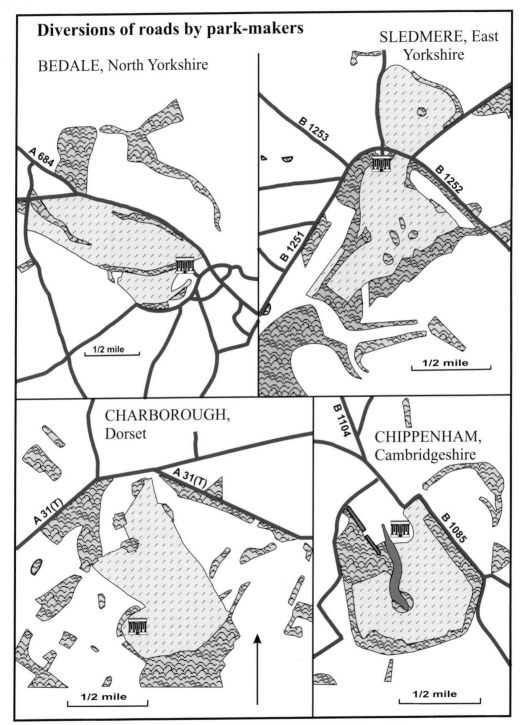

Diversions of roads by park-makers

BEDALE, North Yorkshire

SLEDMERE, East Yorkshire

A 684

B 1253

B 1252

B 1251

1/2 mile

1/2 mile

CHARBOROUGH, Dorset

CHIPPENHAM, Cambridgeshire

A 31(T)

A 31(T)

B 1104

B 1085

1/2 mile

1/2 mile

Map 5.7   The diversions of roads by park-makers. The maps portray examples of the diversion of routeways by the makers of landscape parks. The parks are shown in the lighter tone, with associated woodland in the darker tone.

driveways complete with avenues of trees, add dignity to the approach to their mansion, as well as providing evidence of the social concern of the owner. (Bettey, 1993 p.117)

Whether or not they were better-housed than most other villagers of England, the effect of most aspects of model village life was the humiliation of the occupants. At Old Warden in Bedfordshire, transformed by Lord Ongley in the middle of the nineteenth century, the cottages were elaborate parodies of Gothic and Swiss styles, whose occupants, it was reported in 1895, were obliged to adorn the scene clad in red coats and high hats.

Parks were exclusive preserves, and the pursuit of the exclusive ideal quite frequently involved the eviction and diversion of roads, tracks and footpaths used by the public at large. Fortunately from the point of view of the emparker, the people who would arbitrate on such transformations were men of the same ruling classes, the grander of them probably themselves the makers of parks. At first, the diversion of a highway was a costly affair requiring an Act of Parliament or the issuing of a writ in the Court of Chancery. However, with numerous turnpikes being created and parks increasing in size and number a new law was adopted in 1773 which greatly eased and cheapened the process:

> All that was now required was the agreement of two county magistrates, men from the same social group as the park-maker and, as often as not, his neighbours and friends. Road closure orders make amusing reading, for they always maintain the polite fiction that the proposed change is for the good of the general public. A road so effected is always described as superfluous to local requirements, as an unnecessary burden on the parish, or as inconvenient in some way. The replacement, of course, is always

of better quality, and more direct. Seldom is the real reason for the change expressly stated. (Williamson, 1995 p.104)

Given that the creation and expansion of a large park might involve the closure of five to ten rights of way, Williamson speculated that several thousands of miles of thoroughfare must have been lost to emparking (p.105). The roads affected might endure as carriageways, but generally pains were taken to obliterate the traces of the destroyed thoroughfares and settlements.

The closure and diversion of roads continued into more egalitarian times. At Charborough in Dorset, where a brick wall creates a 'polite seclusion' and monumental gateways proclaim the status of the owner, two messages are inscribed on a gateway. One boasts of the instrumentality of J.W.S. Sawbridge Drax MP in completing the new road between Wimborne and Dorchester in 1841–2, while the other announces the closure of the former road through the park in 1841.

Parks and gardens as relict features

The same economic and social circumstances which have led to the decline of great houses have affected parks and gardens. In terms of landscape archaeology, the significance of disparking should not be underestimated. Garden earthworks, like the huge terraces at Strixton in Northamptonshire, may be encountered despite the absence of any prominent historical accounts or local knowledge of their origins. Such monuments are very common, and the interpretation demands an understanding of fashions in gardening extending back to the medieval period. Like the landscapes surrounding it, the park itself can be likened to a palimpsest, with traces of former patterns, perhaps beginning with the ridge and furrow of the preceding ploughland, sometimes showing faintly through. According to the dictates of

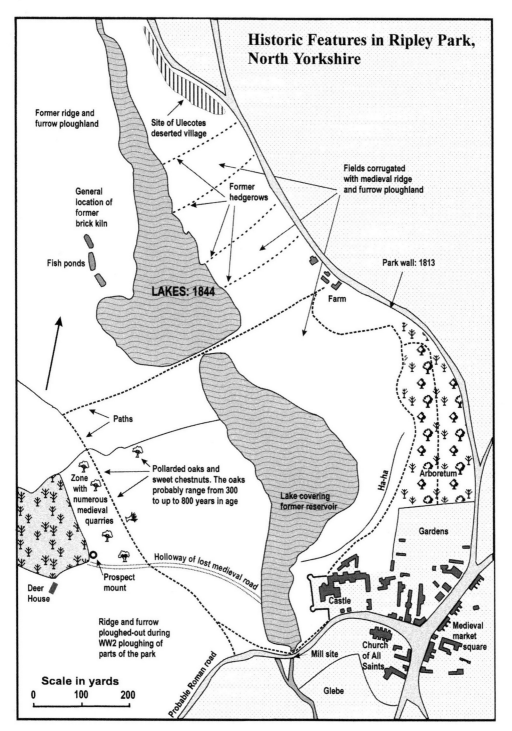

Map 5.8   Historic features in Ripley Park, North Yorkshire. Parks are likely to reveal much more than aesthetic features, while the landscaping may date from various periods. This map of a section of the Tudor deer park at Ripley is based on the author's current research.

Table 5.3   Interpreting features of former parkland

Element	Characteristic features
Gardens of the sixteenth and seventeenth centuries	
Earthworks	Large quantities of earth dug and moved to create straight-faced formal garden terraces, usually south-facing with paths at different levels and motte-like mounts providing views beyond the confines of a walled garden as well as mounds with spiral walkways and pyramidical mounds. Some parks and gardens had associated water gardens with artificial ponds in geometrical shapes.
Boundaries	Walls, palings or hedges around the park. If originating in a medieval deer park then substantial earthworks. Parch-marks or other indicators may denote the course of the wall of a walled garden.
Trees	Avenues of trees, notably limes, of which some members may survive, sometimes planted in former deer parks. Old field and hedgerow trees incorporated in new parks.
Routeways	Formal walks around the garden. Gravel paths in knot gardens could show up as crop-marks or parch-marks.
Gardens of the late seventeenth and early eighteenth centuries	
Earthworks	Terraced flower beds and raised walkways. Large mounts, round, square or octagonal, sometimes topped with trees. Also smaller mounts, sometimes in groups. Square beds and lawns in the garden. Enclosure banks sometimes set around tree plantations. Beyond the terraces there might be a 'wilderness', an area of woodland. Deserted village earthworks—but these often obliterated along with the related holloways.
Trees	Long avenues of trees, often limes, horse chestnuts or beeches, sometimes pine. Areas of woodland, some irregular and compact, some geometrical in form, with regimented block plantings sometimes being employed. Some wood-pasture-like patterns. Old field and hedgerow trees incorporated in new parks.
Routeways	Networks of straight pathways radiating from the house to the limits of the park. These may have vanished from the countryside but remain as rides cutting through former parkland woods.
Other	Straight canals, sometimes filled by diverted streams or rivers. Possible diversion of water for fountains. Construction, at considerable cost, of semi-geometric lakes, often in opposition to local terrain, and rectangular ponds.

Table 5.3   Interpreting features of former parkland—continued

Element	Characteristic features
Gardens of the eighteenth century	
Earthworks	Ha-has or trenches to exclude livestock from the vicinity of the house and any adjacent gardens. Villages removed, leaving house platforms, holloways, boundary ditches and ridge and furrow. Holloways of diverted roads. Great efforts sometimes made to conceal these traces.
Routeways	Paths winding through woodlands. Courses of closed-off roads.
Trees	Irregular tree clumps, but avenues still occasionally planted. Tree belts planted to obscure any views of the workaday world. With the growing popularity of pheasant shooting, woods with the high edge-to-interior ratios which the birds liked were favoured and small, serpentine or island woods also made it harder for poachers to go undetected. Pre-existing trees incorporated in new parks.
Other	Streams diverted, if necessary, to create winding lakes and sheets of water retained by dams.
Gardens of the late eighteenth and early nineteenth centuries	
Earthworks	Terraced gardens and flower beds near the house return. A few village removals but some cottages and farm buildings brought into the park. Numerous road diversions leaving holloways where the roads not filled-in or re-used as carriage ways.
Trees	Screens between park and working countryside sometimes removed and sometimes planted. Fashion for collecting exotic trees, grown as specimens and in groups. Pre-existing trees incorporated in new parks.
Other	More than mere earthworks may survive from Victorian gardens—enclosing walls, buildings, intact or in fragments, pieces of hardware and naturalised plants.

fashion and the purse and tastes of the owner, landscapes shaped according to one vogue would tend to be remoulded to conform with another. Sometimes all traces of the former patterns would be obliterated by spade and barrow, but elsewhere evidence might survive. Sentiment or frugality might preserve a straight avenue of limes after the arbiters of fashion favoured curves, or an old fishpond might be reshaped to follow a more ornamental existence.

The living park can be a significant preserve of landscape history. From 'Capability' Brown to the obscure or anonymous, park-makers would tend to incorporate useful features from the preceding landscapes into their plans. In the newly created and otherwise featureless park, any mature trees were of great value, so that old pollards would be gratefully preserved. Sometimes the countryside affected had existed in an early enclosure mode, with

Table 5.4   Investigating garden remains

First question	*Do the features represent the remains of a garden?* Ponds might have been associated with a fishpond complex. Platforms terraced into a hillside might represent the sites of buildings rather than garden terraces.
Second question	*Where are the boundaries of the garden?* Look for traces of banks, buried wall footings, or the parching of grass above such footings.
Third question	*Do the features display a symmetrical plan?* Symmetrical layouts were in vogue between about 1550 and 1650. Later designs involved more curves and less formal arrangements. If the lay-out is symmetrical then existing features can be used to detect or replicate vanished features which balanced them.
Fourth question	*What was the source of water?* A natural spring or stream might still be apparent, but in some cases water would have been artificially introduced by diverting waterways or using gravity to convey a water supply to a conduit house.
Fifth question	*Did the boundaries move?* The changing fortunes and ambitions of the owners would often be expressed in moving boundaries to enlarge or reduce a garden, with staff costs being cut if a garden was reduced. Look for banks and alignments that could represent successive shifts in the boundary.
Sixth question	*Where was the house that the garden served?* The alignment and disposition of features should give some clue relating to the position of the house, e.g. a formal garden would be precisely aligned on its house, and normally roughly to its south.

slightly curving hedgerows punctuated by oak, elm or ash standards surrounding packages of former selions. Within parkland one will sometimes see ancient trees arranged in rows—not because the designer of the park wished it so, but because standards were preserved after the grubbing-out of the intervening hedge shrubs. Taylor noted that parks are one of the most important agents of preservation for all periods: 'Most lowland parks preserve large areas of medieval ridge-and-furrow but often include the remains of former farm-steads, medieval moats, watermills and a host of other types of site' (1983 p.63).

It is not unusual to encounter what might be described as hybrid countrysides in which characteristics of parkland and work-ing countryside are interdigitated. Thus circular groupings of trees planted on domed mounds may stand in a sea of ploughland, or large standards, perhaps of exotic species like horse chestnut or Turkey oak, may punctuate a network of fields. In such circumstances, two possibilities arise: either a park has contracted or ceased to exist, leaving behind a residue of land-scaping features, or else the process of landscaping has been extended beyond a park and into the surrounding cultivated countryside. The fluctuating fortunes of parks during the last 150 years or so can easily be established by studying any tithe maps or enclosure maps which record the earlier contents and outlines and then following the pattern of development through successive editions of the Ordnance Survey 1:2,500 and 1:10,560 maps.

Embedded in various countrysides are features such as earthworks, ponds and lakes and tree groupings which have been inherited from a former phase of landscaping associated with a park or a garden. Interpretation of such features may involve a survey of the earthworks which may link them to one of the standard systems of artificial garden features, like terraces, prospect mounds, walkways, canals and so on. Aerial photography may reveal more about the extent and nature of the features, while the relevant archives may produce maps and plans showing the recreational area in its original form.

The remains of former gardens are among the commonest of earthworks, as well as sometimes being among the most difficult to disentangle. Some of the problems and procedures are sketched in Table 5.4. Normally, a thorough understanding of the features and their relationships can only be gained after a large-scale survey of the site concerned, say, involving a triangulation with tapes. Following such a survey, unexpected aspects are likely to emerge as well as the reasoning that underlies the design.

REFERENCES

Aston, M. *Interpreting the Landscape* (London: Batsford, 1989).

Bassett, S. 'Continuity and fission in the Anglo-Saxon landscape: the origins of the Rodings (Essex)' *Landscape History* 19 (1998) pp.25–42.

Beresford, M.W. *History on the Ground*, 2nd edn (London: Methuen, 1971).

Bettey, J.H. *Estates and the English Countryside* (London: Batsford, 1993).

Bonney, D.J. 'Pagan Saxon burials and boundaries in Wiltshire' *Wiltshire Archaeological and History Magazine* 61 (1966) pp.25–30.

Defoe, D. *A Tour Through the Whole Island of Great Britain* (Harmondsworth: Penguin, 1971).

Everett, N. *The Tory View of Landscape* (New Haven: Yale University Press, 1994).

Faull, M. and Moorhouse, S. (eds) *West Yorkshire: An Archaelogical Survey to A.D. 1500* (Wakefield: West Yorkshire Metropolitan County Council, 1981).

Fleming, A. 'Early medieval polities in Upper Swaledale' *Landscape History* 16 (1994) pp.17–30.

Finberg, H.P.R., *Gloucestershire* (London: Hodder and Stoughton, 1955).

Ford, W.J. 'Some settlement patterns in the central region of the Warwickshire Avon' in P.H. Sawyer (ed.) *English Medieval Settlement* (London: Arnold, 1979).

Gregson, N. 'The multiple estate model: some critical questions' *Journal of Historical Geography* 11 (1985) pp.339–51.

Hadley, D.M. 'Multiple estates and the origins of the manorial structure of the northern Danelaw' *Journal of Historical Geography* 22 (1996) pp.3–15.

Hook, D. 'Charter bounds of the South West of England' *Local Historian* 27 (1997).

Hoskins, W.G. *The Making of the English Landscape* (Harmondsworth: Penguin, 1970).

Jones, G.R.J. 'Multiple estates and early settlement' in P.H. Sawyer (ed.) *English Medieval Settlement* (London: Edward Arnold, 1979).

Muir, R. and Amos, J. 'Nidd, the death of a village' *Local Historian* 28 (1998) pp.208–216.

Nightingale, M.D. 'A Roman land settlement near Rochester' *Archaelogia Cantiana* 65 (1952) pp.150–9.

Reed, M. 'Anglo-Saxon Charter Boundaries' in M. Reed (ed.) *Discovering Past Landscapes* (London: Croom Helm, 1984).

Roffe, D. 'Pre-Conquest estates and parish boundaries: a discusion with examples from Lincolnshire' in M.L. Faull (ed.) *Studies in Late Anglo-Saxon Settlement* (Oxford: Oxford University Department for External Studies, 1984).

Sawyer, P.H. 'Anglo-Saxon settlement: the documentary evidence' in T. Rowley (ed.) *Anglo-Saxon Settlement and Landscape*, British Archaeology Reports 6, pp.108–19.

Sheail, J. *Rabbits and Their History* (Newton Abbot: David and Charles, 1971).

Stamper, P. 'Woods and parks' in G. Astill and A. Grant (eds) *The Countryside of Medieval England* (Oxford: Blackwell, 1988).

Taigel, A. and Williamson, T. *Parks and Gardens* (London, Batsford, 1993).

Taylor, C. *The Archaeology of Gardens* (Aylesbury: Shire, 1983).

Veale, E. 'The rabbit in England' *Agricultural History Review* 5 (1957) pp.85–90.

Williamson, T. *Polite Landscapes* (Stroud: Alan Sutton, 1995).

Williamson, T. and Bellamy, L. *Property and Landscape* (London: George Philip, 1987).

CHAPTER 6

Landscapes of Belief

Belief has been an important factor in landscape development, but its effects may be more difficult to understand and recognise than those that derive from economic or political causes. The needs to extract food from the land or to defend a community against the actions of outsiders have always been apparent to all. Religions, however, tend to leave monuments that are far more ambiguous than a system of fields or a distribution of strongholds. The 'ritual' category has, for some time, provided a convenient repository for all those patterns, artefacts and constructions that the archaeologist can not understand. The sockets which once held standing stones, deposits of pottery and burnt bone, the presumed mortuary houses or cremation trenches at ritual sites may all be studied in the greatest detail and with the latest of technologies, but they will not reveal the nature of the god involved or even the outlines of the beliefs of the worshippers. Given these problems of interpretation that are associated with the archaeology of religion, where the study of landscape and its history are concerned, two questions seen relevant. Firstly, how may landscape help to shape and condition belief? Secondly, how have religion and religious organisation influenced the evolution of cultural landscapes?

Landscape and belief

Religion, one suspects, was closely influenced by place. Some Neolithic and early Bronze Age monuments embodied phenomenal amounts of valuable labour and they contained the remains of ancestors who were, presumably, highly venerated. Consequently, it seems that their positioning within the landscape would have been considered with great care. The particular factors influencing decisions about settings and siting may generally be undetectable, but in a few cases the significant aspects can be recognised. In the Cleveland Hills it appears that special places in the physical landscape were developed for the practice of rituals. They were defined and enhanced by cross-ridge dykes: linear earthworks which severed the tips of elevated promontories and spurs to produce a series of symbolically detached and lofty platforms, as at Ingleby Greenhow, Glaisdale and Danby (Vyner, 1994 pp.27–8).

It would be strange indeed if the sense of place did not play an important part in the location and siting of religious monuments. Sense of place is, however, to some degree a subjective phenomenon: it cannot be expressed and gauged with precision by the professional archaeologist or historian, while its indefinable qualities commend it to the charlatan and the lunatic fringe interloper. The objective approach cultivated in the universities is admirable for most purposes, but the exclusion of emotion from intellect and symbol from reason in Western science does not equip us to recognise and relate to sense of place factors which may have motivated our distant forebears (Walter, 1988). The academic study of the relationship between landscape and human behaviour is in its infancy, though Appleton's (1990) prospect-refuge theory, which claims that we favour landscapes which provide us with

Figure 6.1   A stupendous ritual monument such as Avebury in Wiltshire must plainly have exercised great spiritual magnetism—but it was also a thunderous proclamation of the might of the priesthood, elite or monarch that commanded its construction.

opportunities to see without being seen, is at least a beginning.

If some religious monuments were associated with features of the visible and immediate landscape, others may have had links to features that were far more remote. The long barrows and other tombs of the Neolithic may perhaps have been orientated on the rising moon, though a little before 3000 BC, many tombs were sealed and the old ceremonial centres and meeting places may have fallen into neglect, while subsequent religious monuments seem to have favoured the sun. The reality is likely to have been much more complex than this. Drawing upon analogies from Madagascar, Parker Pearson and Ramilisonina (1998) have discussed parallel ceremonial monuments and the division of landscapes into ritual zones. Under the process of 'lithicization' (the transformation of a monument from wood to stone) the conversion symbolised a passing from the realm of the living to the realm of ancestors: 'Thus the changing of a monument from wood to stone is a marking of the movement of the living through death to ancestorhood, as the ceremonial places which were once

Figure 6.2   Castlerigg stone circle plainly occupies a platform ringed by loftier fells—but we may never discover the detailed place and ideological factors which urged its builders to select this particular spot.

associated with the living became places devoid of living people where the ancestors now reside' (p.324). Thus he argues that late Neolithic Britain was essentially shared by two communities living side by side, the living and the spirits of the dead: 'Contrary to recent speculations by archaeologists, New Agers and other groups, the great stone monuments, once built, were largely the domain of the spirit world into which the living rarely entered' (p.324). A zonation of the landscape around Stonehenge was proposed. The great stone circle was regarded as an abode provided for the spirits of the ancestors which was seldom

visited by the living and it was surrounded by the domain of the ancestors. This was surrounded in turn by a zone between 1 and 2 km wide which functioned as a liminal zone containing early Bronze Age barrows, and beyond this was the domain of the living, containing the huge wooden cere-monial circles of the living, Durrington Walls

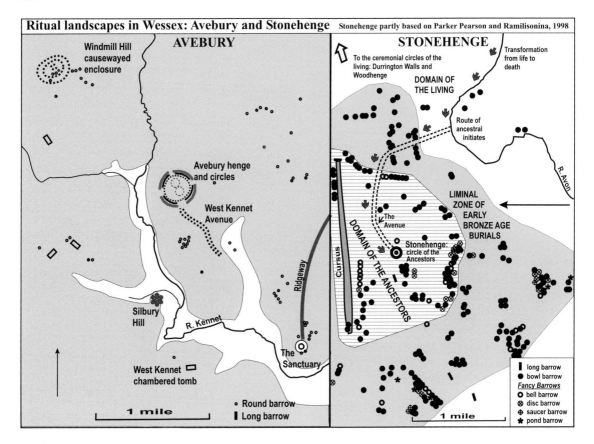

Map 6.1   Ritual landscapes in Wessex: Avebury and Stonehenge. Neolithic and early Bronze Age ritual features attracted the interest and religious monuments of Bronze Age communities. Partly based on Parker Pearson and Ramilisonina (1998).

and Woodhenge. To the south of these circles of the living, the River Avon formed a corridor for the transformation from life to death, and the Avenue, leading from the river to the stone circle, then provided a routeway for initiates into ancestorhood. Whether the ritual landscapes around Stonehenge and Avebury were regarded as functioning in quite this way, one does not know, but concepts such as this are valuable reminders that neighbouring monuments, such as the henge at Avebury, the West Kennet tomb and Avenue, Silbury Hill and the Sanctuary, are unlikely to have existed in

isolation. Rather, they must have been complimentary components in a ritual landscape which encompassed them all.

Since the 1970s, much interest has concerned the supposed alignment of prehistorical ritual monuments on astronomical events. Such notions were recently tested on North Mull by Martlew and Ruggles (1996), who found that:

> the evidence from the stone rows suggests the hypothesis that their builders did not regard the alignment of the stones on a specific horizon point as a single, isolated focus of interest. Rather, they may have been interested in the entire track of the full moon low in the southern sky in relation to distant hills on the horizon, perhaps linked to ceremonies around the time of the summer solstice . . . the location of the stone row would be chosen

with respect to a significant stretch of the horizon across which the moon could be observed. (p.129)

Two major considerations appear to have governed the selection of locations for stone rows. Firstly, a prominent peak should be seen in a position associated with the rising of the southernmost moon, towards its major standstill limit. Secondly, a relatively distant horizon was required in the south and to the west of south, so that having risen at its southernmost point, the moon should be visible until it set. In ways such as these, the terrain characteristics of the physical landscape may have been incorporated in ancient ritual landscapes, where they were exploited for prediction and ceremonial purposes. Claims concerning 'megalithic science' have sometimes been ill-founded, while one may never be able to prove the significance of any particular alignment. Nevertheless, research such as that accomplished on Mull can be employed to explore the nature of ritual landscapes in many other places: 'Location and visibility seem to be important attributes of a landscape that is defined in a ritual context, and where landforms are relatively unchanged from prehistoric times they are still available for analysis' (p.130).

Some places proved to be particularly compelling to the creators of ancient monuments, so that near the junction of Wensleydale and the Vale of York one has the Thornborough trio of great henges, built on the line of a cursus, and another trio at Sutton Moor, nearby, which along with the Nunwick and Cana henges form a chain of ritual sites extending northwards for 11 miles from the (possibly younger) standing stones known as the Devil's Arrows (Burl, 1991). In locations such as this the locality itself appears to have exerted a magnetism—though whether this magnetism concerned the particular qualities of the terrain or else features of the cultural landscape, such as proximity to a dynastic headquarters or elite cemetery, one does not know.

Much of our understanding of the more distant past derives from excavation reports, and this may explain the strong tendency to regard sites and monuments in isolation rather than as components in ritual landscapes—landscapes which have their own history and spatial structure. Those studies which have considered prehistoric religious monuments in their broader landscape context have tended to be concerned with the tomb as a spiritual central place serving a surrounding clan or tribal territory. The Woodwards (1996) attempted a more sophisticated analysis and studied early Bronze Age round barrow cemeteries in relation to three main monumental complexes in Wessex: the South Dorset Ridgeway, Avebury and Stonehenge. An underlying structural principle of circularity was identified, evident in curved settings and arcs in the cemetery layout, the shapes of the barrows and of the post circles which lie beneath them, and the shapes of the older timber and stone monuments on which they focus. These ancient monuments were still revered by the barrow-builders and it was found that:

On the Dorset Ridgeway, development was clustered and hierarchical; barrows were arranged around a series of monuments and the richest barrows lay nearest to the monuments. In a similar scarped landscape around Avebury the barrow layout was much more uniform than this, and conceived on a larger scale. Finally, at Stonehenge, in an area of much more even topography, the layout involved two concentric circuits, apparently of equal status in terms of richness of grave goods and incidence of fancy barrows. A common denominator of all these patterns is that the barrows seem to have formed a major component of a ritual landscape. The barrows were sited at set distances from the monuments and the monuments were placed such that many barrow sites were clearly visible from them. Thus the barrow settings appear to have defined a reserved inner sanctum. (p.288)

It appeared that during the early Bronze Age: 'there may have been an underlying symbolic principle, based on the concept of circularity, that pervaded the realms of monument building, funerary activity, and the placing of visible structures in the human environment. This concept formed a distinct contrast with the prevalence of linearity now isolated in many Neolithic contexts' (p.189). The Bronze Age barrow arcs, lines and rings around the pre-existing monumental complexes in Wessex suggest a strong continuity of tradition and reverence for the focal Neolithic ritual centres, which must still have been revered (though at Stonehenge, the last of the stone settings were being erected at the time when the cemetery rings were being established). Although the old ritual centres attracted later barrows, a respectful distance was often observed. In the case of Stonehenge: 'The most impressive barrow cemeteries . . . are all located so as to be just visible from Stonehenge, placed at the limits of visibility. The remainder, numbering several hundred, are placed so as to lie further outside this area of visibility from Stonehenge. This "envelope of visibility" from Stonehenge provides a zone which was largely free of the physical remains of the Early Bronze Age dead' (Parker Pearson and Ramilisonina, 1998 p.318).

In numerous cases, a member of one generation of religious monuments has plainly attracted the establishment of a representative of another, as at Knowlton in Dorset, where the medieval church, always isolated, was placed inside one of a set of three henges. As with this case, thousands

of years and several major shifts in belief could separate the juxtaposed monuments. This was also the case with the Roman theatre established inside the henge at Dorchester, or the deposits of pottery and bone placed in the ditch at Wayland's Smithy Neolithic chambered tomb in Wiltshire in Roman times. In other cases, the re-use of a site for ritual purposes did not follow a long phase of neglect, as with the establishment of Roman shrines inside Iron Age hillforts, which happened at Chanctonbury Ring in Sussex and Maiden Castle in Dorset. There are also cases of the appropriation for ritual uses of non-religious monuments; in the middle Saxon period, churches were established inside disused Roman forts at Brempton and Bewcastle in Cumbria (Newman, 1984) and Saxon churches also appeared in the forts at Bradwell, Felixstowe and Reculver.

Neolithic tombs were commonly re-used, as was the case with the great round barrow, Duggleby Howe, in the Yorkshire Wolds, where several intrusive burials had taken place before the domed mound became absorbed into a Bronze Age cremation cemetery, with 43 cremation burials being inserted into the skin of the mound. During the Roman occupation coins and pottery were placed in various ancient tombs, like Walkington Wold in East Yorkshire. Burials in barrows became increasingly numerous as the Roman period progressed, and there was also great interest in caves. Saxons particularly favoured round barrows as burial places, but they also made burials within or beside Roman villas and temples.

According to Williams, an explanation for these practices can be found in early literature:

In the Saxon epic *Beowulf*, in the *Life of St Guthlac*, and elsewhere, we read of people going to ancient barrows to make contact with supernatural forces. Similar stories are found in Scandinavian and Irish

literature. I would argue that ancient monuments were re-used because their antiquity encouraged their association with supernatural and ancestral powers, and that they became the focus of new local cults to these ancestors and deities'. (1997 p.6)

He added that by the involvement with ancient monuments people were establishing and maintaining relationships with the supernatural world 'perhaps as a source of spiritual and political authority. Social identity and status, control of land and even the success of crops may have depended on the ritual veneration of these ancient sites' (p.6).

During the conversion to Christianity the spiritual and superstitious reasons for

Figure 6.3 Lanyon Quoit in Cornwall is composed of stones re-erected in 1824 on the site of a Neolithic chambered long barrow. Although the manner of the rebuilding may be inaccurate, the tomb exists as a potent symbol of megalithic beliefs, though New Age converts and discriminating observers will interpret the monument in quite different ways.

perpetuating religious and ritual practices at favoured places were combined with others of a more political and pragmatic nature. Not only were efforts directed at the conversion of the respective royal families, but also a continuity of worship was established at places revered by the pagans. In an oft-quoted letter written in 601 to Abbot Mellitus, later to become Bishop of London, Pope Gregory urged that pagan temples and

Figure 6.4   The hilltop church at Brentor on Dartmoor is dedicated to St Michael, the archangel. The churches with this dedication in England number around 600 and a high proportion are sited on hilltops, perhaps revealing an association with pagan worship.

sacred places not be preserved, but rather sanctified with holy water; Christian altars should be set up in them so that in these familiar religious surroundings converts would more easily be won to the new faith. He concluded by remarking that should a man wish to climb, he should do so by steps rather than by leaps. Dimly-remembered

pagan practices endured throughout the medieval period and even beyond, with the incorporation of seemingly blatantly pagan displays of 'green men' or shiela-na-gigs within the fabric of churches and the persistence of pagan symbolism in folk dance. In the more immediate aftermath

Law makers continued to find it necessary during the seventh century to forbid the worship of heathen gods, even in Kent where Christianity was strong. In Essex the old temples were repaired and pagan worship was resumed during the stress of a great plague in the 660s; Raedwald, king of East Anglia, erected pagan and Christian altars in the same temple during the early seventh century, while Bishop Wilfred, landing in Sussex after a visit to Gaul in 666, was set upon by heathens led by their priest, who attempted unsuccessfully to bind the bishop's hands by his magical arts. (Bettey, 1987 p.13)

Churches plainly associated with the sites of pagan worship include Rudston, near Scarborough, built on an elevated platform beside a towering prehistoric monolith. The Rudston stone stands at a place where four cursuses loosely converge, though it probably post-dates the supposed ceremonial avenues. Other juxtapositions of Christian and pagan centres include La Hogue Bie, Jersey, where a Norman chapel was built on the crest of a Neolithic chambered tomb, directly over the burial chamber and sharing the same orientation, and St Martin's, Guernsey, where a prehistoric carved stone idol stands at the entrance to the churchyard. Until its destruction in the nineteenth century a monolith stood by the church at St Mabyn in Cornwall. Churches associated with prehistoric burial mounds are found at Berwick in Sussex, St Issey in Cornwall, Edlesborough in Buckinghamshire, Fimber in Yorkshire, and various other locations. Pagan shrines devoted to the worship of Iron Age gods on remote, hilltop sites at places like Brean Down and Lamyatt Beacon, near Bruton, in Somerset were Christianised around the middle of the fourth century (Rahtz, 1982–3).

In terms of the characteristics of places, water appears to have been significant in both pagan and early Christian times:

The importance of water in both pagan and Christian ritual is paramount and it is not therefore surprising to discover that springs have received more reverence than other cult features . . . The christianisation of springs which were formerly venerated by pagans usually took the form of blessing the waters and appointing a saint to preside over them, who was frequently chosen for his local associations. Cornwall is particularly rich in these, good examples being St Breward's Well at Camelford, St Ruan's Well at Grade, St Cranhocus' Well at Crantock, and St Gundred's Well at Roche. (Rodwell and Bentley, 1984 p.30)

Holy wells were particularly influential in the siting of early churches (Rahtz and Watts, 1979), and may be found inside the building, in the churchyard or at its perimeter or nearby. Rodwell noted that 'In deciding where to place a church, proprietary or otherwise, superstition and ancient custom played their part, as they always have done in religious matters' (1989 p.154). The church at the original site of Ripley village, North Yorkshire, occupied a seemingly appalling site on a stone-revetted platform terraced into the face of a river bluff. Springs rising here may provide a ritual-based explanation for its situation. Some 1,179 holy wells have been counted in Wales and around 600 are known in Scotland, though the late Victorian estimates of 40 wells in Cornwall and 67 in Yorkshire must considerably underestimate the true totals. A significant minority of pagan wells attracted Christian foundations; in some cases the pagan deity presiding over the well was converted to a saint, so that the Celtic child-eating Annis could re-emerge in dedications to St Anne, while the Celtic goddess Elen became St Helen. The appearance of the holy well can vary from that of a spring to a dark swamp overhung by trees and ivy, as at St Madron's Well in Cornwall. At Dupath in Cornwall a baptistry or well house covers the well, and it resembles a conduit house supplying fresh drinking water, like the one at Alnwick Abbey (Northumberland).

Water exerted an important locational attraction for practical as well as ritual purposes where medieval monastic foundations were concerned. Springs or streams were needed to provide drinking water, for sanitation and to feed ponds and power mills, while an effective drainage system was needed to remove excess water.

The ideal in practice meant a gentle south-facing slope with a stream running below. The church could then be built to the north of the cloister, with the stream draining the claustral ranges of buildings to the south. In reality there was often

Table 6.1   Place-names and ritual landscapes

Place-name/place-name element	Significance
Barrow, Berrow, Burrow (OE *beorg, beorge*)	Denotes a mound of earth, i.e. a barrow, though Barrow usually derived from *bearu*, a grove.
Tumulus pl. *tumuli* (Latin)	Appears on OS maps to mark barrows of Neolithic and Bronze Age date.
Cairn (Gaelic *carne*)	A pile of stones, sometimes covering an ancient burial.
Quoit	Used in Cornish dialect to denote a megalithic tomb, often a portal dolmen.
Well (OE *wiell, wella, wælla*)	A spring or stream, sometimes a holy well.
Font (OE *funta*); Keld (ON *kelda* and OE *celde*); Burn (OE *burna*); Beck (OE *bekkr*); Brook (OE *brōc*)	These all signify springs and streams which may, in some cases, be linked with pagan worship. 'Spring' itself was frequently associated with coppiced woodland rather than a stream.
Holywell	Appears in names like Helliwell, Holwell, Holybourne etc., while Helen Hill may derive from the Celtic goddess Elen.
Lann or *lan* (Cornish)	Refers to oval enclosures associated with early Christian foundations. Generally *lan* pre-dates *eglos* names, but outside Cornwall, in Wessex, oval enclosures with churches can represent the enclosures of *burhs* or Saxon fortified towns.
Merther (Cornish)	A saint's grave.
Eccles (Latin *ecclesia*, Cornish *eglos*, OE *ecles*)	Thought to indicate the sites of very early Christian churches associated with the survival of Christianity in post-Roman Britain.
-minster (Latin *monasterium*)	Settlement associated with a minster church, e.g. Yetminster, Charminster, Iwerne Minster.
Plu (Cornish)	A parish.
All place-names associated with water	A very high proportion of early churches—more than half of the minsters in the case of Hampshire—have place-names associated with situations by rivers, springs and wells. Such names are particularly common in dry chalk country.

great ingenuity employed in laying out the buildings to make the best use of the locally available water supply, with many examples of the claustral plan being reversed, with the cloister on the north side of the church, if this meant that a more efficient drainage system could be devised. (Aston, 1993 p.90)

Between 1066 and the mid-thirteenth century, the number of monastic establishments increased tenfold, to around 600. The sites selected for the multitude of new houses were not determined so much by the physical character of the landscape, but more by reference to the pattern of land ownership and the tenurial arrangements of the period: 'As the status of the founders of monasteries moved down from the Crown, in the pre-Conquest and early medieval periods, so the choice of site became less of an easy option. The foundation process went from a wide variety of extensive lands from which to choose, to more a case of finding somewhere reasonable in the locality' (Aston, 1993 p.110).

Influences on the landscape

Religious beliefs and practices impact upon the landscape in various ways; religious buildings and structures exist as small-scale components of the landscape, while the organisation of worship and of the property of religious institutions can have far-reaching effects. Most religious structures are easily recognised, but some, along with various prehistoric monuments, are less obvious or confusing.

Religious institutions normally exert their effects upon landscape by influencing patterns of boundaries, settlement, land-use, communications and exploitation, while the religious buildings and structures *themselves* are normally more modest components of landscape. In some cases, however, they can be the dominating features in the visible landscape, as in the Avebury locality in Wiltshire, with the henge and stone circles complex, the West Kennet avenue and West Kennet chambered tomb, Silbury Hill and the Windmill Hill

Table 6.2   Ritual monuments and physically similar structures

Monument	Might be confused with
Neolithic long barrow	Morrainic or fluvio-glacial deposit. Pillow mound. Embankment from a rifle range.
Round barrow (usually Bronze Age)	Motte mound. Windmill mound (though some mills were built on barrows). Degraded prospect mount. Mounds erected to mark boundaries. Mounds of dross associated with back-filling of pre-Industrial Revolution mine shafts.
Neolithic/Bronze Age monolith	Medieval or later boundary-marker. Medieval or later way-marker. Gate post. (A monolith might be re-used as any of these.)
Preaching cross	Medieval territorial boundary-marker, e.g. limits of monastic estate, warren or sanctuary. Medieval market cross.

Figure 6.5   For the landscape historian the medieval monastery is most meaningful in terms of its relationship with the surrounding territory. The immense late-twelfth-century cellarium at Fountains is almost 100 m (300 ft) in length and was originally partitioned to provide stores or cellarage, offices and the frater. It reminds one of the produce pouring in from the estates and the needs of the large monk and lay brother community.

causewayed enclosure in relatively close proximity, as well as the various less prominent Bronze Age burial mounds. Whole landscapes associated with religion could also be found surrounding some of the greater medieval monastic houses. At Rievaulx there were some 27 different buildings located in the inner and outer courts of the monastic precincts, including mills for fulling and for corn, workshops for smiths, plumbers and tanners, and domestic accommodation for corrodians, who paid to be cared for by the monastic community.

Religion achieved its greatest influence upon landscapes through the activities of medieval monasteries engaged in managing their estates. Such estates embraced a complexity of resources, including mills, markets, fisheries, quarries, minerals, livestock, crops, granges and lodges. In several places it will be possible to locate resources like routeways, farms, fisheries and mines and thus attempt to recreate the outlines of the monastic landscape, as accomplished by Williams for Wales (1990). The dynamic for the monastic estate was provided by the grange system, which was devised by the Cistercians and imitated and adopted by other orders: 'It was supremely well-equipped for the development of the less intensively settled areas, such as the forest lands, marshlands and uplands of many

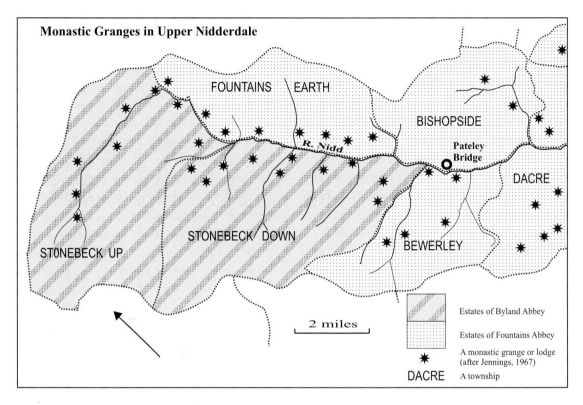

Map 6.2   *Monastic granges in Upper Nidderdale.*
The nucleated settlements and many of the
farmstead sites in the upper dale are associated with
monastic granges of Fountains and Byland abbeys.
Based on Jennings (1967).

parts of Britain. It was a flexible instrument for it could be an administrative, pastoral, arable, or industrial unit depending on the area in which it was situated' (Aston, 1993 p.139). Many granges continued to exert an influence upon the landscape long after they had been let out to lay tenants and after their founding monasteries had been dissolved. Frequently they endure as farmsteads and some, like Kilnsey in Wharfedale, Middlesmoor and Ramsgill in Nidderdale, or Healaugh in Swaledale, developed during the post-medieval centuries into small villages.

There were, however, subtle differences between the different monastic orders, some of them of a doctrinal nature—and these differences could find expression in the landscape. The Benedictines had a long connection with the English landscape and people, and Benedictine estates were often intimately associated with the prosperous and well-peopled countrysides. These estates tended to consist of villages and their associated lands, and although the monks kept separate home farms, the tenanted lands and the demesne were closely interdigitated. The Cistercians, in contrast, had an ascetic ideal and sought remote sites and to be divorced from laymen, often improving their isolation artificially by evicting peasant communities from the vicinity of their houses and granges. There were contrasts, too, in the scale of estates and the intensity with which they were exploited. In contrast to the great Cistercian houses of Yorkshire, Mount

Figure 6.6   Wimborne Minster in Dorset, one of many churches in the county deriving from an early minster foundation. It is dedicated to St Cuthberga, sister to Ine, an eighth-century king of Wessex, though the visible fabric spans the periods from the Normans to the fifteenth century.

Grace, a Carthusian house, worked only a small estate and derived most of its income from rents from gifted land. Like the Cistercians, the Carthusians tended to be ascetic and isolationist, but they did not make the transition to deriving great fortunes from estate management on the grand scale. Also in contrast to the Mount Grace example was the case of Glastonbury Abbey, an extremely rich Benedictine house with lands in seven counties; four years before being dissolved the annual income of the monastery was a massive £3,300 (Bond, 1998 p.5).

With their spires and steeples as landmarks punctuating the vistas of fields and trees and usually signalling the presence of settlement nearby, churches are more significant features of the landscape than the modest dimensions of their groundplans might suggest. Almost all medieval churches must have been altered and rebuilt on several occasions, so that some of the best clues to the antiquity of worship in a particular place may derive not from the architecture of the building, but from its surrounds. If the churchyard is elevated in relation to the adjacent ground and there is a sharp break of slope at its boundary, then the enclosure is likely to be ancient, a condition which is also suggested by broad

Figure 6.7 Fragments of late Saxon and Norman carved stonework incorporated into the walls of the medieval successor church at Grantchester in Cambridgeshire.

boundary ditches or boundary banks topped with veteran pollards. 'When recording boundaries careful attention must be paid to banks, ditches, kinks in hedgerows, changes in walling material or alignments, and evidence for former entrances since these are all clues to the history of the churchyard as an enclosure' (Rodwell, 1989 p.143).

Churches and landscape history

The church, more than any other building, was intimately associated with the affairs of the surrounding community. No matter how unjust or extortionate the conduct of organised religion may have been, the local church was a place where the anxieties, celebrations, entertainment and tragedies of the neighbourhood were collectively experienced. The church was a public

Figure 6.8   *The medieval church helped to shape*
popular culture, not only through the more purely
religious activities but also by disseminating
ideology and codes of conduct. The walls of the
church could be like great billboards that issue
warnings of the Last Judgement or conveyed gentler
images like this St Christopher carrying the Child
Christ at Little Missenden in Buckinghamshire.

building which gave a physical expression to
the affairs of the community. Its size was
tailored to the size of its congregation.
When the number of worshippers rose then
the quest for extra space would be embodied in extensions to the nave, while
when it dwindled the time could come for
reductions in the floor space which might
result in an abandonment of side aisles, a
shortening of the nave and a lowering of its
roof.

During the decades following the Roman
withdrawal from Britain in 410, Christian

Figure 6.9 The architecture and masonry of the church could serve as political statements. The exceptional carvings produced by a craftsman of the Herefordshire school at Kilpeck in that county proclaimed to a contemporary onlooker the triumph of the Normans, but also the endurance of pagan beliefs, as represented by the 'green man' character with vines issuing from his mouth.

congregations appear to have endured in numerous larger settlements, such as Dorchester, Exeter and Gloucester, and also in various rural localities. During the second half of the century, Christianity seems to have gained strength and pagan shrines were Christianised. Traces from this early

Table 6.3   Evidence contained in the name, parish and fabric of a church

Feature	Significance
Dedication	Dedications to obscure Celtic saints, like St Kew, may identify the founders of ancient churches. A high proportion of minsters were dedicated to St Mary, while many early hilltop churches were dedicated to St Michael.
Parish	Churches which were formerly minsters tend to have retained parishes a little larger than those of their neighbours.
Cross shafts or grave slabs incorporated in the wall fabric	These are materials taken from the site on which the church was built. The cross might derive from worship there before there was a church and the grave slab could be from the tomb of an early priest. Any carved decoration should be datable.
Fragments of decorated masonry incorporated in the walls	This material is likely to derive from a previous church. The decorative styles employed may reveal the age of the predecessor.
Windows, doors and arches	Their proportions and decoration will be datable, but they *cannot* be used to date the building. The walls in which they are set could be older, but they too could be the last link in a building succession.
Roof creases visible externally on the tower or on the wall containing the chancel arch	These reveal how the roof of a nave and/or chancel has been lowered, perhaps to create a less imposing building and one that was cheaper to maintain. Could indicate a declining congregation.
Differences in the thickness of walls	This usually denotes different phases of construction.
Roman brick or masonry incorporated in the walls	This will normally denote the building of the church close to a ruined Roman building, often a villa, at a time when its walls were still standing or when the rubble from fallen walls was still not overgrown.
Blocked arches	At an elevated level these will denote refenestration, while at ground level they are likely to reveal the reduction of the building and removal of chapels or aisles.
A chancel that is shorter than it is wide	This will probably have been shortened to economise on maintenance costs in a parish with a declining population/prosperity.
Straight joints in masonry	These indicate junctions between work of different periods, though new work was sometimes keyed in to the old.

phase of Christianity seem few and hard to recognise, with small, flimsy churches perhaps being erected on hilltop sites and by springs and watercourses that had some-times been associated with pagan worship. In the late sixth and seventh centuries, monasteries were established in rural settings in the south-west and evangelical

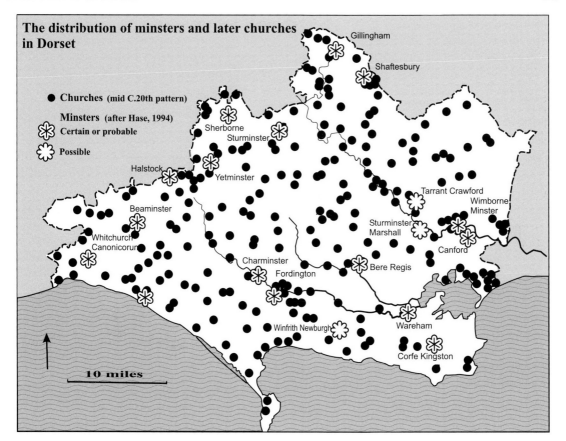

The distribution of minsters and later churches in Dorset

● **Churches** (mid C.20th pattern)

Minsters (after Hase, 1994)
✳ **Certain or probable**
✺ **Possible**

Gillingham

Shaftesbury

Sherborne
Sturminster

Halstock
Yetminster

Beaminster

Whitchurch
Canonicorum

Charminster
Fordington

Tarrant Crawford
Wimborne Minster

Sturminster Marshall
Canford

Bere Regis

Winfrith Newburgh

Wareham

Corfe Kingston

10 miles

Map 6.3   The distribution of minsters and later churches in Dorset. The pattern of minsters is based on Hase (1994).

work was accomplished in the surrounding areas. These early centres of worship were sometimes erected at the sites of Roman villas, as at Cheddar in Somerset, though flat, well-watered sites in the productive areas which must have supported most population were also favoured. Factors common to many of these early minster sites were situations beside rivers and dedications to St Mary. The possession of parishes larger than those of neighbouring churches can still lead to the identification of such minsters. Sub-Roman churches established in regions where pagan Saxon influences became dominant were likely to perish, though churches in areas which fell under the control of Saxon converts to Christianity, in places like Dorset and Somerset, would survive. After the establishment of a Saxon ascendancy in Wessex, the kings chose to build churches away from old villa sites and

situations were chosen which lay very close to the royal *burhs* or fortified towns (Hase, 1994).

Following the conversion of the pagan Saxon kingdoms, minsters were established between the mid-seventh and mid-ninth centuries by the respective kings upon royal estates which formed the economic, administrative and judicial centres of the subordinate districts of the kingdoms.

In Wessex it looks as if there was a conscious policy to ensure that every *regio* had a church, a royal church . . . Such a policy ensured that every settlement was clearly in some specific *regio* and *parochia*, so that every settlement was subject to a specific royal reeve, advised and assisted by a specific, and almost equally royal priest. At the local level, political, social, economic and religious life would thus have been controlled by royal agents, subject to a king advised by a close-knit group of aeldormen and bishops. (Hase, 1994 pp.53–4)

According to Blair, the overemphasis on European examples has resulted in a misplaced emphasis on royal centres as the nuclei for later lay settlement. At first, he believes, the only developed nuclei were monastic and the subsequent royal centres latched onto them. He writes:

Recent interest in the development of towns from pre-urban 'hierarchical centres' has generated two rival models, one emphasising royal palaces, the other emphasising minsters. Some very important and well-known sites can be interpreted in alternative ways, depending on which camp one belongs to. Was the massive ninth-century stone building excavated in Northampton a palace hall or a minster refectory? Was the palace which Philip Rahtz found at Cheddar the nucleus of the site, or was it merely grafted on to a pre-existing minster? (Blair, 1998b p.130)

Between the 660s and the 750s many religious establishments were founded, often on sites enclosed by re-using prehistoric earthworks, with river and coastal situations being favoured. Gradually, these minster sites could be secularised as aristocrats settled in the vicinity and lay settlements developed around them to become small market towns. The *burhs* were often monasteries that were fortified and then developed urban and commercial functions. Sometimes it is still possible to recognise the central location of the original monastery and the more peripheral siting of the

royal and commercial sites (Blair, 1988 and 1998a).

Each mother church was responsible for organising and providing ecclesiastical services for its tributary area, though the system of minsters became disrupted in the centuries bracketing the Norman Conquest as multitudes of new churches appeared, each serving a single estate or parish. Gradually, the initiative in matters of worship slipped from the minsters to the estate churches as lay lords established churches at the gates of their homes, as lands were granted to greater churches which then created churches on the estate and as the communities of the minsters themselves began to establish new churches in outlying localities.

In terms of the sites selected for the earlier Saxon churches, in some cases hillforts or other prehistoric enclosure sites were chosen, while in other cases such places existed nearby but appear deliberately to have been avoided, as at Amesbury in Wiltshire. Sometimes churches were erected directly outside the enclosures of Roman settlements, as with Dorchester, and sometimes they were erected within the enclosures, as at Reculver or Dover. They appear frequently to have been established at places close to, but not upon Roman roads, as at Kirk Hammerton in North Yorkshire or Nursling in Hampshire. In Wessex: 'it seems clear that the early West Saxons built their mother churches, where possible, near, but not adjacent to, Roman roads—often at the nearest permanent spring to the road . . . It is the siting of the church near the spring or stream that caused the Saxon and later town to move away from the Roman towns at Andover, Alton and Wimborne Minster: the Roman towns at these places were at the crossroads of the Roman roads, the later towns were around the church, a mile or two away' (Blair, 1998a p.58). When associated with

Table 6.4   *Types of churches in medieval England*

Type	Characteristics
Parish church (ecclesia)	Responsible only to its bishop. Had its own incumbent who was provided with land in the form of a glebe and was supported by tithes.
Dependent parochial chapel (capella)	This also had its own incumbent etc., but was required to pay a portion of its tithes to another church and might only have had limited rights of burial.
Chapel of ease	Had no incumbent or glebe and was served by salaried chaplains. Was not responsible for the cure of souls and seldom had rights of burial.

Saxon *burhs* the West Saxon minsters appear to have been placed at the gates of the fortified townlet, near a river or stream and facing the market.

In Cornwall the situation was rather different. Here, parishes are named after saints rather than settlements or other places. The saints could be obscure local missionaries or merely benefactors who had helped to endow a church, though the churches were frequently associated with small settlements, which in many cases presumably developed around them once they were established. Names linked with churches are often associated with the elements *lann-* and *eglos*, respectively denoting a religious enclosure and a church. Cornish parishes are not related to manors or to tithings but are named after saints and seem to derive from an earlier territorial arrangement.

By the late twelfth century the process of church creation was, in most parts of the country, almost over, and it would remain dormant until industrialisation generated a need for new urban and rural churches. In some sparsely peopled upland areas, however, the pattern of churches was still far from complete, and the former existence of vast parishes, like those associated with Grinton in Swaledale or Helmsley in the North York Moors, testifies to the effects of environmental factors as well, in some cases, as those of the Harrying of the North and the creation of Forests. Within the established parishes, churches were repeatedly redeveloped, and many of the changes incorporated in their fabrics reflected changing conditions in their localities. It is notable that only rarely were churches completely demolished and begun anew. Normally, changes would be incorporated in stages as developments in liturgy, in the prosperity of the locality or in income encouraged alterations. Thus the local church existed and exists as a complex assemblage of building works of different ages, some recognisable to the educated eye and some undetectable. Meanwhile, below ground level, an even greater complexity of phases will probably exist in the form of successive footings which chart the expansion and/or contraction of the building.

Many types of changes reflect the enlargement of the building in order to accommodate a growing congregation—such as would commonly have occurred during the phase of population growth during the thirteenth century. It is possible to recognise periods when there great eruptions in church building—periods when the products of the previous eruption were frequently erased. There was the building of minsters in the period 650–850; the construction of field, estate or parish churches around 950–1150; the replacement of hundreds of Saxon churches in the Norman period, for both religious and political reasons; and then a massive (re)building drive in the thirteenth century:

> The thirteenth century was . . . marked by a period of numerous massive enlarge-

Figure 6.10   The church reflected the affluence or poverty of its setting. Hubberholme church in Langstrothdale, North Yorkshire, was a remote chapel of ease of Arncliffe church in Littondale and served a dispersed community of rather impoverished farmers. It was so far from the beaten tracks that instructions from bishop and archbishop did not always reach it.

ments of narrow Norman churches. Chancels were lengthened, chancel arches were heightened and porches added. It was at this period, rather than later, that the wholesale removal or destruction of Saxon or Norman work took place. Many churches in England, if examined carefully, can be seen to be basically thirteenth century in form if not in detail. (Taylor and Muir, 1983 p.67)

The need for more space in the nave would have been the most pressing problem as population rose, and this could have been accomplished by lengthening the church, either by pushing the nave westwards or the chancel eastwards. Alternatively, the nave might be widened, with the construction of side aisles or transepts. Evidence of these enlargements should be recognised in the fabric of the church in the form of discontinuities between the older and the newer work and, possibly, slight misalignments. It is plainest in aisles where buttresses with integral plinths terminate at the junction of new and old work: 'Early medieval aisles were quite narrow, while later ones could easily be as wide as the nave. It was therefore common practice for Norman aisles to be more or less doubled in width in later centuries, and the tell-tale evidence for this having happened is sometimes discernible in the west end of an aisle: there may be a straight joint or a discontinuous plinth' (Rodwell, 1981 p.65).

The evidence of expansion contained in the fabric of a church may be confirmed and clarified by documentary sources, for

If a church was rebuilt on its original site at any date after 1250, a good many traces

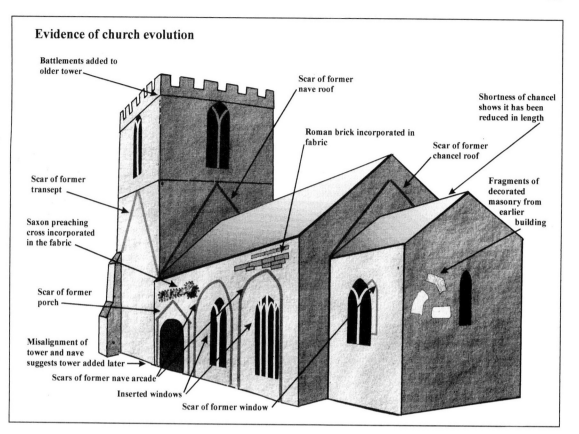

Evidence of church evolution

Battlements added to older tower

Scar of former nave roof

Shortness of chancel shows it has been reduced in length

Roman brick incorporated in fabric

Scar of former chancel roof

Fragments of decorated masonry from earlier building

Scar of former transept

Saxon preaching cross incorporated in the fabric

Scar of former porch

Misalignment of tower and nave suggests tower added later

Scars of former nave arcade

Inserted windows

Scar of former window

Map 6.4   Evidence of church evolution. The drawing shows some of the diagnostic features which may assist an interpretation of the history of a church.

are usually left in records. An episcopal licence (what would now be called a Faculty) would be required, such as Bishop Charlton granted to Queen Isabella in 1330 for the rebuilding of Churcham (Heref.) . . . When the building was complete it would require consecration and this, too, would be entered in the episcopal register: for example, the mandate for the consecration of the church at Colmorton [Chelmorton], newly rebuilt by Sir Gerald Braybroke Knight . . . The expenses of consecration would be met by the parish, and might be accounted for in the churchwardens' accounts . . . or, if the parish church defaulted, presentments and subsequent action would appear in visitation entries in the register. (Owen, 1976 p.24)

Evidence relating to the alteration or rebuilding of churches comes from a variety of other sources. Wills described bequests of the kind commonly made to finance or contribute towards repairs, improvements and enlargements to the building. In terms of responsibilities, the rector had responsibility for the chancel, while the parish was obliged to repair the nave and belfry. Parishioners could maintain a fabric fund, receiving bequests and selling candles or ale to raise money. Large projects could require a special church rate which might be recorded in diocesan records.

The evidence of blocked arches at ground

Figure 6.11   The size, form and fabric of the church mirrored the economy of its setting. Long Melford church in Suffolk was built towards the end of the fifteenth century, with monuments to the local benefactors, the Clopton family, being prominently displayed. The village had grown rich during a cloth boom which followed the settlement of Flemish weavers there during the fourteenth century. (An eighteenth-century brick tower was encased by the present structure at the start of the twentieth century.)

level in the walls of a church will tell of the reduction of the building, and depending on their position, the arches concerned may have corresponded to the nave arcade or might have marked the entrances to side chapels leading from the chancel. In times of economic hardship, a defective tower might be demolished rather than repaired, with the strengthened construction of the walls in the west end or crossing perhaps denoting a former tower. A chancel which is shorter in its east–west dimension than it is from north to south is likely to have been reduced, perhaps to avoid expensive repairs when the congregation was impoverished or declining.

In numerous parishes the church provides the best physical indicator of the social and economic history of the locality. Changes to its layout and fabric can be related to three groups of causes: *the evolving nature of ritual*, as expressed, for example, by the building of Lady chapels during the medieval heyday of the cult of the Virgin Mary; *the quest to enhance the building and to compete with the magnificence of neighbouring churches*, as manifest, for example, in the heightening and embellishment of towers; and *local and national socio-economic circumstances*, as exemplified in the enlargement or shortening of naves and chancels. (Local traditions and preferences in building would also affect the appearance of a church, as with the round towers of East Anglia or the broach spires of Mid Anglia.) Where a church lies ruined one can be confident that the congregation either dwindled beyond the point at which a church could be supported, or that a shift of settlement or a realignment of communal arrangements resulted in the migration of worshippers to another church. Although local economic and demographic decay normally explains the ruination of a church, there are a few exceptions—as with Roudham St Andrew in Norfolk, abandoned in 1734 after the ashes from a workman's pipe accidently ignited the thatch of its roof (Batcock, 1991 p.51).

The extent to which the structure of an abandoned church remains prominent in the landscape depends upon more than the robustness of the building and the length of its abandonment. In some parishes during the medieval period the church was the only stone building of substance. It incorporated a mass of valuable building materials, and was likely to be robbed right down to its foundations. This likelihood increased in stone-poor regions where expensive stones had been imported by barge, sled and wagon. However, in the poorest of the regions, the chalklands, where churches were generally built of flint gathered from the litter of nodules in the ploughsoil, the building was unworthy of robbing and was quite likely to survive. Isolated churches

very frequently mark the sites of deserted medieval villages and thus provide valuable information about the evolution of the cultural landscape.

In some cases, however, they are not indicators of deserted settlements. The parish concerned may always have had a dispersed pattern of settlement, as in numerous upland and 'woodland' localities, or else the nucleated settlement that once accompanied the church still flourishes in a different location. This was the case with the hilltop settlement at Comberton in Cambridgeshire, which migrated from its church to a lower, crossroads site, presumably being attracted by the growth in traffic on the roads below. In a small number of cases, the church may have commandeered a deserted location which had been associated with pagan worship—although the number of hilltop churches sited in this way was probably exaggerated. Dedications to St Michael are often associated with hilltop churches. There are more than 600 examples of dedications to the Archangel in England and he may have been a popular substitute at Christianised pagan sites for Mercury and Hermes and other gods charged with guiding the dying and the dead. He maintained his popularity after the Reformation because he was a biblical figure and did not owe his canonisation to the Vatican.

The presence of a ruined and isolated church may prompt research that uncovers the history of decline in a parish, as at Little Ringstead in Norfolk, where the single cell surviving may be the chancel of a once-larger church. The village was depopulated by the pestilence epidemic of 1349, after which the church was probably abandoned, though it continued in use as a chapel until the sixteenth century and was converted into a barn in the century that followed (Batcock, 1991 p.51). A familiar pattern was for a church to survive the demise of its village for some time, before eventually being abandoned. At Saxlingham Thorpe, in Norfolk, the village perished in the late medieval period; in 1685 one of the church-wardens illegally sold the church bells and in 1687 the church was officially abandoned and was declared to have been ruined for the last two decades (pp.126–7). There are very rare occasions on which a ruined church may signify the growth rather than the decay of prosperity in a locality, as with the case of Thorpe-by-Norwich. Here, the rise in population resulted in the construction of a larger church on a different site to the north in 1866, with the old church being reduced to a 'picturesque' ruin in 1881 (p.51).

In the graveyard of the deserted church, providing the soil conditions are not too acidic, the skeletons of the former community may be preserved. They provide sizeable and datable assemblages of people from a particular locality such as will allow scientific studies to be made of health, working conditions and nutrition. Comparative studies between such assemblages allow investigations of mortality in town and country. Thus, work on bones from Wharram Percy and St Helen's, York, showed that the low-class city-dwellers suffered higher rates of sinusitis, a condition associated with atmospheric pollution (Mays, 1998). It was also shown that there were more females than males in the urban parish, while the reverse was the case at the parish in the Yorkshire Wolds: were country-women leaving and seeking work in York?

REFERENCES

Appleton, J. *The Symbolism of Habitat* (Washington DC: University of Washington Press, 1990).

Aston, M. *Monasteries* (London: Batsford, 1993).

Batcock, N. *The Ruined and Disused Churches of Norfolk*, East Anglian Archaeology Report 51 (Norwich: Norfolk Archaeology Unit, 1991).

Bettey, J.H. *Church and Parish* (London: Batsford, 1987).

Blair, J. (ed.) *Minsters and Parish Churches: The Local Church in Transition, 950–1200*, Oxford University Committee for Archaeology: Monograph 17 (Oxford: Oxbow, 1988).

Blair J. 'Minster churches and settlement formation in Anglo-Saxon England', paper given to the International Medieval Congress, Leeds (1998a).

Blair, J. 'Bampton: an Anglo-Saxon minster' *Current Archaeology* 160 (1998b) pp.124–130.

Bond, J. 'The Glastonbury abbey and estates' *Society for Landscape Studies Newsletter* (Spring/Autumn 1998).

Burl, A. 'The Devil's Arrows' *Yorkshire Archaeological Journal* 63 (1991) pp.1–24.

Hase, P.H. 'The church in the Wessex heartlands' in M. Aston and C. Lewis (eds) *The Medieval Landscape of Wessex*, Oxbow Monograph 64 (Oxford: Oxbow, 1994).

Martlew, R.D. and Ruggles, C.L.N. 'Ritual and landscape on the west coast of Scotland: an investigation of the stone rows of northern Mull' *Proceedings of the Prehistoric Society* 62 (1996) pp.117–31.

Mays, S. 'Human skeletal remains at Wharram Percy', paper given to the International Medieval Congress, Leeds (1998).

Newman, R. 'The problems of rural settlement in northern Cumbria' in M.L. Faull (ed.) *Studies in Late Anglo-Saxon Settlement* (Oxford: Oxford University Department for External Studies, 1984).

Owen, D. 'Documentary sources for the building history of churches in the middle ages' in P. Addyman and R. Morris (eds) *The Archaeological Study of Churches*, CBA Research Report 13 (London: Council for British Archaeology, 1976) pp.21–5.

Parker Pearson, M. and Ramilisonina 'Stonehenge for the ancestors: the stones pass on the message' *Antiquity* 72 (1998) pp.308–26.

Rahtz, P.A. 'Celtic society in Somerset AD 400–700' *Bulletin of the Board of Celtic Studies* 30 (1982–3) pp.176–200.

Rahtz, P.A. and Watts, I. 'The end of Roman temples in the west of Britain' in P.J. Casey (ed.) *The End of Roman Britain*, B.A.R. 71 (1979) pp.183–210.

Rodwell, W. *The Archaeology of the English Church* (London: Batsford, 1981).

Rodwell, W. *Church Archaeology* (London: Batsford, 1989).

Rodwell, W. and Bentley, J. *Our Christian Heritage* (London: George Philip, 1984).

Taylor, C. and Muir, R. *Visions of the Past* (London: Dent, 1983).

Vyner, B.E. 'The territory of ritual: cross-ridge boundaries and the prehistoric landscape of the Cleveland Hills, northeast England' *Antiquity* 68 (1994) pp.27–8.

Walter, E.V. *Placeways* (Chapel Hill NC: University of North Carolina Press, 1988).

Williams, D.H. *Atlas of Cistercian Lands in Wales* (Cardiff: University of Wales Press, 1990).

Williams, H. 'Ancient attitudes to ancient monuments' *British Archaeology* (1997) p.6.

Woodward, A.B. and Woodward, P.J. 'The topography of some barrow cemeteries in Bronze Age Wessex' *Proceedings of the Prehistoric Society* 62 (1996) pp.275–91.

CHAPTER 7

Villages, Hamlets and Farmsteads

As the last quarter of the twentieth century approached much had been written about the origins and nature of rural settlement—and only a small proportion of it was of any real worth. By the millennium, however, the understanding of these themes has advanced so far that we can answer most of the questions about what happened and when in relation to settlement origins, even if we do not yet understand all the whys. It has also been recognised that villages are extremely complex. They cannot be interpreted in terms of simple morphological or developmental models. Instead, they display a wide spectrum of individuality and they gel and then evolve in manners that can be difficult to detect. Above all, they are not 'timeless' and 'stable'. Rather, they are vulnerable, fragile and extremely responsive to changes in the local, regional and national economic and social environments. Recently, the significance of smaller settlements, the hamlets and farmsteads, has been appreciated, leading to a better understanding of dispersed settlement and its contribution to the evolution of 'village England'.

Dispersed settlement

A variety of interpretations exists concerning the roles played in the development of settlement patterns by farmsteads and hamlets. Drawing upon his experiences in Devon, Hoskins argued for a very deeply rooted continuity in the occupation of farm sites, a view supported by more recent studies in Cornwall. Other authorities have argued that farmsteads are the remains of

hamlets that have contracted, and it has been shown that nucleated settlement can disintegrate to produce dispersed settlements. Equally, it now appears plain that widespread processes of nucleation occurred in England during the middle-to-late Saxon period. This process seems to have been strongest in a central belt of nucleated settlement running diagonally across the country from Northumberland and Durham to Dorset.

Previously, the settlement tradition, particular in the uplands, had been a dispersed one, with village-sized nucleations being present but uncommon within countrysides dominated by farmsteads and hamlets. The features that were characteristic of prehistoric and post-Roman settlement were not typical of medieval villages. Any prehistoric sites encountered which have substantial surface settlement traces are very likely to have been recognised and recorded already, although the identification of new sites on the basis of air photograph evidence, mainly crop-marks, is continuing at quite a rapid pace. Earthbound observers may still detect unrecorded prehistoric settlements, and not only as a result of the discoveries of concentrations of ancient pottery in the course of field-walking. In the northern Dales and uplands, for example, sites on knolls or slopes which enjoyed broad, panoramic views and which are associated with access to a source of water, litters of stones and patches of nettles are worthy of inspection. It is useful to remember that during the Iron Age and much of the Bronze Age, people in England occupied mature agricultural countrysides

Figure 7.1   The nature of dispersed settlement is encapsulated in this pattern of dwellings near Darley, North Yorkshire.

that had experienced several phases of exploitation, over-exploitation, retreat and re-colonisation. The wildwood was restricted and most of the panoramas seen were fieldscapes stippled with hamlets and farmsteads.

Dispersed settlement had a very long history in England and was seemingly the norm for all regions until around the time of the Viking raids. One must wonder, therefore, whether the dispersed settlement encountered today represents the vestiges of a pattern preceding the foundation of 'village England'? Certainly excavations seem to reveal a transition from hamlets and farm-

steads to nucleated forms of settlement, but the picture is complicated and various processes took place:

It can hardly be disputed that many nucleations have medieval roots . . . but it is in practice surprisingly difficult to prove precisely what settlement form or pattern existed in a particular decade or even century for the many thousands of named and documented places known from medieval taxation records and Domesday Book of 1086 . . . Still less is this possible for the thousands of localities attested by place-names whose linguistic origin—Anglo-Saxon, Scandinavian or Anglo-Scandinavian—suggests their presence long before they are first documented in Domesday Book or even in Anglo-Saxon charters. (Roberts *et al.*, 1996 p.76)

Table 7.1   Comparing prehistoric and medieval settlement

Criterion	Prehistoric	Medieval
Permanence	Would normally be abandoned after a few decades/centuries of occupation.	Would be abandoned in the face of special crises or opportunities. Otherwise the villages were intended to be permanent.
Mobility	Footloose: a migration of the settlement to another site nearby was commonplace.	Would sometimes drift to a new site in response to special stimuli.
Structure	Do not generally have well-defined structures or plan components. Straggles or seemingly random scatters of dwellings normal.	Structures, involving greens, toft rows, streets, churches, manor houses etc. are usually well-defined.

These researchers estimated that there are at least 10,000 localities where nucleations have existed. This is based on the 7500 nucleated settlements that existed in England in the mid-nineteenth century, plus approximately 2,500 deserted settlements. The existence of a hierarchy of settlement has always been recognised. To the chroniclers of the Dark Ages, a *domus* was a house, a *vicus* a group of buildings, perhaps a large hamlet, and a *castella* was a lesser settlement, perhaps a small hamlet. Medieval writers seem to have regarded the *vicus* as a market town that was lower in importance than a town or *urbs* or *civitas* or city.

Figure 7.2   A small, circular Bronze Age dwelling situated within a compound at Grimspound on Dartmoor.

Confusingly for us, 'town' was formerly used to describe most rural settlements from a village to a cluster of associated hamlets; 'hamlet' could have its present meaning or could describe a subdivision of a northern township; and 'thorpe' was also a name attached to small, subordinate settlements. In Cornwall, a *lys* was an administrative focus, a *ker* was a fort or round (a circular defensive enclosure), a *tref* appears to have been the basic settlement unit, a large farm dating from after the fifth century, a *bod* was a minor or seasonally occupied hamlet, and a *ty* was a house

If documentary study were able to reveal the processes at work turning a country of dispersed settlement into one in which villages frequently dominated the rural settlement patterns then, arguably, it would have done so by now. Rather, the answers are emerging from archaeology, the Raunds project in Northamptonshire being an important case in point. The county lies in the central province of nucleated settlement and is associated with villages composed of rows of tenements arranged in a regular order. The villages are frequently found to be standing on frameworks of boundary ditches that were superimposed on the landscape in the tenth century in a replanning of the countryside based on rectangular acre plots. For example, West Cotton originated around AD 950 as small settlement with a hall and a watermill which were established on a site divided into regular acre, half-acre and quarter-acre plots defined by ditches which were set out using a unit of measurement of 16 feet. Before becoming deserted the original planned layout of West Cotton was obscured, with the re-orientation of manorial build-

Figure 7.3   Kilnsey in Wharfedale is one of a minority of villages whose origins are known: it evolved from a grange of Fountains Abbey.

Figure 7.4 Bainbridge, North Yorkshire, developed at the foot of a Roman fortress following the establishment there of a community of nine foresters of the Forest of Wensleydale, each with a dwelling and 9 acres of land, some time before 1227.

ings in the thirteenth century, the appearance on the site of peasant tenements (leading to the adoption of the 'Cotton' name) and the insertion of a central triangular green (Chapman, 1998). Oval enclosures of the early Saxon period may be associated with later estate centres in Northamptonshire, as at Higham Ferrers and Daventry, where it is possible to detect such enclosures fossilised within the later nucleated centres (Foard, 1998).

Oval enclosures were an element in the early settlement of the Levels of the Somerset coast and appear to have been the

Figure 7.5   Old Byland, North Yorkshire, is a planned settlement arranged around a rectangular green and was created in the 1140s to house a community evicted by monks of a convent at Hood who went on to found Byland Abbey.

primary settlement and agricultural foci in the reclamation of areas following their inundation by a marine transgression in the fifth century. These enclosures were ditched and embanked and they could be the nuclei from which subsequent medieval settlement developed. The reclamation of surrounding areas seems to have been organised from these places and the villages that followed often developed at their edges, with their churches sometimes being within the oval enclosures. In other cases, the enclosures may have names associated with religious centres (Rippon, 1997). Archaeological work at the planned medieval village of Shapwick, near Glastonbury shows that the

nucleated settlement was preceded by a 'lost' church located, perhaps at a former pagan site, well outside the area where the village developed. Shapwick gained its own village church in 1330. Historical research revealed that Shapwick probably had a minster and that by Domesday it was the *caput* or chief place for a number of estates in the Polden Hills. Several of the associated fields and furlongs had habitative names (i.e. ones that are associated with settlement), like Chester, Cot, Croft, Wick or Worthy, and these furlongs contain scatters of pottery of Roman and tenth century date. The evidence suggests a dispersed pattern of settlement that was reorganised to produce a planned village set out to a ladder-like plan with a brook forming the central axis of the settlement. The junctions of the streets forming the 'rungs' and the brook seemed to have the main concentration of tenth century finds. It is possible that following St Dunstan's reorganisation

Table 7.2 The coincidence of major aspects of change

Period of change	Nature of change
AD 850–1050 continuing to 1200	Nucleation of settlement in many regions with village formation and abandonment of hamlets.
AD 850–1050 continuing to 1200	Establishment of open field farming systems in most lowland localities, over-running pre-existing fields.
Ninth century onwards	Replacement of the minster church system of ecclesiastical organisation with another, based on parishes.

of Glastonbury Abbey and the tenth century expansion of the Wessex economy, monks may have reorganised the settlement pattern, removing peasants from their dispersed holdings and concentrating them in villages (Selkirk, 1997).

It is becoming plain that, around the period of the Viking raids or perhaps shortly after, there was a quite widespread re-organisation of settlement in England, associated with the abandonment of dispersed farmsteads and hamlets and the resettlement of their occupants in (regulated) nucleated villages. These traumatic changes in the countryside were roughly paralleled by other revolutions affecting the organisation of agriculture and of worship, as summarised in Table 7.2.

The link between the nucleation of settlement in many regions and the establishment of open field systems of farming is not coincidental, 'but arises from the functional connection between them. If land in a defined territory was to be laid out in great expanses of arable, then any small settlements scattered about the landscape could

have formed an obstruction and their inhabitants would have been encouraged or forced to move to a central place' (Lewis *et al.*, 1997 p.203).

Dispersed settlement is no less complex than nucleated settlement. According to established wisdom, three forms of dispersed settlement can be found in areas in which nucleated settlement predominates: as surviving relics of an ancient pattern of dispersed settlement which precedes the introduction of villages to the region; as archaeological traces of an ancient dispersed pattern which has now almost entirely vanished and which was largely gone by Domesday; and as a secondary form of settlement resulting from the colonisation of land in the centuries before AD 1300 by colonists from pre-existing nucleated villages in the adjacent, more fully exploited areas (Taylor, 1995).

Taylor also describes how dispersed settlements could be created on medieval fields, with selions being converted into tofts. Small settlements could form when large landowners carved off portions of manors to create sub-manors or separate long lease-holdings.

Hamlets with regular plans could have resulted from such initiatives and 'Lordly control might also have been necessary if such settlements were established within existing arable with all the subsequent disruption both to the fields themselves and to the access arrangements that this would have involved' (p.33). It seems, in fact, that dispersed settlements could develop in a variety of ways, depending upon local circumstances. In East Anglia, medieval increases in the pressure of population upon resources resulted in a migration from villages to greens and commons, where pasture and common grazing were more readily available and where new hamlets formed. In the neighbouring East Midlands, where the regulation of land was stronger, this was less apparent (Davison, 1990 p.67).

Table 7.3   Significant elements in settlement place-names

Element	Meaning
-ton (OE *tūn*)	A small estate or a lord's enclosure.
Cot,-cote(s) -cot (OE *cot*)	Cottage, but more often a sheep house in the northern uplands.
-thorpe (ON *thorp*)	Subordinate settlement.
-wick (OE *wīc*)	Various meanings. Sometimes an outlying farm or a building used for particular purposes. Particularly in the West Country, -wick and –wickham names are often close to Romano-British settlements. Wick names can also denote sheep farms.
-worth (OE *worth*)	Enclosure.
Carl-, Charl- (OE *ceorl*)	Settlement for slaves, probably founded to accommodate the churls of the manor.
Barton (OE *beretun*)	Outlying grain farm subsidiary to main settlement or manor.
-burgh (OE *burh*)	Stronghold, but could be no more than a moated manor.
-chester (OE *ceaster*)	Site associated with the Roman occupation.
-ham (OE *ham*)	Homestead, settlement, but can derive from OE *hamm*, a meadow. –hamton is a home farm.
Stow, -stow (OE *stow*)	Holy place, assembly site.
-toft (ON *topt*)	Site of a house plot.
-stoke (OE *stoc*)	Secondary settlement, holy site.
-stead (OE *stede*)	A place or site. –hamstead is a homestead.
Tref-, tre- (Cornish *trey*)	Large farm.
Lys- (Cornish *lis*)	Hall, court, administrative centre.
Bod- (Cornish *bod*)	Minor hamlet.
Ker- (Cornish *ker*)	Fortified homestead.

Deciphering village England

It is now known with certainty that such Anglo-Saxons as may have settled in England in the fifth century and subsequent periods did not establish a dense scatter of nucleated villages from which an assault upon the surrounding 'wildernesses' could be launched. Instead, a dispersed settlement pattern was developed during the early Saxon period, with many similarities to the choice of locations favoured by indigenous people. From the ninth century onwards, many locations experienced an implosion of

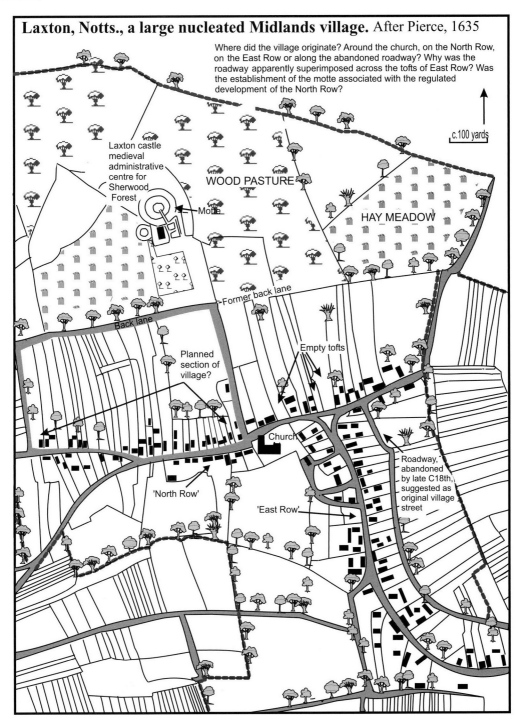

Laxton, Notts., a large nucleated Midlands village. After Pierce, 1635

Where did the village originate? Around the church, on the North Row, on the East Row or along the abandoned roadway? Why was the roadway apparently superimposed across the tofts of East Row? Was the establishment of the motte associated with the regulated development of the North Row?

c.100 yards

Laxton castle medieval administrative centre for Sherwood Forest

Motte

WOOD PASTURE

HAY MEADOW

Former back lane

Back lane

Planned section of village?

Empty tofts

Church

Roadway, abandoned by late C18th, suggested as original village street

'North Row'

'East Row'

Map 7.1   Laxton, Nottinghamshire, a large nucleated Midlands village. Large villages often have very complicated structures. The text on the map introduces some of the questions raised by the layout. Derived from a survey by Mark Pierce in 1635.

settlement, as outlying farmsteads and hamlets were abandoned and people gravitated to newly created villages standing in the English vales and plains like the great collective farms of the latter-day Ukraine.

The main areas affected show some correlation with the areas best-suited for the cultivation of grain, while the period of the changes was one in which documents containing precise descriptions of territorial boundaries proliferated. Might it be, there-

fore, that some challenges of an ecological nature underlay the changes, and that as land became scarce and more closely guarded so a new system of rural production was instituted to improve the efficiency of peasant agriculture? Certainly, the switch from scattered individual holdings to 'collectivised' or communal farming will have allowed simpler and more effective arrangements for the fallowing of land and the pasturing of stock on open field land after the harvest. All the new arrangements could not have occurred spontaneously; they had to be masterminded. The new villages were, therefore, planned creations, with their housing provisions, their road patterns, church and administrative centre (manor) all designed and positioned as part of a strategy determined, one can only assume, by the lord and his officials.

Map 7.2   Two polyfocal villages. These two North Yorkshire villages formed in the fairly recent period. In Birstwith the forces of growth and nucleation were insufficient to produce a continuously built-up form, though in Darley expansion associated firstly with water-powered industry and secondly by modern housing developments bridged the gaps between the discrete agricultural hamlets which are the oldest components of the village. From Muir (1999).

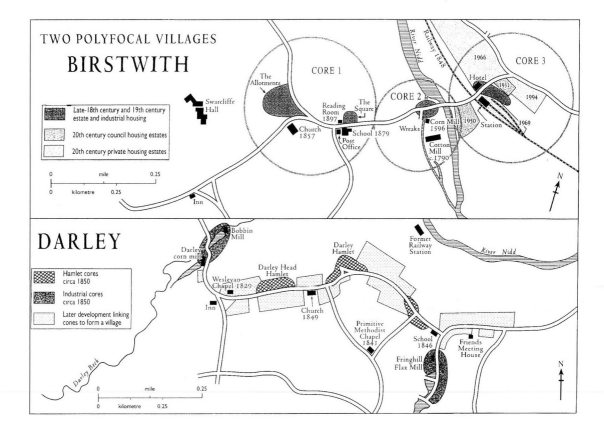

Until well past the middle of the present century, simple stereotypes were used to classify and interpret villages: nucleated or linear, green or lacking a green and so on. Subsequently, the simplistic perceptions of the past have yielded to more sophisticated interpretations (Taylor, 1992). During the last quarter of a century, much more effective concepts have been applied to the task of interpreting villages.

Firstly one should attempt to discover whether, and to what extent, a village is 'polyfocal'. The concept of polyfocality was devised by Taylor (1977) on the basis of extensive fieldwork in Dorset, Cambridgeshire, Northamptonshire and elsewhere in southern and Midland England. He showed that many, probably most, villages have not grown by the accretion of settlement around a single nucleus or core. Instead, villages tend to consist of a partial or complete amalgamation of previously discrete territories associated with different centres. Churches, manors, priories, greens, ponds, hamlets and various other foci could each attract settlement that would later be assimilated into a single village. In this way, the individual nuclei could represent stages in the transition from dispersed to nucleated settlement that is described in the preceding section.

In the most obvious examples of polyfocal villages the original components are plainly defined, as with Culworth and Brime in Northamptonshire, the two foci being linked by a market-place inserted between them in 1264. Usually, the situation is more difficult and one must look at the village landscape on the ground and in maps of different ages. A search is made for bounded units which may previously have been free-standing, like a minster church and its precinct, an assemblage of toft rows forming a planned settlement component or a collection of dwellings surrounding a former green. Once the fundamental components of a polyfocal village have become established, some surge of energy is needed to fuse them together. Frequently, this derived from rural population growth, though in cases like Darley in North Yorkshire the early phases of water-powered industrialisation allowed the expansion which brought the different settlement elements into physical contact (Muir, 1999).

A second consideration for those engaged in researching village morphology is the possibility—not so remote as one might suppose—that the village has shifted from its original situation (Taylor, 1978). In times when the only building of real value and permanence in a settlement was its stone church, mobility was a more acceptable option and settlements would drift or be relocated in order to exploit new opportunities. Research shows that frequently these opportunities concerned market locations, with villagers being resettled in roadside locations which were considered to have better trading potentials, often after their lords had obtained market charters. This may have happened at Ripley, North Yorkshire (Muir 1998), where the village was moved from an economically unattractive situation terraced into the face of a river bluff and redeveloped astride an ancient routeway. It also took place at Caxton in Cambridgeshire:

There is no doubt that the village has moved from its original site to a more commercially attractive position. Its earlier site is still clearly marked by the almost-isolated parish church, a network of existing and abandoned lanes, earthworks of former closes and extensive spreads of early-medieval occupation debris. The village itself lies 500 metres (545 yds) to the north-east of the church, on either side of the Old North Road. None of the sites of the three early-medieval manor houses is in this village, all are now-abandoned moated sites which lie some distance from it . . . In 1248 . . . Baldwin de Freville was granted a charter to hold a weekly market at Caxton. It is therefore a possibility that Caxton was moved from its original site to the main through road of the area, as a deliberate attempt by de Freville to benefit from the commercial possibilities of the road. (Taylor, 1982 pp.24–5)

The obtaining of a market charter could lead to changes in the layout of a village without any shift of location being involved, for example with the enforced demolition of dwellings to create a space to accommodate a market square or green, as must have happened at Masham, North Yorkshire, where the rectangular market square overran Saxon burials. In East Anglia, as has been seen, settlement shifts appear to have been associated with a shortage of common pasture, resulting in settlements being re-established around greens (Wade-Martins, 1975).

As well as the drifts that were associated with the re-siting of villages, there were others that involved a re-orientation upon a fixed site. These realignments were frequently associated with changes in the relative significance of routeways of different kinds, whether between water and road transport or shifting priorities within the road network. Hampsthwaite, North Yorkshire, for example, developed along a Roman routeway leading to a fording place on the River Nidd which locally became part of the main York to Lancaster road. Hostelries for travellers were established and this cross-valley orientation persisted until fairly modern times, when movement *along* the river valley became more important than travel *across* it. In the twentieth century, new housing development followed this valley axis and the village developed a cross-like layout produced by the intersection of new and old axes (Muir, 1999).

Evidence of settlement shifts comes in a variety of forms. The existence of a church or of church ruins in a place outside the village is suggestive, particularly if settlement earthworks or concentrations of pottery are associated with the church. A survey of charter evidence may allow a partial reconstruction of the earlier geography of the locality. One might find descriptions of the courses of routeways, allowing discoveries to be made about places which were upon or not upon roads at particular periods in time, as when, some time between 1157 and 1173, Bernard, clerk of Ripley, North Yorkshire, gave the monks of Fountains Abbey a road 40 feet wide from the bridge on Ripley Beck beside the house of Thomas of Ulecotes to the causeway of Dalbec near their grange at Cayton (Fountains Chartulary p.154). Where a move has involved a drift rather than a 'jump', the stages in the migration may be apparent as pottery scatters of successive ages tracing the drift across the village fields. Efforts can be made to reconstruct ridge and furrow and furlong patterns, in an attempt to discover if a shifted village has been superimposed upon an established field system. Changes of orientation can be reflected in the building composition of the settlement, with the older buildings being concentrated on one alignment and the newer buildings, on another (unless the switch occurred at a period earlier than any surviving buildings). Normally the church will be the oldest building in the village and it is likely to reveal an association with the older rather than the younger alignment.

A third consideration in interpreting villages is that many settlements have shrunk or display signs of shrinkage. The earthworks of tofts or of closes associated with holloways or still-surviving roads and lying outside the currently settled area of a village are very likely to reveal a phase when the settlement was more extensive. Occasionally, it may be possible to relate the contraction to a specific misfortune that

Figure 7.6   The ruined flint-walled church marking the site of Egmere deserted medieval village in Norfolk. By 1603 the village here had dwindled to just one household and in the previous year the church and chancel were said to have been decayed and profaned by the lord of the manor, Sir Nicholas Bacon.

Table 7.4   Evidence of village evolution

Factor	Evidence
Polyfocal structure	Different nuclei, like greens, manorial complexes, units of planned development etc. are embedded in the village layout.
Settlement shifts	Evidence of church buildings, settlement earthworks and pottery concentrations at the original village site. Old documents locate the village elsewhere than on its current site.
Shrinkage	Settlement earthworks *beyond* the bounds of the currently settled area. Gaps in the rows of dwellings lining the roads. Detached churches and greens.
Planning	Settlements composed of toft rows with back lanes paralleling the through road. In the larger settlements grid-iron plans with right-angled road intersections reveal planning. Elongated greens that contain the through road or triangular market greens at road intersections may be found. Sections of planned development may be inserted into unregulated villages.

caused a significant reduction in the local population—such as environmental disruption or enclosure. In the case of Grinton in Swaledale the contraction affected what appears to have been a section of planned medieval development added to the existing village (Muir, 1999). Shrinkage occurred at all periods, and it may be detected in medieval documents—such as those concerned with the Poll Tax or manorial surveys—which record the population of settlements, and it may be picked up in the maps of the post-medieval centuries.

Where the decline of a settlement was relatively recent and related to factors such as Parliamentary Enclosure or the creation of landscape parks then estate, Enclosure, tithe and early Ordnance Survey maps may chart stages in the retreat of settlement. Shrinkage also affected lesser settlements, so that hamlets of the 'green' type have frequently contracted to farmsteads—and with the enclosure of the green, only the place-name, like Clapham Green, North Yorkshire, remains to reveal the former situation. Shrunken village sites should be approached with an open mind and one should be sure that the evidence of desertion discovered adjacent to an existing village relates to dwellings and closes that were originally once part of *that* village and not of a different and completely defunct predecessor on the site. Taylor (1992 p.12) showed that earthworks directly attributed to nearby Coombe Keynes, in Dorset, were actually those of the lost settlement of Southcombe, a component of the polyfocal settlement of Coombe Keynes.

Finally, regulation or planning can have exerted a considerable effect upon a village landscape. Such regulation could occur at any time or several times in the history of the settlement, it might affect all or just a part of the village, and it could be plainly evident in the layout or virtually invisible. Whatever the period of the planning, regulation was always more likely in settlements which were entirely controlled by a single landowner. The influence of the lord upon the landscape could take a variety of forms. Firstly, there were the less deliberate instances associated with the establishment of settlement cores around different manor houses, contributing to the emergence of a polyfocal village. Secondly: 'In the period around the time of Domesday Book we presume the slaves were being settled on holdings of land, and this provided the lords

with the occasion to measure out plots for peasant houses on part of the demesne, ideally near to the manor house' (Lewis *et al.*, 1997 p.205). While slaves could easily have been settled wherever the lord or his agents chose, it is not clear how villeins and free tenants also came to be established in the agricultural dormitory villages erected on the demesne.

As to the nature of the medieval village founders,

Perhaps the type of lord most likely to have pursued order and efficiency might have been the numerous lesser aristocrats, thegns in the pre-Conquest period, knights and minor gentry in the succeeding centuries, whose small manors gave them the incentive to make the most profitable use of limited resources, and

Figure 7.7   The shrunken village at Little Minting in Lincolnshire. Gaps have widened between the groups of dwellings and the earthworks of empty closes fill most of the scene.
© Cambridge UC (CFI 84).

whose continued residence on the spot made them knowledgeable of the local terrain. They had both an interest and the ability to re-organise in detail the land and peasant holdings. (Lewis *et al.*, 1997 p.207)

The contribution of the local lord must have varied from place to place. In some cases a thoroughgoing reorganisation of the estate will have involved a creation of new, planned villages, while in others, the establishment of a manor, a church and, perhaps,

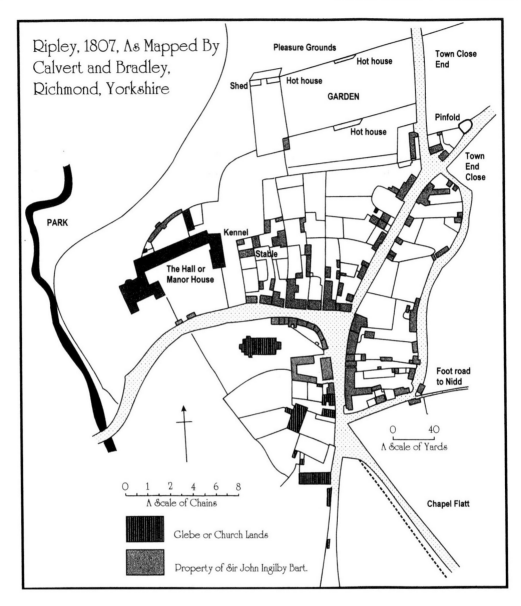

Map 7.3 *Ripley as mapped in 1807. The village appears to have a planned structure, perhaps dating from the relocation of a much earlier settlement and its development in association with a market grant. The roads leading southwards cut ridged ploughland. Within a couple of decades of this map being drawn, Ripley was substantially rebuilt by its owners, the street layout being largely retained, but the pattern of houses being completely transformed. From a map by Calvert and Bradley of Richmond, North Yorkshire, 1807.*

a settlement for slaves may have stimulated the tenants to complete the creation of a nucleated village.

Certain types of regulated settlements are easily recognisable, but there remains the probability that other settlements were reorganised in ways that leave no obvious traces. They may have been built to curving and undisciplined plans, or else the planned alignments may have been masked with the passage of time. Mevagissey, in Cornwall, is a late medieval planned settlement origin-ally organised around a rectangular green beside the harbour, though the subsequent encroachment of buildings upon the green masked its origins (Taylor, 1983 p.188).

The conventional hallmarks of planning include the organisation of dwellings and house plots into 'toft rows', in which the dwellings were aligned along a roadside and their tofts ran backwards from the road to terminate at a common boundary line. Back lanes, running parallel to the through-road and forming the rear toft boundaries, are also a feature of planned villages, as are right-angled intersections. Greens were frequently included in the package, some-times as elongated rectangular features flanking the through-road, and sometimes as triangles accommodated in the fork of a road. '[A] regular plan demands the estab-lishment of at least four, but more usually eight principal points: these form the pegs for a series of principal lines . . . In practical terms pacing would be sufficiently accurate to establish linear distances, but laying out even a reasonable set of right angles can pose difficulties . . . It is probable that rural

communities used land rods, which varied from locality to locality, as basic modules' (Roberts, 1987 p. 196). Roberts (1972) considered that a land rod of 20 feet (6.1 m) was employed to lay out the village of Middlestone in Co Durham and, as described, West Cotton in Northamptonshire began around 950 as a small settlement on a site divided into regular acre, half-acre and quarter-acre plots. Some regulation of rural settlements took place before the Norman Conquest. By 1175 the creation of regular nucleated villages in north-east England seems to have been accomplished, many of these places being created in the rehabili-tation of estates in areas where earlier settlements had been devastated by the Harrying of the North. The creation of planned settlements continued through the medieval era and into modern times, when a range of industrial factory villages were founded.

In addition to those settlements that are completely regulated, sections of planned development were sometimes inserted into apparently unplanned or 'organic' settle-ments. These additions and redevelopments

Table 7.5   Forms of village greens

Origin of the green	Diagnostic features
As a space provided to accommodate a medieval market. Often dating from the thirteenth century, but up to the seventeenth century in the northern uplands.	Could have a regular rectangular or triangular outline. May nest between two lanes as though intervening housing was demolished. Might retain a market cross or cross base.
An original feature of a planned village, particularly in north-east England: ribbons of green flanking a through-road, providing grazing for the local livestock.	Plainly incorporated into the layout of through-road and toft rows. The green may be reduced by encroaching buildings or front gardens.
An area of common pasture which has attracted settlement around its margins. Sometimes an area colonised, encircled and detached from a larger common.	Irregular shape with the surrounding dwellings arranged in a straggling linear form. May display earthworks resulting from mining or digging clay on an old common.
A tiny piece of common land in a road junction or roadside used to accommodate public utilities like a pinfold, stocks, whipping post or lock-up.	As described to left.

could be for commercial or residential purposes. At once perhaps the most and least obvious planned addition to a village landscape may be the village green itself. During the two centuries or so following the Norman Conquest there was an intensification in commercial activity and at the level of the village this was expressed in the purchase of the necessary charters by lords seeking to prosper from charges or 'fines' levied on market traders. 'Hundreds of villages, all over England, acquired these market grants which date mainly from the thirteenth century, when trade was at its most buoyant. Few of the markets succeeded and hardly any survived the economic decline of the fourteenth century. Yet many left their mark on the villages. Numerous lords created market places in their villages and these often altered the shape of the village entirely' (Taylor, 1983 pp.159–60). Apparently it was common, when a suitable open space beside the through-road was lacking, for rows of dwellings to be demolished to free land for a market venue, as may have happened at Sheriff Hutton, North Yorkshire, after the Nevilles secured a market charter in 1378. Cottenham, in Cambridgeshire, may have originated in the ninth or tenth century as a small planned village, and in the twelfth century it gained a planned extension associated with a triangular green (Ravensdale, 1974 p.122).

Deserted settlements

Since the 1960s, the results of air photography and local archaeological and historical surveys have shown that deserted villages are very numerous. Rather than being regarded as stable, the village must be re-appraised as a form of settlement that was extremely responsive to prevailing circumstances. Whereas before the Middle Saxon period, desertion was the virtually inevitable consequence of settlement, medieval settlements were permanent, yet frequently prone to perish or diminish in the face of environmental or cultural hostility. These hostilities took a variety of forms, with the most commonly attributed causes of desertion—pestilence and war—actually being relatively unimportant. An understanding of the nature of deserted settlement remains will be greatly assisted if one can identify the reasons why the place was abandoned. Different causes for desertion tended to occur at different times, so that if the cause is identified an approximate date for desertion may sometimes be deduced.

Little is known about the villages and hamlets destroyed in the Harrying of the North (though perhaps the distribution of early medieval churches may assist in revealing the pattern). In any northern locality that is known to have been acquired by the Cistercians, monastic evictions must be considered as a possible cause of village desertion. Occurring before the formation of villages had reached completion, this was one of the earliest causes of extensive desertion. A few settlements, like Herleshow near Fountains Abbey, were removed because they intruded upon the solitude of the new Cistercian foundations, but many more were cleared away as the monks established networks of granges and lodges upon lands donated by the aristocracy (Donkin, 1964).

On the whole, the environmental and cultural conditions of the twelfth and thirteenth centuries favoured the village, with the climate being mild and fairly dry, while marginal lands were being colonised and the reorganisation of rural population into nucleated settlements was still continuing. At the start of the fourteenth century a new climatic regime, associated with cloudy, cool, cyclonic conditions, was established. While the new physical conditions produced a retreat from the agricultural margins and inundations of coastal settlements, the century also witnessed firstly an incursion of Scottish war bands into northern England and then the arrival of the Pestilence or Black

Figure 7.8   The earthworks of dwellings, tofts and ridged ploughland at the site of the deserted village of Argam in East Yorkshire, destroyed by the Cistercian monks of Meaux and Bardney abbeys. © Cambridge UC (CBQ 82).

Death in 1348. Against a background of agricultural retreat and economic contraction, the outbreaks of Pestilence removed 40 per cent or more of the population.

Relatively few villages, however, emerge as plague victims. Plenty had their populations severely diminished by the Black Death and some were temporarily abandoned. Most retained a population or else were resettled after a period of desertion. The Pestilence did, none the less, pave the way for desertions on a massive scale during the Tudor centuries. A situation of labour surplus had been transformed into one in which labour was scarce, more expensive and less tractable. Faced with a community of fractious tenants and labourers, many lords were tempted to evict the arable population and reorganise their estate as a

pastoral concern, grassing over the communal ploughlands and pulling down the villages as part of a wider shift from arable farming. The impact of such Tudor evictions on rural England was immense, with some parts of the country, like the Yorkshire Wolds and parts of the Midlands, still deriving much of their landscape personalities from village desertion. Throughout lowland England, the Tudor clearance is the most likely explanation for any unattributed village desertion. From the Elizabethan era

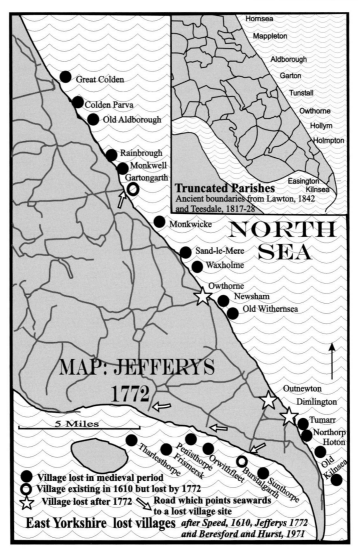

Map 7.4   East Yorkshire lost villages. Villages inundated by the retreat of the Holderness coast. Based on Maps by Speed, 1610, Jefferys, 1772, and information in Beresford and Hurst (1971).

until well into the nineteenth century, emparking was a significant cause of depopulations, with the villagers domiciled in the intended territory of the new park either being rehoused, often in a showpiece village outside the park gates, or else put on the road. Subsequently, the reorganisation of tenancy patterns, Parliamentary Enclosure or the abandonment of mining or quarrying

in a locality could lead to desertion, but never on the scale of the Tudor clearances.

Where they survive as earthwork features, deserted medieval villages are likely to display several distinctive components:

Holloways (hollow-ways)   The courses of former roads are likely to be hollowed or worn into the countryside to produce a flat-bottomed trough. The degree to which the old road was incised would depend on the toughness of the underlying geology, the amount of traffic which used the road and the length of time the road was in use, as well as the nature of the traffic—the ratios

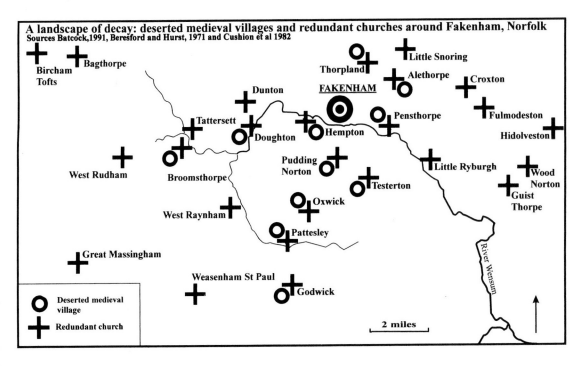

A landscape of decay: deserted medieval villages and redundant churches around Fakenham, Norfolk
Sources Batcock,1991, Beresford and Hurst, 1971 and Cushion et al 1982

Bircham Tofts
Bagthorpe
Dunton
Tattersett
Doughton
West Rudham
Broomsthorpe
West Raynham
Great Massingham
Weasenham St Paul
Godwick
Pattesley
Oxwick
Pudding Norton
Testerton
Hempton
FAKENHAM
Thorpland
Little Snoring
Alethorpe
Croxton
Penthorpe
Fulmodeston
Hidolveston
Little Ryburgh
Wood Norton
Guist Thorpe
River Wensum

O Deserted medieval village
✝ Redundant church

2 miles

of pedestrians, farm animals, shod livestock and tumbrils or wagons. Erosion by passing traffic was most effective on convex slopes, so that routeways that were scarcely hollowed on level ground became quite deeply incised into hill and valley sides. Sometimes a holloway may be traced for some distance beyond the former village, suggesting its origin/destination, while the discovery of a holloway does not necessarily imply the presence of a deserted settlement nearby. Lesser holloways may intersect a main village through-road and it is necessary to decide whether these were contemporary side-roads or subsequent additions to the pattern of routeways. Back lanes were often found in villages, as were tracks serving as access ways to the surrounding fields.

House platforms Holloways and house platforms are usually the most obvious indicators of deserted settlements. The platforms, marking the areas where dwellings once stood, take the form of horizontal shelves that are most easily seen on sloping ground. These shelves can be pronounced or

Map 7.5   A landscape of decay: deserted medieval villages and redundant churches around Fakenham, Norfolk. The map shows one of the most remarkable concentrations of deserted villages. Developed from Batcock (1991), Beresford and Hurst (1971) and Cushion et al. (1982).

else be difficult to interpret until the most favourable vantage point is found: when they are roughly at eye level, a horizontal line of parched grass or shining grass stems may render the platforms quite obvious. On the surfaces of shelves, a search for rectangular features can reveal the outlines of dwellings, with corners and the little dips which were entrances often being the most obvious features. Other dips may mark the pathways that linked the homes to the roads. Pottery fragments of different ages found amongst the soft earth of molehills or outside rabbit burrows will be invaluable for dating the period of occupation.

Other features Ditches, appearing as shallow, narrow troughs, often defined the house plots or closes within a village. Greens normally appear as level areas beside or in the angle of holloways. They sometimes contain ponds, clay pits or quarries.

Associated features The earthworks of features associated with the manorial economy often lie beside those of the former village itself. Fishponds were rectangular or trapezoidal in form, shallow, and they existed as scoops or, more commonly, as ponds contained by earthen banks. Frequently a short chain of ponds, which progressively increased in size, would be built, allowing fish to be netted and moved from pond to pond, as they grew larger. Such ponds could be fed by streams or springs, and sluices, perhaps surviving as nicks in the earthworks, allowed water levels to be regulated. The manor house—or the houses of other substantial members of the village community—could be surrounded on four, or fewer, sides by wet moats, existing now as substantial, steep-sided troughs that may or may not still contain water.

REFERENCES

Batcock, N. 'The ruined and disused churches of Norfolk' *East Anglian Archaeology Report 51* (Norfolk: Norfolk Archaeology Unit, 1991).

Beresford, M.W. and Hurst, J.G. *Deserted medieval villages* (London: Lutterworth Press, 1971).

Chapman, A. 'Raunds', paper given to the International Medieval Congress, Leeds (1998).

Cushion *et al.* 'Some deserted village sites in Norfolk' East Anglian Archaeology Report 14 (Norfolk: Norfolk Archaeology Unit, 1982) pp.40–107.

Davison, A. *The Evolution of Settlement in Three Parishes in South-East Norfolk* East Anglian Archaeology Report No. 49 (Norfolk: Norfolk Archaeology Unit, 1990).

Donkin, R.A. 'The Cistercian grange in England in the twelfth and thirteenth centuries, with special reference to Yorkshire' *Studia Monastica* 6 (1964) pp.95–144.

Foard, G. 'Planned villages or planned towns', paper given to the International Medieval Congress, Leeds (1998).

Lewis, C., Mitchell-Fox, P. and Dyer, C. *Village, Hamlet and Field* (Manchester: Manchester University Press, 1997).

Muir, R. 'Villages in the Yorkshire Dales' *Northern History* 38 (1998) pp.1–16.

Muir, R. 'The villages of Nidderdale' *Landscape History 20* (1999) pp.65–82.

Ravensdale, J.R. *Liable to Floods* (Cambridge: Cambridge University Press, 1974).

Rippon, S. *Severn Estuary* (Leicester: Leicester University Press, 1997).

Roberts, B.K. 'Village plans in County Durham: a preliminary statement' *Medieval Archaeology* 16 (1972) pp.35–6.

Roberts, B.K. *The Making of the English Village* (Harlow: Longman, 1987).

Roberts, B.K., Wrathmell, S. and Stocker, D. 'Rural settlement in England: an English Heritage mapping project' *Ruralia I, Pamatky acheologicke—Supplementum* 5, Prague (1996) pp.72–9.

Selkirk, A. 'The Shapwick Project' *Current Archaeology* 8 (1997) pp.244–54.

Taylor, C. 'Polyfocal settlement and the English village' *Medieval Archaeology* 21 (1977) pp.189–93.

Taylor, C. 'Aspects of village mobility in medieval and later times' in S. Limbrey and J.G. Evans (eds) *The Effect of Man on the Landscape: The Lowland Zone*, CBA Research Report 2 (York: Council for British Archaeology 1978) pp.126–34.

Taylor, C. 'Medieval market grants and village morphology' *Landscape History* 4 (1982) pp.21–8.

Taylor, C. *Village and Farmstead* (London: George Philip, 1983).

Taylor, C. 'Medieval rural settlement: changing perceptions' *Landscape History* 14 (1992) pp.5–17.

Taylor, C. 'Dispersed settlement in nucleated areas' *Landscape History* 17 (1995) pp.27–34.

Wade-Martins, P. 'The origins of rural settlement in East Anglia' in P.J. Fowler (ed.) *Recent Work in Rural Archaeology* (Bradford-on-Avon: Moonraker Press, 1975).

CHAPTER 8

Reading the Fieldscape

Fields are the most obvious features of the countryside—and it is often the obvious that is overlooked. Their shapes, sizes and patterns are the distinctive products of different stages in the long agricultural exploitation of the landscape, while the names that they carry can sometimes provide confirmation for a pet theory or open a window on an unexpected chapter in landscape evolution. Previously, research into the study of fields was unbalanced. Huge amounts of earnest attention were paid to the problems concerning the origin of open field systems, and theories were defended with passion. While this debate continued across the decades, relatively little attention was paid to the many other questions concerning fields, and the realisation that many parts of the country are underlain by vast networks of co-axial prehistoric fields has come fairly recently. Also, the detailed surveying of small-scale features of the working countryside is now giving a better understanding of farming at the local level and of the differences between agriculture in the various regions and localities.

Fields exist for a variety of reasons:

a. to divide a land unit into functional sub-units suitable for use at a given level of technology;
b. to give a physical expression to aspects of the property system;
c. to confine livestock in suitable groups and to prevent them from destroying crops or interfering with each other.

A study of field sizes and shapes in a country like England, with a history of agriculture extending back for almost 7,000 years, reveals a great diversity of types. This reflects the ways in which changes in the nature of farming produced a response in the fieldscape. Factors which would affect field patterns are summarised in Table 8.1.

Prehistoric fields

The existence of prehistoric fields and farming has been known for a long time; discoveries of polished axes of flint and stone and the recognition of the mis-named 'Celtic' fields as prehistoric fields verified the facts. It has taken significantly longer for an appreciation of the dramatic extent of ancient farming and the large-scale planning often associated with its development to dawn. The traditional view of prehistoric farmers as people dwarfed by the wilderness is evident in this extract from a relatively progressive account of 1945: 'There were homesteads and settlements, however flimsy, with their cultivated plots; there were conspicuous entrenchments cutting the chalk; there were domestic herds not only noticeable in themselves, but helping also to keep vegetation in check and hill-tops open, and with their good stone axes men could even nibble away a little at the fringes of the forest' (Hawkes, 1987 p.17). The pre-occupation with pioneering similes masked more remarkable aspects of prehistoric farming. These concerned the way in which a land of forest and marsh was converted into one in which the enclosed fieldscape must frequently have stretched from horizon to horizon—and where power could be mobilised in ways that would extend one

Table 8.1   Factors that affect field patterns

Factor	Effect
Technology	Changes in technology urge changes to the field units. For example the replacement of oxen by horses, which had more stamina, allowed arable fields to be lengthened or joined up. Combine harvesters urged the removal of hedgerows to create huge, rectangular fields.
The system of farming	Private and communal systems of landholding will produce very different field patterns. For example, where livestock are grazed on fallowing communal ploughland then the land must be open and without field boundaries of a sort that would obstruct the animals.
The density of population	When high population densities are being supported, fields tend to be relatively small and intensively worked, while relatively low population numbers limit the systems of farming that can be practiced and favour large field units worked extensively. Under great population pressure, as in the thirteenth century, intensive exploitation can be found on quite marginal land.
The settlement pattern	Forms of farming requiring large inputs of communal labour or the pooling of communal resources were unlikely to develop in areas of dispersed settlement.
The distribution and potency of power	Where power is far-reaching and concentrated in the hands of a ruler or an elite, then efforts to reorganise countrysides under extensive systems of co-axial fields are likely. When there are high levels of local autonomy then field patterns that are both idiosyncratic and finely tuned to terrain details are likely as farmers pursue their own priorities and respect small-scale environmental differences.
Physical geography	Topographical and climatical factors will operate at various scales to condition the field patterns. With increases in the steepness of slopes, medieval ridge and furrow would sometimes be replaced by forms of contour ploughing to create strip lynchets. The creation of water meadows was conditioned by the availability of floodable valley bottom sites, while a susceptibility to wind- or frost-damage restricted the spread of orchards.

network of walls or hedgerows across a pre-existing agricultural country-side.

The revelation that in the Bronze Age there existed countrysides where the grain of the landscape was provided by co-axial networks (in which the constituent fields shared similar alignments) derived from work during the 1970s and 1980s on the field walls or hedge banks on Dartmoor known as 'reaves' (Fleming, 1988). There, systems of fields defined by reaves could be 4 miles in length and up to 18,500 acres (7,500 hectares) in area. It might have been imagined that such fieldscapes were associated with upland backwaters, but soon Williamson would use his technique of 'landscape regression' to identify a co-axial system in Norfolk (Williamson, 1987). In the 1990s, Fleming transferred his attention from Dartmoor to Swaledale, where on the moors around Reeth there were traces of parallel walls around 100 yards apart which formed a large system of land division and resembled the reaves of the south-west

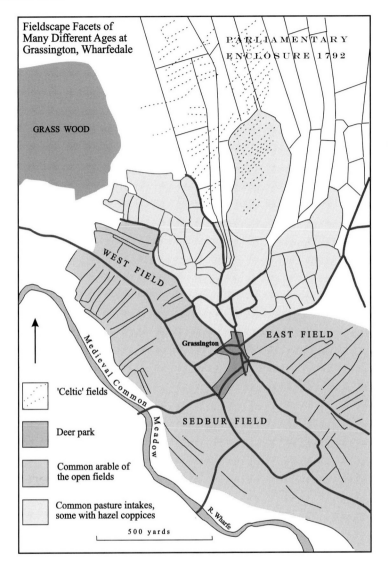

Map 8.1   Fieldscape facets of many different ages at Grassington, Wharfedale. This locality contains a remarkable collection of fossil and living fields, while a short distance away on the southern side of the Wharfe at Linton there are spectacular flights of strip lynchets.

(Fleming, 1998 p.18). Co-axial systems of varying dates can now be recognised in numerous parts of the Yorkshire Dales. In some localities, such as Grassington, late Iron Age field systems are associated with Bronze Age cairns, hinting that the cairns represent a Bronze Age clearance of land and that linked field systems may have been obscured by the late prehistoric patterns. The ability to regulate the patterns of colonisation and land division across vast areas was matched, in the Yorkshire Wolds at least, by the ability to exclude field networks from a huge tract of country, found to be devoid of any field traces, which may have been reserved as common or hunting territory (Stoertz, 1997 p.86).

There was no single form of field system and the surviving evidence of prehistoric

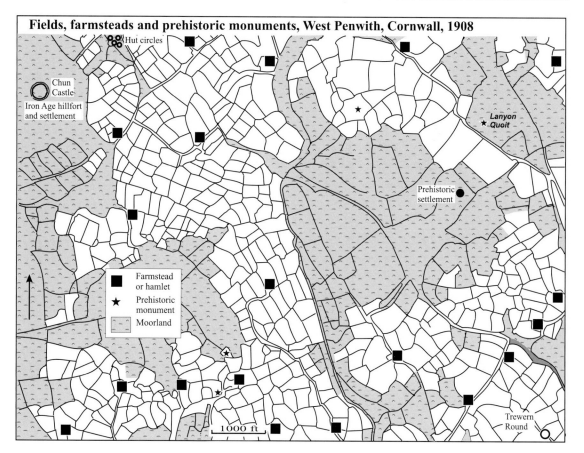

Fields, farmsteads and prehistoric monuments, West Penwith, Cornwall, 1908

Hut circles

Chun Castle
Iron Age hillfort and settlement

Lanyon Quoit

Prehistoric settlement

Farmstead or hamlet
★ Prehistoric monument
Moorland

1000 ft

Trewern Round

Map 8.2   Fields, farmsteads and prehistoric monuments, West Penwith, Cornwall, mapped in 1908. Most elements in the field network are probably prehistoric, and some may date back to the Bronze Age. Evidence from elsewhere in Cornwall suggests that many of the present farmsteads are occupying ancient farmstead sites.

land management—whether it be seen in air photographs or viewed from the ground—varies greatly in appearance just as the fields must have varied in function. Whatever the nature of the remains, their correct interpretation will depend upon an understanding of the then-prevailing system of land ownership and tenure. Differences in these factors will produce differences in field layouts and forms—as the evidence from the historical period plainly shows:

Any field system, and particularly a system of enclosed fields, represents a capital investment in the land; it represents too a commitment of expenditure to make that capital yield an income, whether of subsistence food or cash from surplus production. Well-farmed land, however, always gives more than income: it gives power. As always, the basic question of farming in prehistoric Britain comes down to 'Who owned the land?' (Fowler, 1981 p.47)

Extensive co-axial systems one associates with centralised power structures and grand acts of landscape reorganisation by kings, chieftains or their agents, while local complexes of irregular fields and paddocks seem to tell of semi-autonomous farming households.

Figure 8.1   In the Langdale area of the Lake District melting snow is picking out traces of earlier cultivation in the valley. Favourable conditions can be crucial to detecting former field patterns.

Prehistoric fields may survive in places where the land has subsequently experienced little or no subsequent ploughing. Consequently, they are associated with areas that were marginal to arable cultivation and they may not be typical of those patterns that existed in the richer locations that have experienced ploughing in the modern, medieval and Roman periods. The appearance of a relict field network is unlikely immediately to betray its age: the full lengths of overgrown walls forming the main axes of a co-axial system may not be apparent while the abandonment of a group of small medieval hillside closes may produce sub-rectangular patterns of earthworks quite similar to those associated with the 'Celtic' networks linked with prehistoric cultivation. Some networks are only visible as crop-marks or as soil-marks, while in other cases they are quite prominent in the countryside as viewed from the ground.

Where prehistoric fields are visible in this way they tend to be seen as lynchets or to be outlined by eroded boundary features or defined by a litter of rubble from tumbled walls. Reynolds notes that:

Most commonly these ancient fields are observable on the sides of hills and sloping ground where the rectangles, varying in size from less than a quarter of an acre (0.1 ha) to over an acre (0.4 ha) are marked out by lynchet boundaries. The lynchets are low banks which form through plough action and soil creep on the downhill side of the field. If another field is located immediately downslope the bank is accentuated by soil moving

away from the upper edge of the field. In
effect the lynchet has a positive element
where the soil gathers and a negative
element where the soil erodes away . . .
Excavation of some lynchets has shown
the presence of lines of stake-holes,
indicating that some fields were fenced
probably with interwoven saplings of
hazel or willow (1987 p.17).

Table 8.2 shows that prehistoric fields
exist in many forms other than the well-

known 'Celtic' fields of Wessex. They may be
detected on air photographs or in the field,
but the aerial images are likely to disclose
little about the ages of the features portrayed. From the ground, however, it may be
possible to deduce relative dates, as when
boundaries are seen to be over-ridden by
medieval ridge and furrow or drystone walls
and be destroyed or buried in the creation of
strip lynchets. Difficulties can, however,
result when it is found that similar
earthworks have been created at different

Table 8.2   The appearance of prehistoric fields

Nature of the remains	Examples and probable date
Small, roughly rectangular fields bounded by ditches and double-ditched trackways with grain storage pits associated with circular dwellings incorporated into the fieldscape, all invisible from the ground and emerging as crop-marks in lowland localities.	Numerous examples, mainly Iron Age or multi-period landscapes.
Networks of small, roughly rectangular and trapezoidal fields which are bounded by ditches and which may contain barrow cemeteries, the fields being visible only as crop-marks in lowland areas of arable farming.	Lawford and Mucking, Essex; Bronze Age.
Former walls that bounded networks of small, roughly rectangular enclosures now visible mainly as a litter of rubble distributed in a linear fashion which reflects the old wall alignments.	Grassington, North Yorkshire; probably Iron Age/Romano-British.
Lynchet banks surviving as earthworks on hillsides and outlining systems of small, rectangular fields.	Butser Hill, Hampshire, and Grassington, North Yorkshire; various ages, mainly Iron Age?
Low, parallel banks roughly 25–50 metres apart running up slope roughly at right angles to a river or stream and underlying medieval ridge and furrow in places.	Wharfedale, Wensleydale; parts of co-axial field systems of uncertain age.
Broad, low parallel walls, perhaps originally crowned with hedges, running upslope to similar cross walls in upland areas which may have served as winter grazing areas below the open commons.	Mid-Swaledale; Iron Age, but similar networks were created in the same area in the Bronze Age.
Small, irregular, oval walled enclosures serving as paddocks for associated circular farmsteads, forming small, 'frogspawn-like' groupings in open upland country.	Burton Moor, North Yorkshire, and the granite moors of the south-west; Bronze Age.
Low banks of earth and stones, perhaps originally hedged, defining very extensive networks of co-axial fields.	The reave systems of Dartmoor; Bronze Age.

periods in time: remains of small huts with associated enclosures seen in upland areas of prehistoric farming might, for example, be medieval shepherd huts with associated sheepfolds (Horne and MacLeod, 1995 p.35). Ancient field systems can also be identified through cartographical analysis. Williamson (1987) employed a technique of landscape regression in his analysis of an area in south Norfolk which was traversed by the *Venta* to *Londinium* Roman road. Progressively older features were removed from tithe map of *c*. 1840 until the Roman road and a network of field boundaries remained. It appeared that the road had been superimposed diagonally across the

network, causing fields to be divided and corners detached. Given that the Roman road seemed to be an intrusion, it was concluded that the co-axial network of fields must predate the introduction of the road. This interpretation has been challenged. Welch (1992) suggested that the field system might be Anglo-Saxon and have been set out at a time when the Roman road was out of use (though a society that needed fields would surely also need every

Figure 8.2   Medieval ridge and furrow showing the characteristic 'reversed S' plan form at Padbury in Berkshire. © Cambridge UC (MOD).

useful road available to it). More recently, Hinton (1997) argued that the field shapes which survived into the nineteenth century were medieval and wrote: 'Until more evidence is available, however, those of us who are reluctant to believe in long-term continuity in lowland England will remain sceptical about the existence of an early Roman or pre-Roman field system that ignored the grain of the local topography but nevertheless survived for at least fifteen hundred years' (p.12). Even so, it is hard to imagine how the road/field relationship patterns could have formed were the road

---

Map 8.3   Open field system, Gamlingay, Cambridgeshire, as mapped in 1601. This is a 'classic' three-field system with communal meadow, hedged closes around the large village and outlying commons. Many other village field systems diverged from this norm.

not younger than the co-axial system. This technique for detecting prehistoric fields certainly merits more applications.

Medieval fieldscapes

While a few localities of England may have experienced centuriation during the Roman occupation, the pattern which existed until the middle Saxon period was essentially a prehistoric one, with countrysides divided by co-axial networks or by more localised divisions into small, roughly rectangular hedged (or walled) enclosures. Then, the reorganisation of this pattern and the introduction of open strip fields with plough ridges in many places would create a form of countryside that might evolve, but that would exist until long after the close of the Middle Ages: 'The open and commonable fields of much of the English Midlands remained in use for most townships until

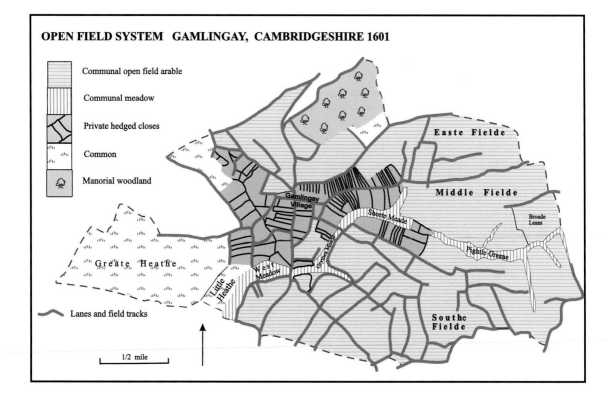

OPEN FIELD SYSTEM GAMLINGAY, CAMBRIDGESHIRE 1601

- Communal open field arable
- Communal meadow
- Private hedged closes
- Common
- Manorial woodland
- Lanes and field tracks

Easte Fielde

Middle Fielde

Broade Leaes

Shorte Meade

Pightle Greene

Gamlingay Village

Greate Heathe

Little Heathe

West Meadow

Southe Fielde

1/2 mile

the seventeenth century and for upwards half of them until the eighteenth century when they were enclosed by private Parliamentary acts' (Hall, 1994 p.94). Aspects of the open field system can be dated from historical and archaeological sources. The characteristic features of ridge and furrow are mentioned in charters of the tenth and eleventh centuries and a Wiltshire charter of 963 described 'single acres dispersed in a mixture here and there in common land' (Hooke, 1981 p.58). Words like 'furlong' (*furlang*), 'furrow' (*furh*) and 'acre' (*aecer*) were current in Old English. Ridge and furrow can be seen running under the earthworks of the William's Hill early Norman ringwork at Middleham in Wensleydale and beneath the eleventh century earthworks at Hen Domen, Montgomery. Ridging, which gave open field country its characteristic corrugated texture, was probably undertaken for various purposes, one of them to facilitate drainage. In 1975 Green drew attention to the coincidence of ridge and furrow and land recently affected by mole and tile drainage treatment. Contrary to the opinions of nineteenth century students like Seebohm and the Orwins, ridged open fields did not exist in England in the pre-Saxon period, and neither did they exist in the Anglo-Saxon homelands.

Open field farming seems to have originated in the years around 900, some 400–500 years after the Saxon migrations to England, and to have expanded during the centuries which followed: 'The link between nucleated villages and regular field systems is strengthened by the likelihood that they came into existence at about the same time. Most researchers would agree that the

Table 8.3 Components of open field farming

Unit	Nature and function
Plough ridge, ridge, rigg	An elongated ridge deliberately produced by ploughing with a mouldboard plough, usually in a clockwise direction, working outwards from the middle, and turning the soil inwards (i.e. ploughing in a clockwise spiral). The slightly curving shape in the form of a reversed 's' or 'c' reflects the use of long plough teams of six or more oxen, which had to be swung to the left leading into their turn to the right before the end of the ridge was reached. The typical ridge was 8×220 yards, though ridges around 5 yards wide were also common in some areas, like North Yorkshire.
Ridge and furrow	Ridges were separated by furrows or troughs, which were commonly aligned down-slope to facilitate drainage and which may have given some extra security against famine, with crops surviving in the furrows in dry years and on the crests of ridges in wet ones. The furrows served as drains and also marked the boundaries between adjacent ridges.
Selion, strip, land, rap, stich, paull	Generally, but not necessarily, identical to ridges, for selions could, following amalgamations, embrace more than one ridge. The selion was one of numerous such strips of ground tenanted by a peasant household and scattered throughout the open fields. The scattering gave a household an even distribution of land throughout the fields, which were farmed in a rotation wheat/barley–legumes–fallow. Too many strips in the fallowing field would have deprived the family of crops. Where *solschift* arrangements had guarded the allocation of the selions they were arranged in such a way that each household had the same neighbours in the fields as they did at home in the village. Groups of selions such as those groups forming the glebe or the demesne were defined by narrow ribbons of turf.

Table 8.3   Components of open field farming—continued

Unit	Nature and function
Headland, butt	A long mound at the end of the selions in a furlong which accumulated gradually from small quantities of soil shed by the plough or scraped from it when it was lifted after ploughing. Headlands form at the boundaries of two sets of ridges in different orientations, the heads of one set being smoothed over to form the first ridge of the other set.
Joint	An undulating bank formed of a double row of heads found at the junction of two furlongs with ridges running in roughly the same directions.
Ley	Land that was cultivated and then left to fallow under grass for a number of years.
Yardland, oxgang, bovate	A small medieval farm, with arable land amounting to very loosely 20 acres scattered throughout the open fields in roughly 70 selions or ridges. Taxation assessments seem to have been based on yardlands.
Furlong, shott, flat	A roughly rectangular block composed of parallel and adjacent selions lying within an open field.
Field	A large, unhedged area of land encompassing a collection of furlongs. The field was defined by a surrounding furrow. Normally all the land in a field would be subject to the same rotation, though in the post-medieval period this was not always the case. The number of fields varied; three was common, but two, four, five and six or more could be encountered.
Nucleated village	A dormitory for the farming labour force, facilitating contacts and planning between villagers and removing obstructions to farming in the form of intruding small settlements.

critical period lies somewhere between 850 and 1200 for both nucleation and the formation of the midland system, with a strong likelihood in our area that the change occurred in the first two centuries of the time span' (Lewis *et al.*, 1997 p.203). The system was complicated and existed in several variants, but its components and their relationships can be summarised as in Table 8.3.

Most of the features identified in Table 8.3 can be recognised as earthworks in places where they have been protected under pasture. There are also the cases where the system has been modified. Thus, for example, old headlands could be over-ploughed to join-up conventional ridges, creating new ones with double 'reversed-S'

plans. This might have taken place in response to the introduction of horses to the plough team, which had a greater stamina than oxen and could plough longer selions (Taylor, 1981 p.21). The ridged character of open field farmland tended to become intensified over the years, so that plough-land converted to pasture at an early date— say before the end of the medieval period— is less pronouncedly corrugated than later arable.

Grass, meanwhile, tended to become a more prominent feature of the open fields. Some grassland was created by mutual agreement as cow pasture for the village herd. Balks were bands of greensward serving as accessways, and they became more numerous than the basic needs of access required, while green ends or grass ends were created by converting the extremities of selions and some headlands into pasture. Leys were more extensive, consisting of selions, groups of selions or whole furlongs that were converted to grassland, with a strong tendency to convert from arable to grassland being evident at the end of the medieval period and in the seventeenth century. Areas of ley within the open fields experienced less ploughing, so that they may be recognised within a pattern of earthworks as areas of shallower ridging.

From time to time researchers have speculated about possible links between open field systems and earlier field networks. Taylor suggested that population growth in Saxon England may have led to infields being expanded across outfield lands, with the resultant shortage of pasture urging the development of common grazing rights after the harvest. Meanwhile, 'long strip' fields may have been subdivided according to inheritance practices or to provide sustenance for everyone. 'If this suggestion of evolution is accepted, we have two of the basic features of the later medieval common fields developing out of the earlier Roman and prehistoric systems. However, the ultimate establishment of this medieval form of agriculture was probably related to many other and varied factors' (1975 p.69). At Wharram Percy, in the Yorkshire Wolds, it emerged that: 'The universality of the selions does not mean that the whole parish was simultaneously ploughed. Field-walking has shown that only certain areas near to the villages were manured, suggesting an intensively cultivated infield with a less used outfield. It is striking that not only is this similar to the Roman usage but also many of the areas are the same, as if certain core land was kept in better shape' (Beresford and Hurst, 1990 p.96). There is also the possibility that some furlongs may have been derived from earlier fields: 'On some air photographs taken of areas of later medieval fields, now ploughed out, it is possible to discern traces of large, roughly rectangular closes or fields bounded by ditches, underlying the medieval fields. The boundaries of the ditched fields agree to a marked extent with the 'furlongs' or blocks of strips of the medieval fields, and may be the basic reason for the eventual shape of these furlongs' (Taylor, 1975 p.58). In 1998 it was suggested, on the basis of work by Oosthuizen, that traces of prehistoric farming were not obliterated by the imposition of open fields between the ninth and twelfth centuries and that 'A block of fields with prehistoric boundaries containing the remains of medieval ridge and furrow has been identified in South-West Cambridgeshire—perhaps the first example of prehistoric field boundaries to be recognised in the part of England dominated by the open field "strip farming" system' (Denison, 1998 p.4).

Changes have occurred since the introduction of open field farming in the middle Saxon period. Originally, strips may have extended from the village or farmstead all the way to the township boundary (Harvey, 1983). While the supposed links between Saxon immigration and open field farming have been disproved, similarities between English and German experiences have been noted:

The research on the genesis of the settlement pattern in some parts of Eastern England and in the area of Saxon settlement in Northwest Germany exhibits striking parallels for the eighth and ninth century: small settlements were rearranged into larger ones and the older theory, that strip fields originated in the third to fifth century, can be disregarded for both countries. In Northwest Germany this replanning in the ninth and tenth century is considered to be the result of the following chain of causations: exhaustion of the arable land on the sandy soils (Esch), therefore the introduction of manuring with *plaggen*, which leads to the necessity to give up the ard and use the fixed mouldboard plough, hence the tendency to plough long ridges and furrows ... The English and German research shows that the origin of long strips may have two independent roots: in one case they are an adaptation to the fixed mouldboard plough, in the other case they are deliberately planned and the result of a simple measurement technique no matter what agrarian implement was used. (Matzat, 1988 p.145)

Long strips of up to 1,000 yards in length were allowed to survive in the well-drained countrysides on the limestone of the southern flanks of the North York Moors or the chalk of the Yorkshire Wolds, but elsewhere, drainage considerations may have led to a fragmentation into 220 yard lengths. Norfolk had little ridge and furrow and the system was thought to be absent in Kent and Suffolk, perhaps owing to the post-medieval introduction there of different ploughs and ploughing techniques. The practice of ridging lands continued in some places into the nineteenth century, the last ridging giving rise to straight-sided ridges which can be three times the width of the medieval examples (Hall, 1994 p.98). Very narrow ridges were also produced in the nineteenth century, less than half the width of medieval ridges, while straight-ridged land was also produced by ploughs hauled back and forth across a field between steam engines.

The medieval countrysides of England

Table 8.4   Place- and field-names associated with common fields

Name	Meaning
Field (OE *feld*)	Open ground; unwooded ploughland or pasture, though later associated with open field arable land.
-ersh, -arrish (OE *ersc*)	Ploughland, both before and after the harvest.
Acre, -aker (OE *æcer*)	Cultivated land, sometimes an area equal to a day's ploughing.
Land (OE and ON *land*)	An expanse of ground, less often a selion or an estate.
Gore (OE *gāra*)	Triangle of land left at the corners of an irregular field.
Slade (OE *slæd*)	Valley, marshy valley, sometimes a damp patch in the ploughland.
Breck, birch (ME *breche*)	A breach-land associated with an infield-outfield system of farming which was periodically broken in as ploughland.
Link, lynch, (OE *hlinc*)	A bank or shelf: strip lynchets.
Ham (OE *hamm*)	Meadow, flood-prone meadow.
Mead, mede (OE *mæd*)	A meadow.
Wis-, Wist- (OE *wisce*)	A very wet meadow.
Strode, stroud, storth (OE *strōd*, ON *storth*)	Ground or marsh overgrown with brushwood.

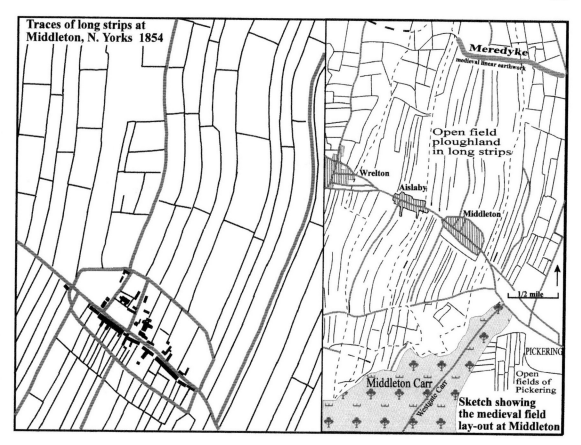

Map 8.4   *Traces of long strips at Middleton, North Yorkshire, 1854. Strips were grouped together and enclosed following agreements between respective holders of land to produce very elongated fields whose curving edges preserved parts of the outlines of the medieval long strips. The smaller map on the right shows how the fields of Middleton were bounded by a dyke to the north and the wet, wooded land of Middleton Carr to the south. The scale bar reveals the remarkable length of the long strips.*

displayed variants of the 'classical' open field system, including small strip fields shared between just a handful of households in areas of ancient or woodland countrysides and infield-outfield systems in the more marginal farmlands. In addition to the arable fields there were the great upland, lowland and wetland commons described in Chapter 2, the privately tenanted tofts and closes associated with the village and its locality, and the enclosed pastures which sometimes intervened between the village and its fields.

Forms of infield-outfield farming were widespread in the Celtic lands and were found in England in places where the resources of good arable land were limited, as in the northern uplands. In the Lake District an infield was still being worked in the mid-nineteenth century at Threlkeld.

Here, there were five households with shares in the eleven selions in the infield, which covered only 14 acres (about 6 hectares). Such systems were not confined to the furthest outposts of the kingdom and an operational infield with outfields were mapped at Carburton in Nottinghamshire in 1615. If infield-outfield systems existed in

Figure 8.3   Pounds or pinfolds, like this example at Raskelf, near Boroughbridge, are reminders of the days when roving beasts were impounded after straying from the commons.

England before the fourteenth century they do not seem to have given rise to very much documentation and this weakens assumptions that such systems were inherited from prehistoric or Roman times. The essential agricultural strategy employed was to concentrate arable production in an infield occupying the best land. This infield was heavily manured and kept in constant production, while areas of outfield land or 'brecks' were periodically ploughed, cropped to exhaustion and then abandoned. Within the infield, features like ridge and furrow were created, but the area under permanent cultivation was much less than in the town-

ships where two- and three-field systems operated.

Strip lynchets are cultivation terraces up to 330 yards (300 m) in length, which can be prominent features in Wessex, the Yorkshire Dales (where they are known as 'raines') and parts of south-eastern England, and which are present but less well-preserved in East Anglia and the Welsh Marches. The lynchets tend to occur in flights that cover hillsides and these hillsides are given a staircase-like profile by repeated episodes of ploughing in one direction that notch the hillsides to create level 'treads' separated by steep 'risers'. The levelled areas allowed an expansion of cultivation from confined sites in the valleys below, while beasts could be tethered on the intervening grassy slopes. Commonly regarded as being prehistoric, most strip lynchets are medieval, sometimes with the corrugations of ridge and furrow on the flatter surfaces of their steps, and they may generally date from the decades of over-population and land hunger preceding the arrival of pestilence in 1348, though a few are probably prehistoric.

In most medieval townships, large numbers of small, hedged or walled fields or closes (i.e. enclosures) would be found. Generally, these belonged to individual farmers, but some could be shared. Some closes would lie beyond the open ploughlands and represent land reclaimed from the waste by assarting, while others would often intervene between the ploughlands and the tofts of the village dwellings, providing enclosed pasture conveniently close to home.

Meadow was essential to medieval communities that needed supplies of hay to feed their stock during the winter after the grass had ceased to grow. The fodder crisis was often kept at bay by storing holly cut from special little woods or 'Hollings' and feeding the leaves to hungry beasts. Branches taken from the upper parts of the trees had foliage that was less prickly. In the English lowlands meadows were normally located beside streams on the lowest ground in the township. They, like the arable fields, were divided into strips, known as 'dales' or 'doles', whose boundaries could be marked by merestones or by hurdles. After mowing around St John's Day (towards the end of June), meadows would be thrown open around Lammastide (at the start of August) and grazed in common by the village livestock. After Candlemas (2 February) the grass would gradually begin to grow again and stock were excluded from the meadows. Periodically the meadow might be ploughed to rejuvenate the grass, though the cultivation of ancient meads has left far less field evidence than has that of arable fields. Stackstands, known as stack garths in the north, can, with great care, be identified as small, slightly raised circular or sub-rectangular earthwork features stand-

ing within areas of meadowland or sometimes aligned along headlands or occupying spare corners of land in open fields. They seem to belong to the medieval or slightly later periods before the widespread construction of durable field barns, though they my have coexisted with primitive barn structures referred to as 'helms'.

Field barns developed during the eighteenth century and were improved in the decades around 1800, becoming essential components of the scenery of the northern dales. They are associated with an ecologically sustainable form of farming. After midsummer, the hay was mown and dried in the sun, then swept into the barn and stored in the 'hay mew' or store area, with some being kept in the loft. A few weeks before midwinter, the surrounding hill pastures would become dormant and stock would be moved into the shelter of the field barns, one of which stood in almost every field in parts of the Yorkshire Dales. There the cattle would remain until late spring, being fed on the hay from the hay mew. Then they would be moved to the more distant pastures while the accumulation of manure was spread across the field to fertilise the growing hay crop. After Parliamentary Enclosure, the large-scale conversion of the Yorkshire Wolds from sheep runs to arable farming around the start of the nineteenth century caused pressing demands for manure to provide the extra fertiliser needed. Given the thin and fragile nature of the chalk soils of the Wolds, these demands required the development of a special type of farm building equipped with foldyards for cattle, the high barns of the Wolds, which became the larger equivalents of the field barns of the Dales. The high barns served 'as outposts from the main farmstead for animals, fodder and equipment and, more importantly, the accumulating animal dung within the foldyard provided a valuable source of manure in a convenient position to be scattered on the more remote fields of the farm' (Hayfield, 1991 p.33).

Post-medieval changes to the fieldscape

England's medieval countrysides, with their expanses of ridged ploughland, communal meadows and vast panoramas of uninterrupted commons, were changed in many ways, so that today we tend to encounter the older patterns as fragments and relics which persist only by the accidents of survival. The Parliamentary Enclosure of communal lands, whether they were common pastures, village greens, furlongs or dole meadows, exerted a profound effect on many countrysides, but other factors were important too. These included the establishment of water meadows and the parcelling out and enclosure of chalk downlands to create large, hedged fields for sheep farming in the seventeenth century.

The breaking up of medieval patterns began in many places long before the close of the medieval period. In Nidderdale the commons of the Forest of Knaresborough surrendered piecemeal to assarting and an investigation of ancient trees there suggests that as the wood pastures vanished so the country people compensated for the loss of timber resources by planting the hedges of their new fields with a high density of pollarded oaks (Muir, forthcoming). Other hedged fields, ones which became more numerous in the closing phases of the medieval period, were created by dismantling the selion patterns in the common ploughlands and collecting adjacent ridges together to form privately tenanted fields. This process of enclosure by agreements between villagers might merely nibble at the details of communal farming, it might seriously erode the furlong patterns and 'privatise' whole fields, or it might even extinguish entire township-wide systems of open field farming. Frequently, it reflected a desire amongst significant numbers of the

village farming community to consolidate holdings and work field-sized blocks of territory rather than be involved in assembling ploughteams in 20 or 30 strip locations dispersed amongst the open fields. Often, however, the old and the new ways failed to mesh. Sometimes, though the land was enclosed and cropped by an individual family, after the harvest the fields would still be thrown open for common grazing by the village herd. In other cases, the hedges and fences marking the new property boundaries cut across the tracks used to get to field or common and heated disputes soon followed.

Fields formed from the unpicking of open field selion networks can usually be recognised even after later ploughing has flattened the ridges, headlands and joints. When new fields were created, the selion packages were defined by walls or hedgerows, and these followed the outlines of the outermost furrows in the group, perpetuating reversed 'S' and reversed 'C' forms and so preserving elements of the distinctive open field patterning. During the Tudor period, numerous townships were wholly or largely depopulated by lords seeking to establish a sheep-rearing economy at the expense of peasant tillage. The fields associated with the evictions could be extremely large. In some cases the hedge-bounded open field could become a single sheep enclosure (Taylor, 1975 pp. 115–17), though such units proved far too large and were subdivided into irregular or straight-sided units sometimes around the size of a furlong.

Medieval meadows were frequently located on low-lying, damp ground. Flood-prone meadows experienced two advantages: firstly, silts, suspended in the floodwater and deposited on the field, enriched the soil, and secondly, in early spring the cool water was warmer than the frigid land and the relative warming encouraged an earlier growth of grass. By the end of the

Table 8.5   Characteristics of different field types

Type	Characteristic
Enclosure by agreement	Curving boundaries of reversed 'S' or reversed 'C' form. Hedgerows may contain veteran timber trees, often pollards. Boundaries conform to furrow outlines where ridge and furrow can still be traced in the pasture.
Tudor sheep pastures	Not easily recognised without documentary support. Possible that a group of such fields may be recognised as lying within a larger unit identifiable as a former open field. Hedges may have been deliberately planted with useful timber (and fruit) trees and survivors will be veterans.
Water meadows	Low-lying land on the floodplain of a river or stream. Evidence of artificial flooding may be found in the shapes of low, parallel ridges or carriers, canals, leats, dams and nicks in the earthworks representing the locations of sluices.
Intakes	Post-medieval intakes often form a zone of rectangular or irregular enclosures between the older closes below and the common or large, geometrical Parliamentary Enclosure divisions above. Sometimes associated with 'breck', 'brock', 'breck' and 'intak' names.
Meadows	Generally located in damp, low-lying areas, meadows were often associated with names like eng and ing, -was (OE *wæsse*, flood-prone land), holme (ON *holmr*, island or meadow), and ham (OE *hamm*, water-girt land or meadow), while 'sykes' can refer to springs, ditches or narrow strips of meadow beside a stream.

Middle Ages, systems which artificially replicated the flooding process had begun to be established. Fitzherbert (1523) advised his readers on how flood sediments would help to level land while the waters drowned any troublesome moles. Sheep were highly favoured in the Tudor period and the two centuries which followed and an advantage of controlled spring flooding concerned the stimulation of an early flush of grass to feed lambs. In Wessex, where flood meadows became numerous, sheep were grazed on the meadows in the daytime and folded to fertilise the ploughed fields at night. Then, when the sheep were removed from the meadows in April, another flooding set the stage for the hay crop. Where springs rose at the foot of a scarp, their waters would be captured in a leat, which would overflow and would soak the land below as they flowed to the river in the valley bottom,

while 'catchmeadows' were watered by streams flowing down from the slopes above.

During the seventeenth and eighteenth centuries, different systems of flood control were developed. Where a system of flooding upwards was employed, a river or stream was dammed, ponding back waters which would inundate the floodplain grasslands lying upstream. Flooding downwards was a more sophisticated technique which involved damming the watercourse and diverting the accumulating waters along a canal or 'head main' which then distributed the water into a system of channels running along the crests of ridges or 'carriers'. From the carriers the waters flooded the meadow and returned to the impounded river.

Intakes were not confined to the post-medieval countrysides, but rather the habit of enclosing land from the margins of

Figure 8.4   A landscape of Parliamentary Enclosure near Pateley Bridge, North Yorkshire. Virtually all the human-made structures seen result directly from the Enclosure of this common.

upland commons continued long after the more generalised assarting movement had lost its momentum. Intaking often involved an illegal alienation of communal land, but in some cases it was tolerated on condition that no manure was applied, which would ensure the abandonment of the exhausted land after a brief phase of cultivation. Intakes could be associated with outfields and sometimes they carry the 'breck', 'brech' and 'brock' names denoting newly broken land, which derive from the Old English *brāc* or *bræc* signifying a breach. As population continued to rise in the post-medieval period, so unenclosed land came under mounting pressure and lords who were no

longer able to enforce the preservation of upland pasture and moor as common would often seek to legitimise the enclosures by taking rents. Some intakes, like those on Greenhow Hill which date from the seventeenth century, were provided to support the ponies and draught oxen used by miners (Raistrick, 1968 p.116). In the Yorkshire Dales a zone of intakes commonly intervenes between the older closes and the common, and in the Lake Districts intakes are frequently seen between the commons of the high fells and the 'inbye' land of long-established walled fields.

Between 1604 and 1914, the dates of the first and last Acts, but mainly in the period *c.* 1750 to *c.* 1850, Parliamentary Enclosure transformed scores of countrysides in England. Landscapes that were the products of a thousand years or more of gradual evolution, with winding lanes and curving hedgerows, had a new, angular geometry superimposed at a stroke. This was a movement that had as its goal the privatisation of common land, and so the intensity of its impact very much depended upon the availability, or otherwise, of communal land, which could exist in the form of open commons, communal ploughland, dole meadows or village greens. In areas of the Midlands, with much land still in open fields, or the northern uplands, with extensive upland commons, the parishes affected could be totally transformed, but in the old enclosed lands of the south-west or the Weald, countrysides might be untouched or affected only in detail.

It was widely accepted by the victims of Enclosure and their sympathisers that the changes to the patterns of landholding would, while benefiting those who could afford the costs of hedging or walling, penalise and impoverish the cottager and small tenant and hasten their departure from the village. At Thornborough in Buckinghamshire the villagers composed a lamentation in 1798:

The time alas will soon approach
When we must all our pasture yield
The Wealthy on our rights encroach
And will enclose our common field.

A more sophisticated indictment was provided in 1821 by John Clare, who saw Enclosure as an assault on justice and the traditions of society and landscape:

There once were lanes in nature's
  freedom dropt,
There once were paths that every
  valley wound,—
Inclosure came and every path was
  stopt;
Each tyrant fix'd his sign where paths
  were found,
To hint a trespass now who cross'd the
  ground:
Justice is made to speak as they
  command;

The high road now must be each
  stint'd bound
—Inclosure, thou'rt curse upon the
  land,
And tasteless was the wretch who thy
  existence plann'd.

To understand the landscapes created by Parliamentary Enclosure it is necessary to understand the processes involved. The shift towards transformation would be set in motion when the leading landowners in a particular parish petitioned Parliament to issue the necessary Act—and this would probably provoke objections from many of those who stood to loose from the privatisation of common land. Parliament could be relied upon to oblige the landed interests (the General Enclosure Act of 1801 simplified proceedings, and the General Act of 1836 permitted enclosure without recourse to Parliament if two-thirds or more of the local interests consented to it). Once Parliament had delivered the necessary Act, one or more commissioners, nominated by the proponents of enclosure, would be appointed to oversee the reallocation of land. Normally they were representatives of the landed classes, the nobility or the Church. They would appoint a surveyor and a valuer, and the enclosure of the common land would proceed upon the basis that those who had shared in the commons would be rewarded with compacted holdings of land which were equivalent in value to the recipient's former share in the open fields and commons.

When the commissioners' allocations were imposed on the parish, changes of two kinds would be produced. Firstly, there were the changes which resulted from the replacement of one network of fields by another, and secondly there were those resulting from the consequences of these, as expressed in the migration of all those small tenants who could not meet the costs of hedging or walling and whose holdings

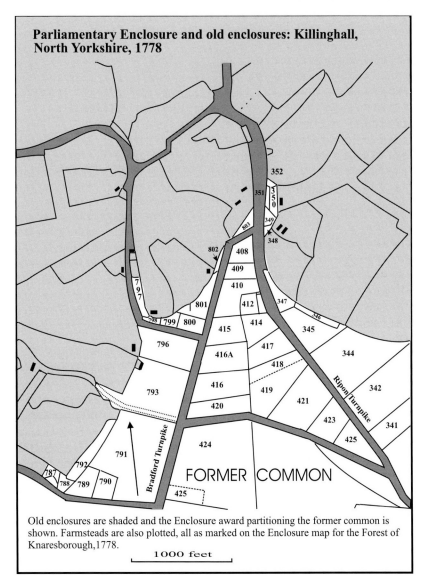

Parliamentary Enclosure and old enclosures: Killinghall, North Yorkshire, 1778

FORMER COMMON

Old enclosures are shaded and the Enclosure award partitioning the former common is shown. Farmsteads are also plotted, all as marked on the Enclosure map for the Forest of Knaresborough,1778.

1000 feet

Map 8.5   Parliamentary Enclosure and old enclosures, Killinghall, North Yorkshire, 1778. This detail from the Enclosure map shows how a common of the Forest of Knaresborough had been partitioned. Many of the divisions would become house plots as settlement gravitated to the sides of the two recent turnpikes which converge here.

were too small to compensate for the loss of rights on the common. The surveyors who produced the blueprints for change facilitated the measurement of land and the demarcation of boundaries by employing straight-line geometry wherever possible. Thus, while the old countrysides may have been harmonious compositions of curves which respected the nuances of terrain and historic ownerships, the new were characterised by their uncompromising, angular geometry. The recipients of holdings were normally required to enclose their new allotments with walls or hedges within one year of the award being made, and generally the specifications were quite precise. At

Burton Leonard, near Ripon, enclosed in 1790, the ditches dividing the allotments were to be 2½ feet deep and 4 feet wide at the top, tapering to 9 inches wide at the bottom, with hedges planted 1 foot from the edge of the ditch and guarded from browsing by post and rail fences. The fences were to be built 2 feet from the outside of the ditches and should remain in place for ten years. On Kirkby Moor, near Kirkby Lonsdale, walls were to be built to a height of 6 feet with topstones set edgewise and not more than 6 or 7 inches deep. Through stones were to be inserted at three different levels and the walls were to stand on foundations 3 feet 6 inches wide (Rollinson, 1978). At Ulceby in Lincolnshire the commissioners appealed for workmen to complete the work of enclosure and for 300,000 good 3 foot tall ash plants and 500,000 quickthorns for hedging (Russell, 1974 p.35).

The commissioners and their agents were able to dictate the future character of the countrysides subjected to their authority. Not only could they specify the pattern of the redistribution of land and the disposition of boundaries, but they could also

determine the nature of these boundaries, the heights and construction of walls and the species content of hedgerows. The changes to the patterns of property ownership set in motion other changes that found expression in the rural landscapes. Field patterns changed as the owners or tenants of small properties faced bankruptcy, while those favoured by the reallocation absorbed small fields and properties into larger ones. Similarly, settlements which were not affected by the award experienced contraction as failed farmers headed for the towns and ports, while others left the village to establish farmsteads nearer the centres of their new, compacted holdings. Meanwhile, in the uplands, countless quarries were opened to provide the materials needed for all the new walls demanded by the awards, while in the vales, mushrooming plant nurseries responded to unprecedented

Map 8.6   Enclosure of moors and wastes, Grantley, Ripon, 1820. The map shows that Lord Grantley, the dominant figure in local society, has done rather well from the reallocation of lands. New Enclosure roads of different widths improve the communications of the locality.

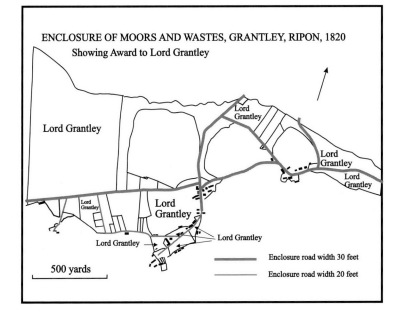

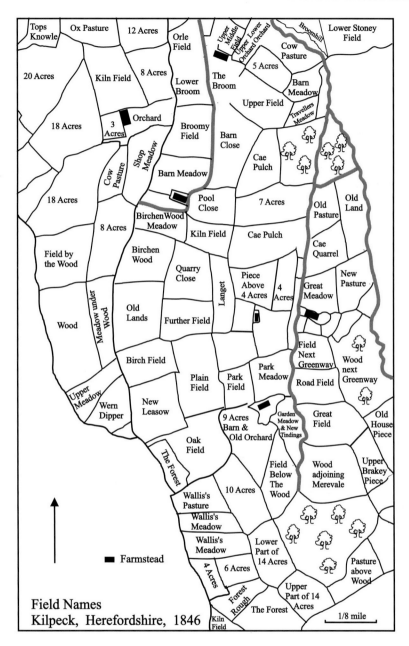

Map 8.7   Field names, Kilpeck, Herefordshire, 1846.
A selection of field-names in a part of the parish of
Kilpeck, as recorded on the tithe map of 1846.

demands for quickthorns and hedgerow trees. The countrysides changed, too, with the removal of some of the resources, like communal osier beds or coppices producing materials for hurdling or thatching, while many narrow lanes and field tracks were regarded as out of place in a privatised setting. Some communal needs remained to be satisfied and places were set aside to serve as sources for the stone, sand or gravel needed in parish road-building works by the local surveyors of the highways.

The nature of the new countrysides was also influenced by the limited spatial extent of each award.

An enclosure Act normally empowered enclosure within a single parish (or part of that parish); it is rare to find an Act authorising the enclosure of two adjoining parishes. One set of commissioners may have enclosed parish A in, for example, 1793–6; another set of commissioners may have enclosed the adjoining parish B thirty years later, while parish C may have been enclosed by agreement in 1617, each implementing different ideas and producing different road plans and field patterns. Roads laid out in one parish may thus stop at the boundary and lead nowhere! More frequently, roads change both their direction and width at parish boundaries. (Russell, 1974 p.31)

Commissioners were powerful, but their fiefdoms were small. They operated at the parochial level and their allocations could convert the parish boundary into a divide between different countryside types. On one side of the invisible line there might be big landowners with big landholdings and large, rectangular fields, while on the other side different commissioners might have created a series of smallholdings to accommodate the smaller fry from the recently extinguished peasant society.

More recently, the destruction of hedgerows to create the vast arenas favoured by mechanised, chemical-industrial farming has removed much of the aesthetic charm from lands now bereft of land-working villagers. A proper understanding of the landscape history of most parishes demands a reconstruction of the medieval patterns of cultivation, though very little evidence that is obvious may remain. Two challenges are paramount: a recovery of the directions of the selions and a rediscovery of the furlong patterns. Some clues may be derived from the survival of ridge and furrow patterns, even if only the edges and ends of some ridges are detectable as the boundaries of later fields. Headlands and joints may also be recognisable as earthworks or in air photographs. While ridge and furrow can be recognised as a banding within fields for some time after ploughing has levelled the corrugations, its proper identification in air photographs may be difficult. The rolling or harrowing of grassland or recent ploughing patterns in fields can cause confusion.

Field-names preserve much useful information about the former uses of land, the contents of a neighbourhood and the evolution of countrysides. Though often now abandoned, the names were formerly commonplace and virtually every field had its name. Frequently, the names were unremarkable, though some can contain gems

Table 8.6   Useful field-name elements

Name/Name element	Meaning
Applegarth	Orchard
Assart, essart, sart	Cleared from woodland
Avenam, Annum etc.	Intake (early)
Balk	A strip of grass in an arable field
Bang/bong	Boundary bank
Barton	Demesne land, outlying grain farm
Brake, breech, breck	Intake or other land broken into cultivation
Carr, moss	Marshy land
Close	An enclosure, often near a settlement
Clough	A ravine

Table 8.6   Useful field-name elements—continued

Name/Name element	Meaning
Conyger	Rabbit warren (early)
Copy, copse, spring	Coppice
Denn	Wood with pannage
Dole, dale, dalt	A share in open meadow or ploughland
Eddish, etch	Enclosed pasture
Ersh, arsh	Ploughland
Fall	Wood
Field	Open country; sometimes ancient rough pasture converted into ploughland
Flat, shot	Furlong
Freeth	Hedge in West Country
Frith	Wood
Garston	Cattle yard
Gore	Triangular piece of land between furlongs
Ground	Land distant from farmstead
Hade, head	Headland
Hag	Wood or assart
Hall, hale	Nook, corner of land
Hamstal	Field near the farmhouse
Hatch	Fenced land
Hay	Hedge, hedged field, deer park or small wood
Held, hel, hill, lench	Slope
Hollins	Holly wood growing winter browse
Holm, wis	Wet meadow
Hope, hoppet	Small enclosure
Ing, eng	Meadow
Intake, inham, inning	Intake, sometimes land enclosed from a moor
Land, loon, selion	A strip; land can be ploughland anciently converted from pasture or an estate
Law, low	Burial mound
Lease, winn	Meadow or pasture
Leasow	Enclosed pasture
Linch, link	Ledge, strip lynchet
Mark, mere, reans, hemm	Boundary
Mead, pre	Meadow
Moor	Marsh or moorland
Over	Sope
Patch, pickle, pightle	Small enclosure
Plash, plachet	Wet ground
Quillet, rap	Narrow strip of land
Raine, linch	Lynchet
Ridding, rode, royd, sarch, stubbs, stubbing	Assart
Ridge, rigg	Ridge, often plough ridges
Sike	Stream, ditch, streamside meadow
Slade	Valley, wet ground
Slaight	Sheep pasture
Slough	Marshy ground

Table 8.6   Useful field-name elements—continued

Name/Name element	Meaning
Storth	Wood
Thwaite	Meadow or clearing
Tye	Large common, sometimes a small enclosure
Wong	Enclosure, garden, meadow
Wray, row, stich, plat	A nook of land

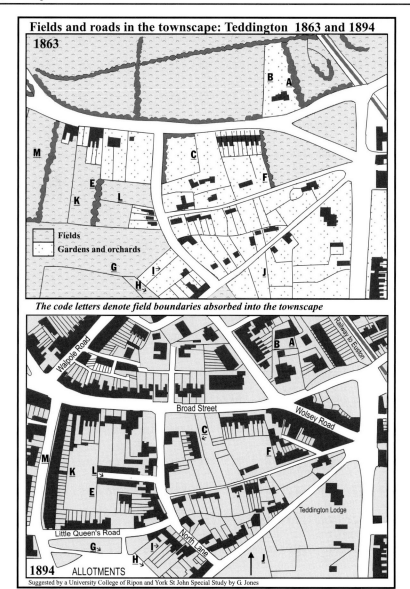

Map 8.8   Fields and roads in the townscape: Teddington, London, 1863 and 1894. Elements from the rural landscape of fields and roads would frequently be incorporated into an expanding town. Maps of Teddington drawn in 1863 and 1894 record the conversion of the locality from countryside into town, but also show how many alignments from the rural framework were preserved. Suggested by a special study by G. Jones, 1998.

of information that are invaluable to land-scape history. The names, however, are not necessarily of great antiquity and changes to a set of field-names could occur at various points in time—for example when a farm

changed hands and the set of names was not conveyed to the new owner or tenant. Some of the commonest field-names are provided in Table 8.6.

REFERENCES

Beresford, M. and Hurst, J. *Wharram Percy* (New Haven: Yale, 1990).

Denison, S. 'Prehistoric boundaries in medieval open fields' *British Archaeology*, 39 (November 1998) p.4.

Fitzherbert, J. *The Boke of Surveying and Improvements* (1523).

Fleming, A. *The Dartmoor Reaves* (London: Batsford, 1988).

Fleming, A. *Swaledale, Valley of the Wild River* (Edinburgh: Edinburgh University Press, 1998).

Fowler, P.J. 'Wildscape to landscape: "Enclosure" in prehistoric Britain' in R. Mercer (ed.) *Farming Practice in British Prehistory* (Edinburgh: Edinburgh University Press, 1981).

Green, F.W.H. 'Ridge and furrow, mole and tile' *Geographical Journal* 141 (1975) pp.88–93.

Hall, D. 'The Origins of open-field agriculture—the archaeological fieldwork' in T. Rowley (ed.) *The Origins of Open Field Agriculture* (London: Croom Helm, 1981) pp.22–38.

Hall, D. 'Ridge and furrow in the English Midlands' in S. Foster and T.C. Smout (eds) *The History of Soils and Field Systems* (Aberdeen: Scottish Cultural Press, 1994) pp.94–100.

Harvey, M. 'Planned field systems in eastern Yorkshire: some thoughts on their origin' *Agricultural History Review* 31 (1983) pp.91–103.

Hawkes, J. *Early Britain* (London: Bracken Books, 1945, reprinted 1987).

Hayfield, C. 'Manure factories? The post-enclosure high barns of the Yorkshire Wolds' *Landscape History* 13 (1991) pp.33–45.

Hinton, D.A. 'The "Scole-Dickleburgh field system" examined' *Landscape History* 19 (1997) pp.5–12.

Hooke, D. 'Open-field agriculture—the evidence from the pre-Conquest charters of the West Midlands', T. Rowley (ed.) *The Origins of Open-Field Agriculture* (London: Croom Helm, 1981) pp.39–63.

Horne, P.D. and MacLeod, D. *The Yorkshire Dales Mapping Project* (Swindon: RCHME, 1995).

Lewis, C., Mitchell-Fox, P. and Dyer, C. *Village, Hamlet and Field* (Manchester: Manchester University Press, 1997).

Matzat, W. 'Long strip layouts and their later subdivisions' *Geografiska Annaler* 70 (1988) pp.133–147.

Muir, R. 'Pollards in Nidderdale: a landscape history' *Rural History* (forthcoming).

Raistrick, A. *The Pennine Dales* (London: Eyre Methuen, 1968).

Reynolds, P.J. *Ancient Farming* (Princes Risborough: Shire, 1987).

Rollinson, W. *Lakeland Walls* (Clapham: Dalesman, 1978).

Russell, R.C. 'Parliamentary enclosure and the documents for its study' in A. Rogers and T. Rowley *Landscapes and Documents* (London: NCSS, 1974).

Stoertz, C. *Ancient Landscapes of the Yorkshire Wolds* (Swindon: RCHME, 1997).

Taylor, C. *Fields in the English Landscape* (London: Dent, 1975).

Taylor, C. 'Archaeology and the origins of open- field agriculture' in T. Rowley (ed.) *The Origins of Open-Field Agriculture* (London: Croom Helm, 1981) pp.13–21.

Welch, M. *Anglo-Saxon England* (London: Batsford, 1992).

Williamson, T. 'Early co-axial field systems on the East Anglian boulder clays' *Proceedings of the Prehistoric Society* 53 (1987) pp.419–31.

CHAPTER 9

Defence in the Landscape

Landscapes, we know, mirror the societies that created them. Encoded there in the forms and patterning of the scene are messages about human vanity and greed, hopes and endurance. Many facets of the man-made scenery derive from economic needs and social behaviour, but there are also numerous features which reflect the darker human capacities for violence, warfare and oppression (Eibl-Eibesfeldt, 1979). Many of these relics of war endure to remind a society now preoccupied with fears of a global nature of the times when enemies might appear on the skyline or emerge silently from familiar surroundings—times when there was no night-watchman state to serve as a community's protector. Other remains are relatively recent, consisting of crumbling concrete slabs, graffiti-daubed shelters and guard posts, or the archaeological shadows of runways and hangars, all of which record decisive landmarks in the nation's history.

Towards a landscape-based approach

A distinctive landscape history perspective on defenceworks has yet to be refined and adopted. The approaches to monuments like castles or fortresses of the landscape historian on the one hand and of the architect or art historian on the other should differ. The former is not as much interested in the castle as a piece of architecture, as in its relationship to the local terrain and the broader cultural landscape beyond. Thus the castle, the Roman fortress and the hillfort are seen, in their different ways, as power centres radiating influence and control across surrounding territories, responding to conditions in the setting and stimulating change. Speculation will then concern the configuration of these tributary areas and the relationships between the dominant and the dominated, the centre and the setting.

Distribution patterns also are interesting and may clarify military policy at the strategic level: the English royal castles of the twelfth and thirteenth centuries were dispersed amongst the baronial castles, reflecting a concern to establish a royal presence in every region. In this way, King John charged an impossible level of relief to Nicholas de Stuteville in 1205 and managed thereby to gain control of the castle of Knaresborough, strategically located in territory dominated by hostile barons. The construction of the royal castle at Orford, in Suffolk, by Henry II in 1165–7 was partly prompted by the need to control the castle nearby at Framlingham, where the treacherous Hugh Bigod had his base. In contrast, the fortresses built by Henry VIII at the close of the medieval period shunned the interior of what was now a unified and internally pacified kingdom, and were strung along the southern coast of England and embodied anxieties about invasion by foreigners from the continent.

Pounds recognised more in the pattern of Norman royal castles than an attempt to counter the baronial threat:

Of thirty-seven royal castles ... established before 1100, no less than twenty were built within or against the defences of a town. In a country as feebly urbanised as eleventh-century England this is a

Figure 9.1   The ownership of a castle is a crucial factor to be considered and royal castles performed a special role in pacifying the realm and dominating their baronial rivals. Orford Castle was built by Henry II around 1165 as part of a strategy to re-impose royal control on East Anglia.

remarkably high proportion. Twelve were in towns of Roman origin, whose defences had survived. Eight were within Anglo-Saxon burhs. All were populous, and, on the evidence of Domesday, large numbers of houses—up to 166 at Lincoln—were destroyed to make way for them. The fact that King William was prepared to destroy, in the aggregate, at least 500 houses—there are no data for either London or Winchester—is proof that he thought it important to secure a site within each town. (1990 p.57)

When Henry II came to the throne in 1154, England contained 50 royal castles, and these were outnumbered five to one by baronial castles (Brown, 1955). Following a rigorous policy of increasing the centralisation of power, by the end of his reign the number of baronial castles was less than

double that of those controlled by the Crown, with numerous baronial strongholds having being taken into royal control. Any stronghold, whether in ruins or existing only as earthworks, should be considered in its territorial and geopolitical context as well as in terms of the effectiveness and evolution of the military architecture employed.

The geopolitical context is continuously changing, so that defenceworks cannot be appraised in terms of current realities, but rather in terms of those that existed at the times when they were built. Settlements flourishing in the modern milieu may owe their existence to factors encountered in a long-forgotten political context. Thus in the Welsh Marches: 'The cardinal factor in town situation has been the desire by lowlanders to command the routeways into the Celtic west. This requirement is expressed by Roman Gloucester and Chester, situated at the heads of the Severn and Dee estuaries;

Figure 9.2   Some Norman mottes were built only to command their immediate locality, but the one at Laxton in Nottinghamshire, later colonised by trees, was associated with the administration of Sherwood Forest.

by Roman Caerleon and Edward I's Flint, in the coastal plains beyond these estuaries; and by Roman Monmouth and Hereford, Anglo-Saxon Shrewsbury, Norman Ludlow and Oswestry, and Plantagenet Montgomery, each close to a strategic valley-way leading towards the Welsh uplands' (Wood, 1962 p.54).

Geopolitical circumstances change, but so too, over time, may those of a physical geographical nature. The physical context is not fixed for all time, and in some cases the topographical setting that we see today differs in crucial respects from the one that existed when fortifications were conceived

Figure 9.3   Strongholds should be appreciated in terms of the setting as it existed during their currency. The Roman fort of the Saxon Shore at Reculver, Kent, close to the ruins of the twin Norman church towers, has been largely removed by marine erosion since the eighteenth century, while the Wantsum Channel which it guarded silted up centuries ago.

and erected. Little sense could be made of the positioning of Harlech Castle were it not realised that when the castle was begun, in 1283, the sea in the Dwyryd estuary lapped the outcrop on which it stands. This enabled the site to be detached from the mainland by rock-cut ditches dug to the east and south, and it permitted freestone to be shipped in from Egryn and lime and limestone from Caernarfon and Anglesey, while

also allowing the castle to be supplied by sea in the event of siege. This occurred in 1294–5, when Harlech was besieged by Madoc ap Llywelyn and the castle was victualled from Ireland by sea. Now the sea is far away and the castle's dock is a railway goods yard. Another great Edwardian castle, Beaumaris on Anglesey, was built after 1295 on a flat, marshy site and surrounded by a broad, tidal moat. Although the setting is now inland and dry, the castle then had a dock that was accessible to sea-going vessels. Similarly, the construction of the Roman forts of *Regulbium* (Reculver) and *Rutupiae* (Richborough) on the northern and eastern seaboards of Kent makes little sense unless one realises that they were once linked by an 'L'-shaped channel, the Wantsum Channel, which separated the Isle of Thanet from the mainland. The Roman forts were positioned to guard either end of the former straits, which disappeared as the flanking salt marshes were reclaimed by the monks of Canterbury priory.

Defenceworks occupy physical settings, but they are also positioned in mental settings that are much harder to recover or define. Henry VIII's preoccupation with anti-invasion defences represented the evolution of attitudes which recognised the English/Welsh as 'ourselves' and others as 'outsiders', and which might equate with the early stages in the development of nationalism. The hillfort expressed the will to defend a community of a different and much smaller and more closely integrated kind, while the castle existed to defend a dynasty and its domain rather than a local society. Military works contain messages about who could or should be defended, about who was included and who was excluded. In this way, the Norman motte and keep made sense only in the context of an alien elite and a resentful and mistrusted peasantry, though in Scotland several tower houses and castles, like the MacLeods' Dunvegan on Skye, outwardly resembled Norman stone keeps but were the homes of clan chieftains who commanded the passionate support of clansfolk living in the surrounding territories. Keeps, the brochs of the Scottish late Iron Age and tower houses of the seventeenth century have distinct architectural similarities, but who could deduce from their appearances the sorts of societies that they represent? It is pertinent to wonder whether landscape historians/archaeologists, encountering fortifications only as earthworks and ruins, could recognise the social and political contexts in which they were created?

Changes in technology have not only transformed the scale and intensity of war, they have also changed its locale. Herz (1957) argued, though with some in-accuracy, that during the medieval period the introduction of gunpowder and large mercenary armies had rendered the baronial fortress obselete. The perimeter of security had expanded from the walls of the redundant fortresses and had come to rest at the limits of the developing territorial state. As nationalism developed and the legitimacy of the state was established under the Treaty of Westphalia of 1648, so sovereign territory came to be regarded as inviolable and defensive strategy focused on the development of a hard outer shell of frontierworks. But during the twentieth century, changes in the technological basis of warfare allowed bomber aircraft and guided missiles to bypass the 'hard' exterior of the state to strike at the civilian populations of the 'soft' interior. The military monuments of the era, like airfields, armaments factories and radio stations, related not to their *local* military geographical contexts but to war as an *international* conflict with cities and industries as its targets.

There is certainly good reason to regard strongholds not only in terms of their geographical and social contexts, but also in relation to the evolution of military technology and science. In this way much of medieval castle development can be explained in terms of a Darwinistic dialectic whereby changes in military architecture were inspired by the need to counter the latest refinements or revolutions in siege technology. The improved castle constructions would then serve as a challenge to prompt innovation in castle-breaking techniques. Beginning with the simple motte, the shell keep represented an attempt to reconstruct the crowning palisade in the more durable, formidable and fire-proof form of an encircling wall. The stone keep or donjon could be regarded as a superior substitute for timber towers which stood atop some mottes, though the greater weight of the stonework often urged that the tower be sited away from a mound, on firm footings. Attacks by sappers on the corners of these towers prompted the construction of splayed bases presenting slopes of masonry several feet thick to the sappers, while the hall keep was a donjon modified to provide greater floorspace for comfortable living. Meanwhile, the bank and ditch defences of the bailey were replicated in a stronger and imposing form in enclosures embraced by curtain walls. With refinements in siege technology it became imperative to exclude attackers from the wall base. Projecting mural towers allowed archers or crossbow-men to sweep the walls with their fire. At first they were built to rectangular plans, as at Framlingham, but their corners were vulnerable to undermining and so 'D'-shaped towers were adopted which presented curved faces to the hostile world.

Increasingly, however, it is being realised that what is seen at medieval castle sites cannot simply be interpreted in terms of the cause and effect interactions of offensive and defensive warfare. Castles were not only strongholds, they were also status sym-bols—the ultimate status symbols, since the possession of a castle was the *sine qua non* of the aristocratic existence. Those who did not have castles imitated the status-impregnated trappings of castle life, having moats dug around their manor houses or crenellating a gatehouse. At East Tanfield, North Yorkshire, the Marmion family, some-time king's champions, packed the adjacent church with the imposing tombs and effigies of the dynasty and built their tower beside it—though the tower was merely a symbol and could be swept with bolts or arrows by any force scaling the taller church tower. Castles were also developed as symbols of elegance, romance and beauty, with their settings being manipulated to maximise the impression on visitors—which returns one, with emphasis, to the theme of the castle in the landscape.

At Framlingham, the elevated castle will have been seen mirrored in a sheet of water. At Bodiam, Sussex, the moat was far wider

than was needed to keep sappers from the wall base: 'Sir Edward Dalinrigge's castle lay at the heart of a complex of gardens and water features such as ponds, the whole being a piece of designed and ornamental landscape, a medieval equivalent of what the earls of Worcester undertook at Raglan, Gwent, in the late Elizabethan period, or what Capability Brown and others created for great estates in the eighteenth and nineteenth centuries' (Kenyon, 1997 pp.8–9). He added the very important observation that: 'The Bodiam survey reminds us that castle studies ignore at their peril the landscapes in which these buildings are situated'. At Bodiam:

> The castle and its moat … form the centre of an elaborate modification of the whole landscape involving the creation of a number of ponds and sheets of water whose positioning has an ornamental impact. More interestingly it is also clear that this modification was at least partly connected with the manipulation of visitors around the site to experience views whose components continually change. Thus the main approach to the castle from the W. would have been along the S. side of The Tiltyard pond [the presumed tiltyard was a pond], giving distant views of the castle across water, thence along the causeway between ponds where only the upper part of the castle was visible, and crossing between further areas of water over a bridge. At this point the climb to the moat dam must have had, indeed still has, a dramatic effect, as the whole castle seems to rise out of its moat. (Taylor *et al.*, 1990 p.155)

In looking at any medieval castle, even one that is apparently well-researched, one should search for aspects that present more aesthetic than military justifications. Approaches could be contrived so as to reveal the building and its setting in the most dramatic and favourable manners, and at Bodiam an elevated viewing platform seems to have been set in ornamental grounds, while on a smaller scale at Steeton, West Yorkshire, the approach road may have been diverted to bring the visitor across water ponded back by a dam and then uphill towards the gatehouse, with the holloway of the original road appearing as a moat backed by a wall. Leeds Castle, Kent, stood in an artificial lake and the gloriette or private royal accommodation was linked to the castle by a bridge. This castle, bought by Edward I as a gift for his wife, Eleanor of Castile, in 1278, was much visited by subsequent queens of England and in the later medieval period it acquired large mullioned windows which confirmed its aesthetic rather than defensive character.

Queenborough Castle, on the Isle of Sheppey, completed in 1365, was the last royal castle to be built. Flanked by the waters of the Thames estuary, with its lofty, circular inner bailey clasped by six towers and rising from the waters of a circular moat above the low wall of the round outer bailey, it must have been an unforgettable sight. This is not to deny the military realities of the fortifications built by the insecure, militaristic medieval aristocracies and the carefully reasoned defensive theories that they embodied. But status, and even romance, were factors too, and in many cases the claims of defence and aesthetics must have coincided: Pembroke Castle standing on its narrow limestone outcrop over the inlets of Milford Haven is still spectacular, as are Nunney, Somerset, and many others— though none perhaps more than Caerphilly, with its elaborate water defences. Kenilworth Castle, in Warwickshire, stood on the side of a valley containing a stream; a long causeway was built which dammed the stream and flooded the valley and further diversions virtually resulted in the castle existing as an island surrounded by shimmering pools, moats and lakes.

At Shotwick Castle in Cheshire, built beside the estuary of the Dee by the Earl of Chester in 1180, a recent survey by the English Royal Commission has produced a reinterpretation of a presumed dock. An exceptionally large expanse of moat seems not to have been constructed to allow ships to moor beneath the castle walls. Instead, a dam barred the area to water traffic on the Dee and the flooded area appears to have been a great ornamental pond. Meanwhile, within the bailey, gardens with raised walkways and a prospect mount were set out. After the Edwardian conquest of Wales in the late thirteenth century, Shotwick Castle may have lost its strategic importance and have been redeveloped as an attractive and prestigious hunting lodge (Denison, 1997 p.4). Designed medieval landscapes such as those described are being recognised in an increasing number of places. The use of sheets of water for visual effect was exploited with considerable ingenuity; vantage points were selected to maximise the impact of the building and its setting, and great care also appears to have been lavished on dramatising the approaches to such castles, sometimes by lengthening the routes concerned and winding them around the most scenic pathways.

Camelot, chivalry and notions of courtly love were not the inventions of romantic Victorian writers. Writing around 1370 in the *Book of the Duchess*, Chaucer described the apartments in a contemporary castle:

> *And alle the walles with colours fyne*
> *Were paynted, bothe text and glose,*
> *Of al the Romaunce of the Rose*

Edward I had opened the alleged coffin of Arthur and Guinevere in 1278 and seems to have been enthused by Arthurian mythology. Given the campaigns in Scotland and Wales, he may have recognised a political advantage in presenting himself as the heir of the mythical king, and Froissart recorded the legend that the royal castle at Windsor

Table 9.1 Strongholds and contexts

Context	Factors to be considered
Topographical	Do tactical or strategic topographical factors help to explain the situation or location of the stronghold? In what ways has the local topography been exploited to maximise its security *or* its aesthetic impact?
Historical	Have any changes in the physical or cultural landscapes served to mask the original function of the stronghold? (These would occur if a coastal fortress were stranded inland or if changes in the transport practices affected a castle which had commanded navigation on a river system. Equally, cultural change would affect a border stronghold if the frontier moved on.)
Re-use	This concerns the way in which a site may have experienced the construction of successive strongholds at different periods in time. One would want to discover whether any exceptional attractions of the site and its setting were responsible, or whether the presence of one stronghold, perhaps with re-usable fortifications or legendary prestige, acted as a magnet to attract a successor?
Economic	How does the location of the stronghold relate to the distribution of wealth and agricultural productivity? Is the stronghold located in one of the areas where the most affluent elements would reside? What resources did it protect? Would the immediately surrounding territory produce the food needed to support a garrison?
Political	How does the stronghold relate to the then prevailing distribution of power? Is its location significant *vis-à-vis* competing strongholds? Is it a component of a system of defenceworks created to meet a particular challenge?
Cultural landscape	Is the stronghold sited so as to control aspects of the cultural landscape like roads, passes, bridging points, navigation? More particularly, how did the presence of the stronghold influence the development of its cultural setting?
Impact on the senses	Was the stronghold established or developed in order to magnify the status of the owner or to impress visitors by the visual impact of a remodelled setting? Did the setting have qualities and potential of an aesthetic character?

had been built by King Arthur. Tournaments were adopted from France in the twelfth century and became so riotous and dangerous that they had to be licensed by the Crown after 1194, with five sites in the kingdom being designated for the contests. Edward III held a tournament to commemorate the knights of the round table in 1344 and had a circular table constructed; subsequently, he founded the Order of the Garter as an order of chivalry which was centred on the chapel at Windsor Castle.

When castles became obsolete they evolved into great country houses set within landscape parks: elegant and grandiose buildings surrounded by carefully remodelled countryside. This description, however, with the addition of a mention of defence, would also fit many castles very well. In seeking an approach to strongholds which is rooted in landscape, one must be aware of traditional stereotypes and how they may affect perceptions of the past. Thompson has described the difficulties encountered by those who retained unrealistic childhood visions of the castle as it existed at the time of the Norman Conquest:

> the average historian could not bring himself to believe that the earthworks belonging to the earth-and-timber structures described by Round or Mrs Armitage would really have to be substituted for the vision of 'cloud-capped towers' that he had imbibed from his early childhood. It offended common sense. The image he cherished derived from the final period of the castle's history when function played less and less part and display or even fantasy ever more part in the minds of the builders. (1987 p.vii)

Today, nobody would dispute that castles of earth and timber were built by the Normans, but while most children have heard of motte and bailey castles, very few people appreciate that more than a quarter of defensive earthworks built at this time were ringworks rather than mottes (Cathcart King and Alcock, 1969). The earthworks themselves can sometimes on careful inspection reveal information about castle-building. At the ringwork overlooking Middleham, in Wensleydale, the inner face of the earthen bailey is a series of straight sections, showing that the earthworks were cast-up around a pre-existing arc of timber buildings (Moorhouse, 1998 pers. com.)

An approach based on landscape history/archaeology would, above all, relate strongholds to their particular setting or contexts, and these contexts exist in many different forms, as illustrated in Table 9.1 and Map 9.1.

In terms of the *topographical context*, a stronghold might be sited *strategically* to guard a geographical province, like a valley, estuary or capital, or *tactically*, say, to take advantage of exceptional terrain, in the way that Bamburgh Castle, Northumberland, colonised Castle Rock, a rugged outcrop by the seashore. Some situations have both strategic and tactical advantages, as with Dover, where the castle guarding the important medieval seaport had a commanding cliff-top position previously exploited by Roman defences and an Iron Age hillfort. Topographical evidence could be significant in another sense, for the fact that a stronghold *disregards* advantageous terrain suggests that it was built with factors other than defence in mind. In this way, Bolton Castle in Wensleydale, which was built in 1378, is overlooked by higher ground and its site was apparently chosen because it had been occupied by the owner's previous manor house. When this is considered, along with the commodious accommodation which the castle offered, its lack of a moat, poor capabilities for wall-flanking fire, lack of gunloops and the creation of garden terraces on the limestone slopes beside the castle, the true role of Bolton as a venue for comfortable living, large-scale hospitality and the proclamation of status becomes apparent.

With regard to *historical factors*, some stronghold locations have been hugely transformed, as in the case of Orford Castle, where a spit of sand and shingle has extended southwards for almost 10 miles since the castle was built, diverting the River Alde and causing the decay of the port of Orford. Over time, the function of a castle could change, and while most originated in the demands of defence, many developed superior residential or administrative roles. Around 20 royal castles became the centres of shrieval administration, most lost any military significance and some were reduced to only the buildings employed by the sheriff.

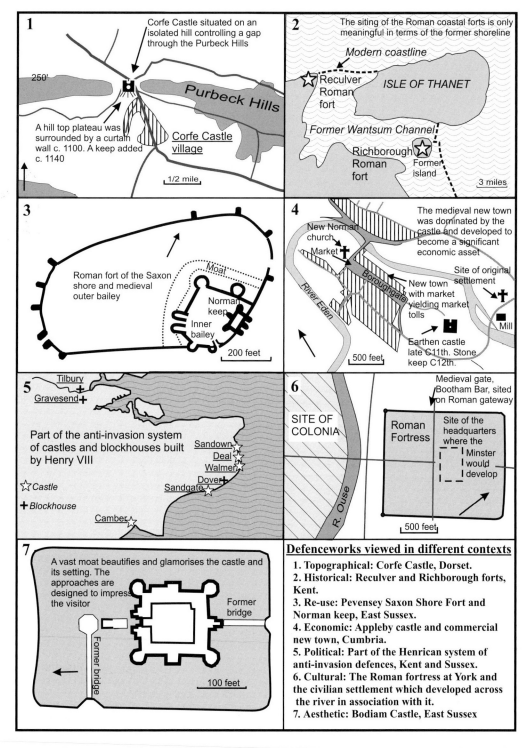

1 Corfe Castle situated on an isolated hill controlling a gap through the Purbeck Hills

250'

Purbeck Hills

A hill top plateau was surrounded by a curtain wall c. 1100. A keep added c. 1140

Corfe Castle village

1/2 mile

2 The siting of the Roman coastal forts is only meaningful in terms of the former shoreline

Modern coastline

Reculver Roman fort

ISLE OF THANET

Former Wantsum Channel

Richborough Roman fort

Former island

3 miles

3 Roman fort of the Saxon shore and medieval outer bailey

Moat

Norman keep

Inner bailey

200 feet

4 The medieval new town was dominated by the castle and developed to become a significant economic asset

New Norman church

Market

Boroughgate

River Eden

New town with market yielding market tolls

Site of original settlement

Mill

Earthen castle late C11th. Stone keep C12th.

500 feet

5 Tilbury

Gravesend

Part of the anti-invasion system of castles and blockhouses built by Henry VIII

Sandown

Deal

Walmer

Dover

Sandgate

☆Castle

✚Blockhouse

Camber

6 SITE OF COLONIA

Medieval gate, Bootham Bar, sited on Roman gateway

Roman Fortress

Site of the headquarters where the Minster would develop

R. Ouse

500 feet

7 A vast moat beautifies and glamorises the castle and its setting. The approaches are designed to impress the visitor

Former bridge

Former bridge

100 feet

Defenceworks viewed in different contexts

1. **Topographical: Corfe Castle, Dorset.**
2. **Historical: Reculver and Richborough forts, Kent.**
3. **Re-use: Pevensey Saxon Shore Fort and Norman keep, East Sussex.**
4. **Economic: Appleby castle and commercial new town, Cumbria.**
5. **Political: Part of the Henrican system of anti-invasion defences, Kent and Sussex.**
6. **Cultural: The Roman fortress at York and the civilian settlement which developed across the river in association with it.**
7. **Aesthetic: Bodiam Castle, East Sussex**

Map 9.1   Defenceworks viewed in different contexts. Each of the seven maps is drawn to reflect a different perspective of a defencework.

Re-use is encountered in many periods: numerous Neolithic causewayed enclosures were redeveloped as hillforts in the Iron Age; various Iron Age hillforts were hastily refortified in the 'Arthurian' era, while perhaps the most celebrated examples are the cases of the Roman Saxon Shore forts at Portchester, Hampshire, and Pevensey, Sussex, which much later served as the outer baileys of medieval castles. At Portchester, an eleventh century manorial site with a hall and stone tower appears to have preceded the medieval castle (Cunliffe, 1975 p.3). (Strictly speaking, we are considering *re-use* rather than *continuity* of use, such as would occur, for example, if a castle were to be continuously redeveloped and updated to accord with current needs, as with Windsor Castle, which originated as a Norman motte and shell keep and currently serves as a royal residence.)

Regarding the *economic context*, Hughes wrote of the situation in Norman Hampshire that

> One particular area of the county which has a marked concentration of market towns and village market centres is the south-east which shows a greater degree of economic development, hence a concentration of wealth, than any other part of Hampshire in the thirteenth century. It is therefore possible that this wealth and prosperity is reflected, for example, in the concentration of twelfth-century earthwork castles at Rowland Castle, Motleys Copse, Rowner, Pinsley and 'Place Wood', Southwick; and in the development of Portchester Castle and the building of the Kings House in Portsmouth. (1989 p.31)

The exploration of the *political context* involves a consideration of the stronghold concerned in terms of the configurations of power and policy which conditioned its construction. The Roman forts of the Saxon Shore were comprehensible only in terms of

a system of fortresses and a strategy of co-ordinating land power and sea power in order to counter a threat of barbarian raiding. To evaluate any single Saxon Shore fort in isolation would be fruitless. The nature of the intended role would be likely to govern the layout of a stronghold, so that the coastal forts which were built by Henry VIII in response to an invasion scare in 1538–40 were designed as artillery platforms for directing heavy firepower at raiders and invasion fleets, with an additional capability for defence against attacks from landward by troops which had come ashore further along the coast. As, say, dynastic power bases they would have been sadly lacking, and they could only deter invasion when combined as integral parts of a system controlling the length of the invasion coast.

Strongholds existed in a *cultural context* as interacting components in cultural land-scapes. Pounds wrote:

> No castle ever stood in isolation. It was always part of a community. Indeed, there were two communities: the one within the castle, the other surrounding it and forming its milieu. Their mutual relations were marked by both interdependence and animosity. How did the people of the town or village view the castle? Was their fear of it modified by their dependence on it for protection and employment? Above all, what were the institutional relations between community and castle? Was the former obliged to perform services or to provide goods? What kind of jurisdiction did the lord of the castle claim over the community, and how did the latter, as it strove for some kind of independence, come to define both its boundaries and its rights? (1990 p.184)

Frequently, castles were built to dominate particular facets of the cultural landscape—a town, a collection of villages or a political domain. The Roman fort at Hard Knott in Cumbria was plainly created to control the

Figure 9.4   Defenceworks must be seen in their human and physical contexts. The Roman fort of Hard Knott in Cumbria, whose encircling wall is seen in the middle distance, was built to command the routeway using the Hard Knott Pass. The fort does not occupy the summit level of the pass, where the climate would have been severe, but is not dominated by higher ground.

routeway from the Esk valley to Ambleside using the Hard Knott Pass. Hillforts are frequently, if not demonstrably, seen as the military, political and dynastic centres of surrounding chiefdoms, while castles were frequently placed to reflect an association with a particular settlement. The Conqueror built two large mottes near the River Ouse in an attempt to dominate York; a Norman

motte and bailey commandeered a quarter of the Saxon town of Wallingford and another motte was built to control Oxford. Communities were perhaps the most important components of the cultural landscape and the relationship between community and stronghold could vary greatly. The Saxon *burhs*, like Wareham and Wallingford, were boltholes that could be used by all the people of the surrounding countryside, whereas motte and bailey castles shielded members of an alien dynasty and their retainers.

Strongholds would often represent a response to the cultural landscape, but the insertion of a stronghold would evoke a strong response from the landscape. For periods before the thirteenth century it may be difficult to recognise the chronology of closely occurring events, but royal Forests were closely associated with castles at places like Pickering and Knaresborough, while medieval castles were normally linked to deer parks (Crawford, 1953). The building of a new castle at Sheriff Hutton, near York, in 1382, was associated with the replanning of the well-established village to one side of the castle and the development of a deer park on the area of carr on the other. Castles and their deer parks imposed organisation and controls upon the local communities, but they also provided employment, increased demand for rural products and would invariably be associated with markets which, to some degree, stimulated local commerce. While the royal castles were often intimately associated with important towns, various examples of 'castle-gate' towns appeared in the medieval period; planned settlements like Ludlow in Shropshire, and New Buckenham and Castle Acre in Norfolk were established in efforts to attract taxable commercial and residential activities to the vicinity.

Finally, the factors associated with *sensual impact* may not always be differentiated from other factors, such as those linked to impregnability. Corfe Castle in Dorset has a visually stunning situation on a narrow ridge, but this situation not only endows it with a sensual impact, but also gives it defensive advantages, while the site commands the gap through the Purbeck ridge, giving a domination of routes into the Isle of Purbeck and of much of south-east Dorset (Taylor, 1970 pp.105–6). Knaresborough Castle must have overlooked the Nidd gorge in a dramatic and commanding manner, but the gorge was surely largely a defensive attribute. Less ambiguous will be the evidence of human efforts to manipulate the immediate setting to produce a powerful impression upon visitors or a tranquil, romantic or stimulating setting for domestic life. The search for such evidence could

involve a reappraisal of earthworks and other human works previously interpreted in terms of military engineering. The measures taken for the diversion and containment of water will merit investigation, as will the possibility of gardens and parks in association with the castle site. Some castles, like Middleham, were served by large numbers of deer parks, and there, as in various other places, the garden earthworks can plainly be seen outside the walls of the bailey.

A landscape history approach should, therefore, seek to appraise and interpret strongholds as subjects existing in a series of physical, historical and cultural contexts. It is not the defencework, or indeed the history of warfare, as such, that interests, but that stronghold's relationship with its different, overlapping contexts. The fort or castle as a piece of architecture and as a stage in the development of a tradition of military engineering can be studied more effectively by others. Yet when it comes to interpreting a stronghold within the context of the ongoing relationship between societies, communities and classes and their setting then nobody is better placed to succeed than the landscape historian and landscape archaeologist.

Working in the field

Any castle that exists as more than a spread of rubble will be the subject of a detailed guide book and various learned papers. Students of the landscape may have much to contribute regarding strongholds as seen in their contexts, but otherwise, in terms of the reading of the landscape, landscape history and non-invasive archaeology will concentrate on those monuments which were undiscovered or misinterpreted. The significance and intensity of a field warfare is not directly reflected in the impact on the landscape. Three decades after the dropping of defoliants during the Vietnam War, large expanses of the Vietnamese landscape remain poisoned. Aerial bombardment during the Second World War hugely affected the urban landscapes of many English towns, and yet the Home Guard of more than 1.7 million men 'left little in the way of recognisable structures; it possessed no purpose-built barracks or drill halls. Home Guard units used whatever local wartime accommodation was available to provide their headquarters, typical examples being hotels, Territorial Army drill halls, auction markets and vicarages. Accommodation had also to be found for the training of Guardsmen in the arts of fieldcraft, leadership, camouflage and weapons drill' (Lowry, 1998 p.10). Regarding the prehistoric period, hillforts provide plenty of opportunities; in terms of the earlier medieval centuries, many ringworks and small mottes probably remain to be recognised, while the treatment of recent and relatively modern military monuments is surprisingly thin.

Hillforts present opportunities for interpretation employing the context factors already described, but they also present many challenges when such techniques are applied. During the last three decades, many debates have concerned the function of hillforts. They were not sham fortifications, and a careful inspection of sites will show how the scale and disposition of ramparts was thoughtfully adjusted to the potentialities and limitations of the local terrain. Thus: 'At Coxall Knoll (Here.) most of the southern defences, standing above the steepest slopes, consist of a scarp and ledge, quite clearly the remains of comparatively slight defences. On the north side the slopes are much less steep and the defences are correspondingly stronger, consisting of three banks and two ditches defending the main enclosure, with a wide-spaced arrangement elsewhere' (Forde Johnston, 1976 p.56). (There has been, in fact, a classification of hillforts according to their topographical situation: Group I, hill-top; Group IV, ridge-top, and so on.)

The entrances were the most vulnerable points on the hillfort perimeter, and at sites like Maiden Castle in Dorset, Hambledon Hill in Dorset, Danebury in Hampshire and Blackbury Castle in Devon great ingenuity was employed in the use of systems of outworks, hornworks or overlapping ramparts. The military engineering embodied in hillforts argues that the monuments had defensive credibility, particularly when the archaeological evidence for palisades, timber gate defences and guard chambers is taken into account, but it does not prove that they were fortresses in the narrowest sense of the word. During the last three decades, alternative or complementary interpretations have arisen, partly from evidence derived from excavations. During the 1970s much attention was devoted to the possible ritual associations of hillforts (Bradley, 1981). Some arguments concerned the coincidence of hillforts and Neolithic causewayed enclosures, as at Carn Brea in Cornwall or Blewburton in Berkshire, though one could employ the same evidence to argue that both types of monuments must be the venues for regional gatherings or 'fairs'. There was also a realisation that early social/ceremonial sites, notably causewayed enclosures, had been the sites of warfare and skirmishes, as at Hambledon Hill.

It had for long been realised that hillforts were not merely bolt-holes, for many contained dwellings, sometimes in small numbers, sometimes in considerable concentrations, while the arrangements of houses could be irregular or highly organised. Finds of carbonised grain in hillfort excavations had aroused interest since the 1880s, and in 1972–4 excavations at Moel y Gaer hillfort, Clwyd, revealed that circular buildings had been succeeded by rectangular 'four-poster' structures which were widely interpreted as granaries (Guilbert 1975). Rectangular buildings and carbonised grain were found in excavations at Croft Ambrey hillfort, Herefordshire, which was excavated about the same time (Stanford, 1974) and where rectangular buildings were also found. In the years around 1980, attention in archaeological circles came, productively, to focus on questions of power and the domination of societies and landscapes. Not surprisingly, there arose notions of the hillfort as the power centre in an agricultural landscape, a place where the grain of the peasantry might be brought as tribute to their chieftain and stored prior to its redistribution as largesse. Guilbert (1981) pointed out the weaknesses of the factual bases for such assumptions (might not the four-posters be garages for chariots?).

Like any other stronghold, to be appreciated the hillfort must be understood within its context. In their efforts to come to grips with the political geography of the hillfort, some enquirers have resorted to geographical techniques now, thankfully, largely discredited, deriving from spatial analysis, central place theory and the ideas of Christaller. Hillforts must have dominated surrounding territories and so one might assume that such territories might be recreated through the practice of dividing space between neighbouring hillforts to produce a mosaic of Thiessen polygons, each once centred on a stronghold. The attractions of such modelling are superficial, the model failing on the counts of period and hierarchy. Firstly, in any theoretical partition of territory between such 'central places' one would need to know which of the hillforts in the region concerned were in use at any specified period (Collis, 1981). Secondly, one would need to be comparing like with like and be operating within the same level of hierarchy; moated manors were on a different plain to baronial castles and presumably there were qualitative differences between greater and lesser hillforts.

There were other differences of a qualitative nature but which may only be revealed by comprehensive excavations. These concern the facts that apparently *similar monuments* could be associated with the performance of distinctly *different functions*. Some were uninhabited bolt-holes, some were towns or villages, some resembled temples and others were communal centres. In a note on recent excavations in the vicinity of the Uffington White Horse and the Ridgeway (Denison 1998), Uffington Castle hillfort was identified as a late-third/early-fourth-century temple or shrine where ritual and feasting were held; Segsbury Camp was a settlement that was crammed with roundhouses during the Iron Age; and Rams Hill, between the two, was another settlement which persisted from the late Bronze Age to the Romano-British period. These, and related problems, reflect the fact that, unlike the modern mind, the prehistoric mentality did not deal in rigid categorisation: spirituality flowed freely through all aspects of life. To a considerable extent it can be said that the ambiguities of the kind described are less apparent in terms of the monuments of the historical age. However: 'Some motte-and-bailey castles must have been built to control centres of communication and suppress local populations, others were no more than links in a chain of signal stations, but whatever their individual purposes they together coalesced to form a defensive and offensive network throughout the whole country' (Clarke, 1983 pp.109–10).

Theoretical approaches may prove deficient, but much can be gained from a painstaking scrutiny of monuments in the field. Detailed fieldwork was advocated by Burrow (1981) for the investigation of the use of hillforts after the Iron Age. It was recognised that the decay or maintenance of existing defences might not leave any recognisable surface trace, but refurbishment probably would: 'This might be expected to manifest itself either by abrupt breaks in the surface profile of ramparts, indicating that a decayed structure has been heightened and rebuilt, or by evidence of alterations to specific features such as gateways, or additions to, or major changes of plan. The identification of *relative sequences* should therefore be a primary aim of fieldwork, hill-forts with complex earthwork defences being the obvious targets for detailed study' (pp.125–6). The redevelopment of a prehistoric fortification was recognised by Taylor at Sturminster Newton, in Dorset: 'Here not only is there a respectable documentary history of a manor house, as well as a standing fourteenth century structure, but there is also an impressive set of large earthworks including a bank and ditch cutting off a spur. However, once more, careful fieldwork has led to the interpretation of the site as a small prehistoric promontory fort, which was later used as a medieval manorial site' (1974 p.72).

The careful study of earthworks could lead to an understanding of the evolution of prehistoric defences, as well as the first identification of some eroded and damaged hillforts, and it could also enable the recognition of unrecorded examples of small mottes, motte and bailey castles and ringworks. After the twelfth century, stone replaced earth in the construction of fortifications, while documentary material identifying the owners of castles, which is often lacking for the first medieval phases, becomes more abundant: 'Unfortunately, for the majority of non-royal, rural castles in Hampshire, as elsewhere in England, it is difficult to document the owner of the castle at the time of its construction or during the subsequent use and decline. One of the reasons for this paucity of information is that between 1086 and the late twelfth century very little documentation survives— a period when earthwork castle building reached its peak, and in the case of many sites, also their decline' (Hughes, 1989 p.39). The stone castles of the thirteenth century,

in contrast, are very largely known and whatever may survive as a monument should be mentioned in a succession of documents.

At Burwell in Cambridgeshire there are the earthworks of a castle built in 1144 by King Stephen as one of a series of fortresses erected along the Fen Edge in an attempt to prevent the devastation of the East Midlands by the rebel, Geoffrey de Mandeville, who had his base at Ely. The castle takes the form of a rectangular platform or island set within a broad, dry moat. But, according to Taylor, there are several peculiar features:

> The interior of the island is extremely uneven with mounds and hollows and with a gap in one side leading into the moat. In addition, on the north and west outer sides of the moat are huge uneven mounds of earth, higher than the interior island and completely dominating it. With the information we can see there, together with the results of an old excavation on the site, it is possible to see that all this represents an unfinished castle. The interior island is a result of spoil being left in dumps prior to the construction of a full-sized mound, while the gap in the side is where the spoil was being brought out of the moat when the work stopped. The moat therefore was not completed which accounts for its appearance and so was never filled with water. (1973 p.122)

At Burwell, and also at Rampton, where there is another unfinished Fen Edge castle, parts of villages were removed in the course of the castle-building works. The earthworks reveal the boundaries of closes disappearing beneath the heaps of spoil, while a holloway is truncated by the moat: 'These remains show that when the castle was built, far from being on an open piece of land it was raised on part of the village of Burwell and presumably a whole street of houses was demolished to make way for it' (p.123). Such earthworks reveal the castle's impact on its setting in its starkest form.

Medieval homestead moats are the defensive features most likely to be encountered and to challenge local researchers in landscape history, they being extremely numerous and occurring in a wide variety of shapes and sizes. The Moated Sites Research Group listed 5,300 moats in 1978 (Aberg) and there must still be a great many such sites which remain unrecorded or wrongly identified. Moat-building may have begun in the first half of the twelfth century and the heyday of the moat was 1200–1325, with the possession of moats seeping down the social order as time progressed. One may imagine these moats as being rectangular features surrounding a homestead and its outbuildings. In fact, moats could be double, circular, 'D'-shaped, three-sided, or even 'C'- or 'L'-shaped. Moats which failed to protect the entire periphery were surprisingly common, while subsequently scores have been partially filled, so that one, two- and three-sided examples are numerous. More surprisingly, some moats did not contain dwellings and appear to have been associated with garden features or orchards. Whatever the purpose or form of moats, their abundance or scarcity within an area would, to a large degree, be related to the ability of the local geology to retain water: they are much more numerous on clay soils than on sands, chalk or limestone. A moat might be filled by occupying a low position relative to the watertable, by springs or by water arriving via an artificial channel, while waters from such a moat could be redirected to fill fishponds or create garden canals.

The functions of homestead moats have been the subject of debate, with the more recent interpretations concerning status being pitted against traditional views focusing on defence. Steane wrote:

Although moats were not formidable defences they were valuable psychological barriers; their water was a necessary insurance against the ubiquitous risk of fire. Their social significance is that they were constructed by all seignorial sections of medieval society; the majority enclosed structures which might be termed 'manor houses'. Others encircled messuages attached to freehold estates which did not have manorial rights; the partially moated state of many sites suggests that the moat was to some extent a status symbol, a fashion originating among the aristocracy and extending downwards through society, to the lesser knights and freemen. The phenomenon of the moated site underlined the separateness and exclusive character of the lord's share of the wealth of the community. It has even been suggested that they might have been used to protect the lord from his own community. (1985 p.59)

Elsewhere, a broad spectrum of credible uses has been advanced, ranging from swan- and fish-keeping, fire control and the protection of produce and supplies against marauding deer (Cantor, 1982 p.139). Taylor took a more forthright position, pointing out that 'at most moated sites the stables and stockyards which would need protection were outside the main moat and bounded only by hedges and fences' (1973 p.127) and adding: 'Moated sites presumably reflect the general prosperity of their owners and the desire to show off this prosperity by imitating the moated castles of the higher ranks of contemporary society' (pp.127–8). One suspects that more than mere showing off is needed as an explanation for the immense popularity of the form, but moats were indicative of the status and aspirations of the family living within and the configuration of a moat may offer clues as to the former occupants. In this way, Palliser described the timber-framed house at Littywood, near Bradley in Staffordshire:

> The most puzzling feature is that it stands within a double moat quite disproportionate in scale for a modest manor-house (the outer is about 650 feet in diameter), but the manor was held directly by the great de Staffords in the early Middle Ages. The original *caput* of the de Staffords has not been located—it was almost certainly *not* Stafford Castle, which was then in royal hands—and it

may be that the massive defences at Littywood encircled the original castle or fortified manor of the barons before they took over Stafford Castle in the thirteenth century. (1976 p.88)

Table 9.2 could be employed with regard to possible moated features encountered in the field.

It might readily be assumed that homestead moats are easily recognised features of the medieval cultural landscape, but often this is not the case (Cantor, 1982 p.138).

Table 9.2   Checklist for moated features

Topic	Relevant areas of enquiry
Place-names	Place-names in immediate locality associated with defence (notably OE *burh*=burgh, borough: a fort)?
Shape	Any indication that the moat has been partly refilled, e.g. to remove one, two or three sides from a rectangular feature? Look for possible missing sections around 10 to 20 feet wide.
Water	How is/was the moat filled: by seepage from adjacent land; by springs; by a natural watercourse or by diversion of water in an artificial channel? Was there a re-use of supplies, e.g. to serve fishponds? Alternatively, was the moat always dry?
Size/status	How does it compare in size to other moats in the area? Are the original owners/occupants known? How might the moat relate to a social spectrum ranging from barons to the upper orders of free peasants? Can it be related to any estate or other land unit mentioned in documents of the twelfth and thirteenth centuries?
Defensive potential	Is there any evidence that defensive considerations were invoked by the moat-builder, e.g. by avoiding terrain which might overlook the site; by commanding a panoramic view, and so on?
Context	*Topographical*: the relationship to superficial geology (water-retaining clay), and to the watertable? *Cultural*: the relationship to communications and settlements; to estates (can the site be linked to a manor or other territorial unit?); to other moated sites within the region (do they tend to cluster?); and to the agricultural resources of the region/locality (how does the moat relate to arable/pastoral land-uses, to woodland and Forest and to areas of intensive/extensive land-use?).
Identification	Eliminate other possible ponds and trenches/depressions, notably fishponds, garden water features and canals. Consider the less obvious possibilities, like deer park hunting stances.

Firstly, where there has been a continuity of occupation through into modern times many occasions will have existed when a moat could be modified or converted. One or more sides might be filled in order to extend the area of gardens associated with the dwelling or to facilitate access, or the moat might be incorporated into the setting of the expanding house as a garden feature among other water features. Alternatively, moats could be redeveloped as prosaic stock-watering ponds, sometimes with two or more fields converging on the water source. Other suspected moats might prove to be manorial fishponds—leaving open a good possibility that the real moat lay close by.

On discovering features of a puzzling nature in the form of earthworks or as crop, shadow- or parch-marks on an air photograph there is a common tendency to presume that they are of prehistoric or medieval vintages. Evidence for all periods

may carefully be perused—except the modern. In fact military considerations during the modern era have resulted in the creation of an assortment of remains which, though sometimes dating from within the lifespan of the researcher or his/her parents, are little-known and unsuspected. After the *Defence of Britain* project was launched by the Council for British Archaeology in 1995, various forgotten devices like the pre-radar coastal sound mirrors for detecting approaching bombers re-entered public awareness, along with the unsuspected hides and communications systems intended to be employed by the British Resistance Organisation. The sites of searchlight or anti-aircraft batteries, radar transmitter stations or decoy airfields are

Figure 9.5   A steel pillbox from the 1939–45 war was sited on military earthworks dating from the Civil War at Earith in the Fens.

among the many recent but largely forgotten manifestations of defence in the
landscape. Some relics of recent hostilities
will easily be identified. Concrete pillboxes,
strings of cylinders, cubes or pyramids in
reinforced concrete which were used as
anti-tank obstacles and abandoned airfield
control towers will not present problems,
but the circular pits containing cylindrical
concrete 'thimbles' used as mountings for
Second World War spigot mortars or decoy
airfield control posts could well be unheard
of and therefore unsuspected. Even so:
'Emplacements for the *spigot mortar* are
among the most durable of anti-tank or
anti-personnel defences . . . Mountings can
be found throughout the country, often by
bridges, road junctions and other crossing
points, and flanking coastal batteries. The
mounting was usually a drum of concrete
. . . domed at the top with a stainless steel
pin set into it. Mountings have rarely moved
from their original locations, though today
they often lie partially buried with only the
pin visible' (Brown *et al.*, 1995 pp.89–90).

Like their predecessors, modern defensive monuments reflect the preoccupations
of the nation—like the frenzy of fortification
which followed the launch, by the French, of
their first iron-clad warship in 1858 and the
ensuing report of a Royal Commission
appointed to advise on the defences of the
country. Military constructions would evolve
in relation to the experiences of warfare: in
the years immediately following 1935, the
numbers of military airfields expanded
rapidly; at first the new airfields were built
with their buildings concentrated in a semi-
circular arc on one side of the airfield, but
experiences of bombing demonstrated that
it was better to disperse technical, residential and administrative buildings around
the periphery of the airfield and surrounding countryside. The modern military works
influenced their settings in a wide variety of
ways, one of the most striking being the
diversion of the A15 five miles north of

Lincoln away from its alignment on the
Roman Ermine Street to loop around
Scampton airfield (with its compact expansion period layout of buildings concentrated
in the south-east quadrant).

Many of the modern military monuments
were built to centrally standardised designs,
and many of them also formed parts of
integrated systems and networks which may
be linked to particular circumstances,
challenges, plans and policies. As part of the
frantic anti-invasion precautions of 1940,
the War Office issued designs for twelve
types of 'pillbox', though the local con-
tractors employed to construct them very
frequently modified the plans. Although
often encountered in isolation, the pillboxes
were generally incorporated in systems of
defence, guarding a potential invasion
beach or seeking to establish a stop line to
check an enemy advance.

The attempt to create 'stop lines' resulted
in an unprecedented campaign to construct
systems of defensive earthworks, mainly as
defences against advancing tanks, with the
earthworks being sometimes, but not
always, supported by pillboxes and concrete
obstacles.

> Tests carried out by the British Army in
> May 1941 showed that the best and
> cheapest obstacle to stop tanks was not
> the concrete blocks that had been
> designed and manufactured in a variety
> of sizes and shapes, but a V-shaped ditch,
> 9ft deep, 18ft wide at the surface, and
> supported either side by two 2ft high
> ramparts. In reality, anti-tank ditches
> were excavated in a variety of widths,
> depths and profiles. Before 1941, most of
> the ditches had a vertical revetted face on
> the defender's side, but with a more
> gradual slope, and a rampart on the
> attacker's side. The rampart would have
> exposed the vulnerable underside of a
> tank to defensive fire. (Foot, 1998 p.10)

The stop lines reflected a policy of static

linear defence which, by the spring of 1941, was replaced by one of defence in depth which involved systems of highly fortified foci or 'nodal-points'. The routes of the ditches, incorporating zig-zags to allow enfilading fire, were surveyed by the Royal Engineers and convenient watercourses were incorporated into the system. The last of the ditches were dug in 1942, after which ditches, which had bisected farms and disrupted drainage and movement, were filled in and by 1945 the infilling was largely complete.

> For the most part, the courses of the ditches are entirely lost. With very few exceptions, there is no known record of their exact positions. Often the ditches ran well in front of the other defences of the stop lines—such as pillboxes and gun emplacements—so even a knowledge of the course of the stop line will not provide the precise location of the ditch. As documentary records are very limited, it is to archaeology that we have to turn— a remarkable fact, given that the generation that built the anti-tank ditches has not entirely passed from us. (Foot, 1998 p.11)

The study of landscape history/ archaeology is deeply concerned with the interpretation of context. Thus, the first step in any investigation is likely to involve the identification of a feature—as a moat, a gun battery site, and so on. Context demands that one then proceeds to locate the feature in its context, the context having its various topographical, geographical, historical, social and cultural dimensions. The explanation of why a defensive or offensive feature was created will be found in a successful exploration of the context, with the features being linked to a particular policy, social development or attitude of mind. Thus: 'Tudor officials sometimes seemed to think that England was an island—Shakespeare's "scept'red isle"—so that no special arrangements were needed for defence of the long landed frontiers which formed the northern and western boundaries of the Tudor state' (Ellis, 1995 p.36) and 'Undefended marchlands were worthless: they needed castles and tenants to protect them. This meant that border lords and gentry continued to live in castles and peles rather than the country houses now favoured by southerners. Thomas, Lord Dacre spent much of his income on building small castles at Drumburgh, Rockliffe and Askerton to protect his estates and on strengthening those at Naworth and Kirkoswald' (p.37).

REFERENCES

Aberg, F.A. (ed.) *Medieval Moated Sites*, CBA Research Report 17 (York: Council for British Archaeology, 1978).

Bradley, R. 'From ritual to romance: ceremonial enclosures and hill-forts' in G. Guilbert (ed.) *Hill-Fort Studies, Essays for A.H.A. Hogg* (Leicester: Leicester University Press, 1981) pp.66–76.

Brown, I. *et al.*, in B. Lowry (ed.) *20th Century Defences in Britain*, CBA Practical Handbooks in Archaeology 12 (London: Council for British Archaeology, 1995).

Brown, R.A. 'Royal castle-building in England, 1154–1216' *English Historical Review* 70 (1955) pp.353–98.

Burrow, I. 'Hill-forts after the iron age: the relevance of surface fieldwork' in G. Guilbert (ed.) *Hill-Fort Studies, Essays for A.H.A. Hogg* (Leicester: Leicester University Press, 1981) pp.122–49.

Cantor, L. 'Castles, fortified houses, moated homesteads and monastic settlements' in L. Cantor (ed.) *The English Medieval Landscape* (London: Croom Helm, 1982) pp.126–53.

Cathcart King, D.J. and Alcock, L. 'Ringworks of England and Wales' *Chateau Gaillard* 3 (1969) pp.90–127.

Clarke, H. *The Archaeology of Medieval England* (London: British Museum Publications, 1983).

Collis, J. 'A theoretical study of hill-forts' in G. Guilbert (ed.) *Hill-Fort Studies, Essays for A.H.A. Hogg* (Leicester: Leicester University Press, 1981) pp.66–76.

Crawford, O.G.S. *Archaeology in the Field* (London: Dent, 1953).

Cunliffe, B. *Excavations at Portchester Castle* (London: Soc. Antiq. Res. Rep., 1975).

Denison, S. 'Ornamental water garden found at Cheshire castle' *British Archaeology* 24 (1997) p.4.

Denison, S. 'Ridgeway hillforts reveal their little differences' *British Archaeology* (1998) p.4.

Eibl-Eibesfeldt, I., *The Biology of Peace and War* (London: Thames and Hudson, 1979).

Ellis, S. 'Frontiers and power in the early Tudor state' *History Today* 45 (1995) pp.35–42.

Foot, W. 'The lost defensive ditches of wartime' *British Archaeology* 37 (1998) pp.10–11.

Forde-Johnston, J. *Hillforts of the Iron Age in England and Wales* (Liverpool: Liverpool University Press, 1976).

Guilbert, G.C. 'Planned hillfort interiors' *Proceedings of the Prehistoric Society* 41 (1975) pp.203–21.

Guilbert, G.C. 'Hill-fort functions and populations: a sceptical viewpoint' in G. Guilbert (ed.) *Hill-fort Studies, Essays for A.H.A. Hogg* (Leicester: Leicester University Press, 1981) pp.104–121.

Herz, J. E. 'The rise and demise of the territorial state' *World Politics* 9 (1957) pp.473–95.

Hughes, M. 'Hampshire castles and the landscape: 1066–1216' *Landscape History* 11 (1989) pp.27–61.

Kenyon, J.R. 'Country houses behind castle walls' *British Archaeology* 22 (1997) pp.8–9.

Lowry, B. 'Hunting the survivors of Dad's Army' *British Archaeology* 40 (1998) pp.10–11.

Palliser, D.M. *The Staffordshire Landscape* (London: Hodder and Stoughton, 1976).

Pounds, N.J.G. *The Medieval Castle in England and Wales* (Cambridge: Cambridge University Press, 1990).

Stanford, S.C. *Croft Ambrey* (Hereford: 1974).

Steane, J.M. *The Archaeology of Medieval England and Wales* (London: Croom Helm, 1985).

Taylor, C. *Dorset* (London: Hodder and Stoughton, 1970).

Taylor, C. *The Cambridgeshire Landscape* (London: Hodder and Stoughton, 1973)

Taylor, C. *Fieldwork in Medieval Archaeology* (London: Batsford, 1974).

Taylor, C., Everson, P. and Wilson-North, R. 'Bodiam Castle, Sussex' *Medieval Archaeology* 34 (1990) pp.155–7.

Thompson, M.W. *The Decline of the Castle* (Cambridge: Cambridge University Press, 1987).

Wood, P.D. 'Frontier relics in the Welsh border towns' *Geography* 47 (1962) pp.54–62.

Index

Note : Locations are listed both under their place-name and their county or area. *Italic* indicates references to material or text in illustrations, photographs, diagrams or tables.